Your Blueprint for Success

Essential Power Words and Workbook

by John A. Chuback, M.D.

ISBN: 9-798390031-81-0

"By words we learn thoughts, and by thoughts we learn life."

– Jean Baptiste Girard

"The beginning of wisdom is the Definition of terms"

– Socrates

"Without knowing the force of words, it is impossible to know more."

– Confucius

"Silence is the language of God, all else is poor translation."

– Rumi

Word:
A sound or combination of sounds that has a meaning and is spoken or written.

Table of Contents

Foreword by Brian Tracy

Your Blueprint for Success

Once upon a time, there was a remarkable person who fantasized about becoming rich and successful. But he was an ordinary person, from an ordinary family, filled with other ordinary people, and he had no real idea about how to get from where he was to where he wanted to end up.

This is his story. It is also my story and your story, and the story of most people who started with little and then went on to achieve extraordinary things with their lives, as you will in the months and years ahead.

John Chuback has invited me to share my own personal experiences in getting from a poor beginning—sleeping in my car, or on the ground next to it—to living in a big house on a golf course with the ocean beaches in the distance. And what we have done, you can do as well, if you want it badly and long enough.

When I was a little boy, I fell in love with reading. At the age of five or six years, I would go down to the neighborhood pharmacy and "borrow" comic books which I took home and read, over and over. Then I would return the books to the store and "stock up" on five to ten more. Over time, I learned to read quite well, and the better I became, the more I read (and read and read and read).

The Great Discovery

Harvard University conducted a series of research studies to evaluate the relationship between the size of your vocabulary and the size of your income. They were amazed to find that, as you learned more words, your income increased. In fact, in one study, they found that if you learned five new words per day, your income would increase 50% and 60% in a year.

They found that each new word leads to other words, which would lead to more new words. As a result, you learned how to understand more and more, and get more and better results. You developed the ability to think better and more clearly, solving problems faster, getting more and better results.

The Great Breakthrough

Once upon a time, at a business seminar, I remember the speaker asking the attendees, "What is the importance of words?" Everyone pitched in and said "communicating."

But he went on and said something that changed my thinking forever. He said, "Yes, but what else?" We were stumped. He then went on to explain that every word is actually a "condensed thought." The more words you know, the more complex thoughts you can create, and the better you can think.

From that day forward, I never worked without a dictionary at hand. And now, with modern technology, I have multiple languages and dictionaries at my fingertips. I have learned to read, write and speak French, German and Spanish, plus smatterings of Italian, Russian, Chinese and Portuguese. In every case, my new knowledge has helped me to learn and earn, more and more.

John Chuback has prepared a feast for you in this book, a banquet of new knowledge supported by an incredible series of some of the most important words and ideas in the English language, words that will help you to think with greater clarity than ever before.

Congratulations! As you read, learn and apply what you are learning— you will feel yourself becoming smarter than ever before. As you master these additional words, you will become more valuable to yourself and others. You will become more intelligent and thoughtful. You will think with greater clarity. You will get more and better results and become a leader in your field.

Good luck! There are no limits.

Introduction

Your **Blueprint for Success** is meant for anyone who wishes to live a life which is both meaningful and abundant. Anyone can read this book and easily extract a treasure trove of practical information and immediately applicable skills. This work is meant to serve as a guide to writing a "virtual novel" about **YOU** living the exceptional life you have always truly desired. This book provides an authoritative list of powerful words that super-achievers know, use, and build their lives around. I have personally compiled this essential list from years of studying personal development literature. These are the terms that reveal themselves again and again in the works of the world's greatest teachers in the field of winning and success training.

First, you will be given the definition of each of these critically important words. Following this, you will find a passage reflecting how I feel many successful individuals utilize these terms to architect and construct extraordinary professional and personal lives. You will learn just how important such words are in planning and achieving great goals. Below the passage, I share with you related quotations by notable individuals from different periods of history, areas of expertise, and cultures. Finally, each entry ends with a call to action. This makes up the workbook component of this "interactive dictionary." Here you will be asked to engage in deep introspective analysis and to "think on paper." Using a separate notebook, take notes as you read and follow the exercises found within the book.

This powerful resource provides you with a blueprint and allows you to see your life as it would appear had all your dreams come true. Are you curious what your life would look like if your level of happiness, health, finances, and personal relationships were truly ideal? Working with this book will allow you to see the rest of your magnificent life in ultra-high definition.

When writing your story, relax. Always assume your success will have no negative repercussion on anyone else. This will free you from thinking too small and setting your sights too low. How would you truly write the story of your future? How would it unfold under ideal circumstances? This is *not* about imagining what you believe you *may* be able to achieve in the real world; this is about thinking way outside of that stifling box. This is about developing a manuscript that reflects what you really and truly desire.

Remember, this is a harmless mental exercise. If you get rich in your novel, no one need become poor. You haven't hurt anyone else. If you have perfect health in your novel, no one need become ill. If you have a beautiful physique in your novel, no one need become disfigured. If you decide in your novel to have loving and lasting relationships, no one need be lonely. Your wanting happiness and an abundant life filled with all the best things will harm no one. These are just ideas. You need not be apprehensive or hindered by guilt or shame. This is an easy trap to fall into. This is simply an exercise in self-exploration. Let your creative mind and imagination run wild. This will help you tremendously to look deep within yourself and assist you in getting on the path to where you really want to go. This is meant to be a liberating and exhilarating experience. This is exciting and joyous. Don't be afraid to put your whole self into it. Let go of your inhibitions completely.

This process is educational, motivational, interactive, inspiring, and instructional. Hopefully, this is the kind of book you can open at any page, begin reading for five or ten minutes, and then go on to have an exceptionally good day, feeling mentally and emotionally fueled and energized. I'm certain it will leave you feeling like your personal wheels of ambition have been set in forward motion.

When time permits, I strongly encourage you to sit down at your desk and work through the written exercises outlined at the end of each definition to get the most out of this robust volume. Make the time to write your life as a true literary masterpiece.

I wholeheartedly believe in the genre of personal development. I have been a serious student of this subject for many years. A disciplined approach to personal development has assisted me immeasurably in creating a richly rewarding and fulfilling life. Although I had an excellent, lengthy, and rigorous formal academic education prior to studying the field of self-improvement, I can unequivocally state that this additional area of scholarship has bettered my thinking about myself, the world around me, and the interplay between the two. This heightened sense of self-enlightenment has improved my life dramatically and in countless ways.

In homage to my many teachers, I would like to pay forward the favor of their invaluable lessons. I can assure you the wisdom collected from countless sources and shared herein is powerful and real. These vital concepts can improve your life immensely, if you embrace them deeply and sincerely. I bid you bon voyage as you embark upon a magnificent journey of self-discovery and personal development.

—John A. Chuback, M.D.

Preface

It has been said that the best way to predict the future is to create the future. I couldn't agree more. This is your chance to do exactly that. How would you like to live? What do you want to do? Who would you like to be? Where would you like to go? These questions come to mind in your life just as they come up when an author begins writing a novel. Authors, like yourself, concern themselves with the basics: Who? What? Why? When? Where? How?

When an author dreams up an idea, their first thoughts are, *"What is my story about, how does it begin? Where does it begin? When does it begin? Who is it about?"*

When a character within a novel embarks upon a journey or any adventure, questions are bound to come up. That's what makes it so interesting. I know I have, many times, felt like I was in a story or a movie. It's fun not only to be a character in your story, but also the creator and writer of your story. It's best not to be an extra in your own movie. Given the chance, why not be the star? Have the courage to play the lead role.

So, how does your success story start? How does the character overcome obstacles and pitfalls? What happens to this character? What are the character's strengths and weaknesses? Where is this character, and where is he or she going? When do things become easier for the character? When does the character begin to change? Who accompanies this character on their journey? Who or what tries to stop the character from victory? How does the experience change the character? Why does this character make the choices they make?

These same questions appear in our own lives, especially when embarking upon a new journey such as after completing certain milestones like high school or college graduation, after obtaining a degree, hitting an important age milestone, or after any kind of major life upheaval.

Sometimes, these "Where am I, and why?" questions pop up in our lives right in the middle of a mundane lunch hour or watching someone enjoy their job, arranging a bouquet, filling the car with gas, or watching a soccer game. *"How did I get here?"*; *"How do I get to where I want to be?"*; *"What do I really want to achieve?"*; *"What is my goal?"*; *"Where do I start?"*; *"When is a good time to leave this job and work for myself?"*; *"Who is living the life I'd like to live?"*; *"Why does it seem so easy for other people and not me?"* Questions arise at any time. Lucky for us, solutions can too.

You are the author of your own story. *Where* would you like your adventure to start? Would it start at a university of your choosing? Would it begin in medical school, or upon the open sea? Would it begin with your idea of embarking upon your own business like a bakery, art gallery, plumbing supply store, or creating a brand-new startup?

I've been asking you a lot of questions, and you may feel bombarded, but don't worry; you are going to take this journey in your success story one step, one thought, one word, one discovery at a time. No one knows you like *you* do, and you will want to use this book to help establish things about yourself you already know, plus learn a few things about yourself you did not know before. This book is also intended to guide you towards making your life one you can be proud of, one that brings you joy and fulfillment through service to others. Ideally, it will be a rich life, abundant in achievement and happiness. Make no mistake, the journey you are on is one of success. Success comes in many varying colors and styles; it is comprised of many different elements. And, since you are the writer and creator of your story, you get to choose exactly how it unfolds.

With this book as your guide, you will be creating the foundation to your success story by utilizing the words provided to help inspire you. This powerful collection of words will act to spark ideas in your creative imagination. In the process, you will also be taught how to transmute these ideas into action. It is this step, the manifestation of thoughts into action, which will actually change your life. This is where the book reveals its true value. Use it to create a blueprint that will guide you towards your best life. Write your story and then live it.

This book is divided into five sections. They make up the elements and blueprints of your success story:

Section One: Using Your Dream to Develop the Main Character
Section Two: Setting Goals to Determine the Setting of Your Story
Section Three: Making a Plan to Succeed and Overcome Obstacles
Section Four: Taking Action and Letting the Plot Unfold
Section Five: Finishing – The Ultimate Payoff of Motivation

Let's begin to write *your* story.

Section One:

Using Your Dream to Develop the Main Character

What words would you use to describe yourself as the character in your dream? Are you creative? Dependable? Courageous? What is your dream? Be honest! This is *your* workbook, so be free to express yourself. Who do you truly want to be? What do you honestly want to do? In the spaces provided at the end of each word entry, go all out and create your new self. Bonus if you have these attributes already! Write those down too!

Craft the individual you want to be, using the traits you would need to possess to make these dreams of yours a reality. Where do you see yourself in five, ten years? Create the ideal you. Use extra paper if necessary. You're going to want more paper. Be truthful and open—and dream **BIG**! Okay, let's get started!

Aspire

verb
Definition: to want to have or achieve something (such as a particular career or level of success).

Individuals who aspire to do more are the ones who push society ahead. By wondering what more they can achieve, they in turn have an impact on society as a whole, even if it is in a small way. If you aspire to build a better business, it is the customer who benefits, along with the business owner, as

1

quality improves. If the business owner looks to expand and open new retail centers, for example, he or she will need to hire more employees and put people to work. Everyone wins when there are new jobs being filled in the marketplace. The true success story, when working ethically, will always have a positive impact on the community at large. As the old saying goes, "A rising tide lifts all ships."

There is a sense of satisfaction that manifests itself in completing goals and aspiring to new heights that is very rewarding. Once you get a taste of this type of accomplishment, it becomes hard to do without. Successful individuals keep testing their limits to see what they can accomplish personally. More importantly, they work to leave behind a legacy helping their fellow man and making the world a better place.

> *"To understand the heart and mind of a person, look not to what he has already achieved, but at what he aspires to."*
> —Khalil Gibran (1883-1931), Lebanese-American artist, poet, and writer

What do YOU aspire to be or do? If you were building a character in a story, what would their dream be?

Concentration

noun

Definition: the act or process of concentrating: the state of being concentrated; *especially*: direction of attention to a single object.

To excel, you must find a way to create an environment and state of mind which is conducive to deep thought and focus. This can be hard work for the novice. The human brain is a highly metabolic organ, burning through glucose like a 747 burns through jet fuel. Although the human brain only weighs approximately three pounds, it utilizes twenty percent of the total oxygen and receives twenty percent of the total blood flow in your body. The brain consumes roughly 120 grams of glucose per day, which is about sixty percent of what the body consumes at rest. In other words, your brain is an incredible supercomputer that requires tremendous energy to keep running.

Just as lifting heavy weights requires the concentrated force of muscular contraction, deep thinking and difficult problem solving requires concentrated neurological function. It is imperative that successful individuals learn to concentrate for long periods of time on challenging issues, ideas, and concerns. It is only through concentration that new ideas will be added to the complex fabric of your consciousness. Do not expect that answers to life's most troublesome dilemmas will effortlessly reveal themselves to you.

Make time and create space to think hard about the various issues facing you in your life. Consider them deeply and routinely if you expect to be a true super-achiever.

> ❝*Concentration comes out of a combination of confidence and hunger.*❞
>
> —Arnold Palmer (1929-2016),
> American professional golfer, businessman, and entrepreneur

Where, in your dreams, lies your concentration? What do you wish to focus on?

Courage

noun
Definition: the ability or strength to do something that you know is difficult or dangerous.

It is difficult to win without courage. The reason for this is obvious. Winning is hard. If it were easy to be highly accomplished or prosperous, there would be no need to write books on the subject or produce and promote seminars on how it is done.

There are countless obstacles to success. These stumbling blocks often require that risks be taken and almost always mandate that an exhaustive amount of hard work be put forth to overcome them. There is virtually always some price that needs to be paid to realize unusual levels of profit and progress. There is an old saying that states, "You have to spend money to make money." This fact in and of itself is enough to take the courage out of most potential winners in life. Most people are taught to be so risk averse when it comes to investing financial resources into projects that have no definite triumphant result that they become paralyzed at this level of development.

Let's look at some specific examples of winners where courage is a necessary ingredient for prosperity or success. Can you have a pilot who is afraid of heights or crashing? Can you have a surgeon who is afraid of blood or being stuck with needles contaminated with HIV or Hepatitis C virus? Can you imagine a great general rising to that exalted position that refused to take his or her place on the battlefield if duty were to call? How about a submarine commander with claustrophobia? Obviously, these examples point out that varying degrees of courage are needed to accomplish many high-status positions in life. It is not so much that these are examples of people lacking in fears and phobias; they are examples of people who must overcome them to succeed. Whether it means risking life, limb, health, or wealth, there are few prestigious posts that are possible to occupy without some amount of grit, daring, and fortitude.

> ❝*Without courage, wisdom bears no fruit.*❞
>
> —Baltasar Gracián (1601-1658),
> Spanish Jesuit, Baroque prose writer, philosopher

Let's look again on this new and improved character you are developing. Do they possess courage? What will this character have to overcome to succeed? What terrifies you and holds you back? What are some ways you can overcome these fears? For courage to prevail, you must face down your fears.

Creativity

noun

Definition: The quality of having or showing an ability to make new things or think of new ideas.

4

Creativity is fundamental to possessing a winning approach to life. Creativity takes myriad forms. You need not be a painter or sculptor to be creative. Being creative may find its outlet in finding unique solutions to problems that inherently arise in business and in the personal sphere. Creativity lends itself to be solution-oriented rather than problem-focused. Creativity is often believed to be innate or reserved for a special few in any society or culture. Although there may be some individuals to whom a creative tendency comes a bit more easily, I strongly believe that it is ultimately a skill like any other that can be learned through proper training and practice. Sadly, too many people are either not encouraged, or worse, discouraged from developing any creative thinking and expression.

In my own life, I have had the good fortune to paint, draw, write poetry, record educational audio programs, and author several non-fiction books. I asked no one's permission to pursue any of these activities. I waited for nobody's encouragement or validation of whether I was capable or qualified to launch into any of these undertakings. I have also dabbled in music by taking some classical guitar lessons, with only modest success, but it did not stop me from trying. I strongly believe the more of these creative outlets you find for yourself, the more likely you are to find something that really clicks.

Furthermore, I feel that all creative processes are somehow linked in our central nervous system and each activity paves the way for the next. In other words, I hold that by drawing, singing, playing the flute, etc., the individual's mind becomes more limber, more dynamic, and more facile when it comes to finding creative answers to issues that may arise in the workplace, for example. Research shows that children who learn a musical instrument improve their aptitude for mathematics. Besides any practical application that creativity may have, it can also be a wellspring of pleasure and add great richness to your life experience.

I strongly advise you to look for areas in the creative realm that appeal to you and explore them. Buy a book on knitting, take a course at the local community or night school on oil painting or pottery. Find an avocation that brings you happiness, and don't be afraid to try as many as you like. These opportunities are plentiful and may make the fabric of your life much more interesting and rewarding in ways you may not at first appreciate.

"*Creativity takes courage.*"

—Henri Matisse (1869-1954), French artist

What things in your life do you approach creatively? What do you like to create? Seven-course meals? How do you use your creativity? If you are not certain, think of it this way: if you were a character in a novel, what creative talents would you like that character to possess? The gift of singing? Being a math whiz, craftily figuring out conundrums? A designer of buildings and bridges?

Curiosity

noun
Definition: the desire to learn or know more about something or someone.

Successful people are curious. They are constantly asking questions. Through questioning everything, learning occurs at an astounding rate of speed. The mind that is not curious to know why things are the way they are will invariably wind up relatively empty. No matter what your field of interest, questions are the pathway to knowledge. Knowledge will be a major factor in developing expertise, and that expertise can be a significant determinant in forging a reputation of excellence. This standing in your field or community will subsequently equate to prominence, influence, and success.

This is a character trait you want to develop. The curious spend their lives uncovering a mystery, and every day can be an unfolding gift, and you will learn so much along the way. Strive to learn about a new thing each day. With the Internet, it should be a breeze. Even if the thing is not particularly something you are instinctively interested in, you will be surprised where your curiosity will take you. Cultivate curiosity. Treasures await everyone who does.

One of my favorite sayings for a long time is, "*I'm not sure we understand everything we know about this.*" I think this sentiment says a lot. To me, it means take nothing for granted. You should be driven to know all the right answers, but more importantly, a true expert knows why the right answers are right. This is the depth of understanding you should constantly strive for if you wish to stand out as a true authority in your respective field. Be curious.

You're a human being, and one who is hungry for an exceptional degree of authority, distinction, and eminence in your business or profession. Feed and stoke continuously the curiosity that will drive the growth and expansion of your personal skill set. This insatiable desire to learn more about your career terrain will make you a "go-to" individual when opportunity presents itself.

> *"Satisfaction of one's curiosity is one of the greatest sources of happiness in life."*
>
> —Linus Pauling (1901-1994),
> American chemist, biochemist, peace activist, author, educator,
> Nobel Peace Prize recipient, Nobel Prize recipient

Where will your curiosity take you on your journey? If you are not sure, then write down what you are curious about. Are you curious about aquatic creatures? Space exploration? Biology? Candy-making? Running your own theater? Horse breeding? What would you like to learn more about? Get creative, and get curious about life! Remember, this is your story!

Dependability

adjective
Definition: able to be trusted to do or provide what is needed: able to be depended on.

Successful people are dependable. That's a fact. I have never known a highly successful individual who was not dependable. I have known many supremely accomplished individuals in my life; all of them are more dependable than the clock on the wall. There is probably no better example of dependability than what I learned in my many years of surgical training. Surgery is a world comprised of extraordinarily dependable men and women.

If a surgeon books a case for 7:30 in the morning, they will be there. It may snow, it may sleet, it may hail—they will be there. Surgeons don't make excuses because people's lives depend on their ability to function at the highest level. Surgeons don't call in sick because they don't feel like working. They don't take the day off because they are tired. They do what they are supposed to do, when they are supposed to do it. The public depends on them, and in almost every case, they stand tall.

Work hard at building a reputation of dependability. This standing in your community or field of endeavor will literally be worth its weight in gold. When someone calls upon you for your services, they want to be assured that you will provide what you say you will, when you say you will, for the price you have quoted. No one likes to be disappointed. Become renowned for your word and your reliability, and you will be on a collision course with success, profit, and fortune.

> **❝We like to say that dependability is more important than ability.❞**
>
> —Bill Belichick (1952-),
> American Super Bowl champion football coach

Are you dependable? Be honest. If not, how will you go about developing this attribute?

Desire

noun

Definition: to long or hope for: the feeling of wanting something: a strong wish.

Desire is fundamental to success. The individual who is to be successful is driven by desire, a want, a need. At the essence of the successful individual's personality is the longing, hope, and want of earning, having, and doing more than he or she has done up until that point. Desire is what pushes people forward and upward. If the individual has no wants beyond what they already possess—whether that be material, financial, physical, emotional, personal, situational, positional, etc.—then there is no driving force toward change and betterment. Desire is the underlying engine that moves the individual toward loftier results. Without this philosophical power plant, there can be no measurable progress in any aspect of the human condition.

Look inside and ask yourself what it is that you truly desire. This is a fundamentally important question. This is part of creating your dream life. This exercise is one of the basics in high achievement. If you get in the car and head out on the road with no destination in mind, where do you think you may end up? Most likely, nowhere particularly important or interesting.

In the worst-case scenario, you may find yourself in a very dangerous neighborhood or sitting idly at the end of some dead-end street.

It is essential that you ask yourself what you want out of life—and be specific. The more specific you are, the more rapidly you will turn your desires into tangible realities. Ask yourself: *Where do I want to live, what country, what state, what town, what neighborhood, what street?* Ask yourself: *What kind of house do I desire? Is it a Tudor, a ranch, a split level, a French style chateau, a contemporary made of steel and glass, a manor made of brick and covered in lush ivy?*

If you don't know the answer to these questions, what do you expect to end up with? The likely answer is that you'll simply make do with whatever comes along. That's no way to live. Don't go through your life drifting aimlessly at sea. As the gifted speaker and business philosopher Jim Rohn used to say, "Set your own sail" for whichever destination you personally desire.

> 66 *The will to win, the desire to succeed, the urge to reach your full potential… these are the keys that will unlock the door to personal excellence.* 99
>
> —Confucius (551-479 BC), Chinese teacher, politician, philosopher

I have had the good fortune of sitting through many interviews in my life, some academic, some professional. A common question an interviewer will ask is, "Where do you see yourself in five years, ten years, thirty years?" What a wonderful question. I'm not sure enough of us know the answer to

9

that question. Asking questions will reflect your true inner desires and are all part of your creating a dream, creating the success story of your life. Don't be afraid to hear the questions; acknowledge them, write them down, or say them out loud. It's okay if you don't come to terms with what you really want right away. Right now, you may feel as though you are on an aimless path, which will likely lead to a place which isn't particularly special. Perhaps you feel you are in that not-so-special-place right now. Don't fret.

Respect yourself enough to ask yourself the tough questions. Then allow yourself the space to seriously consider these questions and write down some answers. This is *your* life, *your* story. Make it spectacular. Be courageous. Recognize and pursue your true desires.

Be sure you take the time to sit down in a quiet place and ask yourself those questions, then write down the answers you come up with. Listen to your inner voice, and be honest with yourself.

Where do you see yourself in five years, specifically? Where will you live? With whom will you live? How will you support yourself financially? What will you drive? Where will you work? What will you do with your free time? What kind of shape will you be in? What will you do for exercise? Where will you vacation?

What will be your level of education? How many hours will you work per week? Will you have children? If so, how many? How many weeks of vacation will you take each year? How much money will you earn? How much money will you have in the bank? Where will you invest your money? Who will be your investment advisor?

These questions are endless. Give yourself time and space to work out the answers. It's a good place to start.

Determination

noun

Definition: a quality that makes you continue trying to do or achieve something that is difficult.

Winners are a determined lot. As Brian Tracy says, highly successful individuals are "unstoppable." Where others may be deterred, the super-achievers continue to forge straight ahead. There are so many obstacles in life, so many potential pitfalls. It seems that every day when we get out of bed there is someone or something attempting to discourage and dissuade us from achieving our full potential. The winning set is not hindered or impeded by these negative forces, and they understand they are simply a normal part of everyday life in the real world. Life is not a rose garden; in fact, as you travel deeper into the garden of life, the more thorns, vines, and thickets you are likely to encounter. Don't let these frustrating and aggravating obstructions impede your momentum in any significant way. A determined attitude is like a razor-sharp machete hacking through this metaphoric jungle of brush, thistle, and bramble.

Determination is that force which keeps the victorious few treading and moving forward. It is a trait worth cultivating. You cannot succeed without it. This is an essential element of the success-oriented personality because the wind will not always be at your back in life. There will be many times when the headwind may seem endless and oppressive, but never stop putting one foot in front of the other. With time, the winds always change direction, and you will enjoy good times when your sail is full and taut. Always find the fortitude and will to proceed in a positive direction, even when the progress seems minimal. Remain determined, and over time, unexpected breakthroughs will allow for sudden bursts of headway in your personal voyage toward an exceptional life.

> ❝*Failure will never overtake me if my determination to succeed is strong enough.*❞
>
> —Og Mandino (1923-1996), American author

Do you have what it takes to move your dream through the rough spots? Only time will tell. Meanwhile, write down what you are determined to do: Get to a healthy weight? To get your doctorate in biology? Travel the globe? Pay off your mortgage? What obstacles do you think may deter you from success? How do you plan on removing these obstacles?

Dream

---

noun

Definition: an idea or vision that is created in your imagination and that is not real; something that you have wanted very much to do, be, or have for a long time.

This is the process of goal setting: taking those dreams and turning them into goals. Having a dream is the very first element in the blueprint for success. Of course, the final step that differentiates success from failure is the ability to act on those goals, setting a plan in motion, and following through on that plan until the dream becomes an actual reality. The only real failure comes from not trying. This is the hard part.

The human imagination is programmed for dreaming, wishing, and hoping for wonderful things to happen, but how many of us can turn those wonderful, far-reaching desires into reality? Sadly, I believe, very few. Study successful people, and you will quickly learn that their success started in a very common way. They had a dream of some sort. They wished to be well educated, or to have a beautiful home overlooking the sea, to marry a beautiful princess, or get swept away by a charming prince.

These kinds of dreams are natural, if not universal, particularly among young people. These are wonderful ambitions. Everyone should entertain such magnificent thoughts. Why not you? Why shouldn't you have a gorgeous new Ferrari, a stable of Arabian horses, or live the quiet life in a cottage by the sea? Someone will enjoy such luxuries in life. Why not you?

You must first believe you are deserving of such treasures. You must have complete faith in your own incredible self-worth. As I said, there are thousands of people who drive Ferraris and own Arabian horses—can they all be so incredibly special? I think not. I think that people like you and me are every bit as good and every bit as deserving as they are. But you must *believe.* If you don't, then any hope of achieving such success will be dashed from the outset. Be a dreamer, a goal setter, and a doer. Do it because you can. No one can stand in the way of your dreams but you. What's your story? Think big. DREAM BIG! And take big action, starting right now. You will be absolutely shocked by your true innate potential and capacity for almost surreal levels of success.

Many dream of a better life. Dreaming is the very first step to obtaining what you want. First come the thoughts, then the deeds.

> ""*You may say I'm a dreamer, but I'm not the only one.*""
>
> —John Lennon (1940-1980),
> English songwriter, record producer, artist, writer, and activist

Write out your dreams right here, no matter how far-fetched they may seem. Your imagination has no limits! Use extra paper if you need.

Drive

noun
Definition: an impelling culturally acquired concern, interest, or longing (a drive for perfection).

Successful people have a drive others lack. To be driven is to feel a compelling need to work at something, even when there is no obvious impetus to do so. Where this innate tendency comes from seems a bit mysterious. Perhaps some is truly genetic, in other words, how one is wired from birth. This may go hand in hand with the so-called "Type A" personality. It is also likely that drive can be fostered, taught, and nurtured from a young age depending on what environmental factors the child is exposed to. These factors are hard to prove or disprove, and, empirically speaking, we have all seen examples of actual individuals who appear to prove or disprove each of those theories. For example, we all know people who were raised in a family of high achievers who amounted to little and had a reputation for being lazy and shiftless. Conversely, we all know stories of individuals who came from meager and oftentimes dysfunctional households who go on to achieve extraordinary levels of success.

The other concept which once again comes into play is that of adding or maximizing existing skills. Drive is a skill. Drive can be cultivated like any other technique in personal capability. This begins with a desire to improve in this space. Once you recognize the value in having exceptional drive, you can work toward developing this important tool. Then, through reading motivational material, attending inspirational seminars, and using day timers and e-schedules to maximize your efficiency and effectiveness, you can begin to build your personal level of stamina and endurance.

This is one of those intangible qualities which is among the most crucial in becoming a super-achiever. It is common to all high-value individuals. Do all you can to become part of this elite group.

> "*Success is almost totally dependent upon drive and persistence. The extra energy required to make another effort or try another approach is the secret of winning.*"
>
> —Denis Waitley (1933-),
> American motivational speaker, consultant, and author

Can you write down some ways you have illustrated having drive? Motivation is important; what spurs you on towards your goal? Financial gain? Helping people? Personal triumph?

Ego

noun

Definition 1: the opinion that you have about yourself; a person's sense of self-esteem and self-importance. 2: the part of the mind that mediates between the conscious and the unconscious and is responsible for reality testing and a sense of personal identity.

There is an old expression that says, "Don't be so humble, you're not that great." The reality is, like it or not, that every winner has a robust ego. That does not have to be a bad thing. Sadly, having a big ego has become synonymous with being a jerk or being full of yourself. Now, this is not to say that some people with enormous egos aren't jerks; some are. But there is a difference between having a healthy ego and being an *egotist*. It is like the difference between being wealthy and being an elitist. The two things are totally unrelated. A military general cannot command troops if he isn't full of confidence. An astronaut cannot strap herself into a spacecraft loaded with tons of highly combustible rocket fuel unless she feels she is as good, or better, than anyone else in the nation to carry out her mission.

The reality is that super-achievers require a hefty ego to fuel the confidence required to do extraordinary things. Where an ego can be, and often is, a major dilemma is when it is possessed by an individual of limited skills and capability. This can be a recipe for disastrous results. For example, strapping yourself into a rocket when you have no idea what the hell you are doing is not a set-up for success.

The individual must have a realistic notion of his or her true ability and never make the dangerous mistake of overestimating it. The ego should follow the person's ability and achievement; it should not be a product of unwarranted narcissism. It's okay if your surgeon or pilot or train engineer feels up to the job, as long as they have the training and experience to back it up. Put yourself in a position to have a well-developed ego through proper education, work, and training. This will allow you to become a leader in your field. Do not, on the other hand, overestimate your true self-worth, as this could result in great loses in every area of your personal and professional life.

"If being an egomaniac means I believe in what I do and in my art or music, then in that respect you can call me that... I believe in what I do, and I'll say it."

—John Lennon
(1940-1980), English singer, songwriter, record producer, artist, writer, and activist

In your success story, what contributes to your character's self-worth? How would you develop that sense of self-esteem? Learning a skill, an art, or gaining knowledge? What thoughts do you put into this character to make them feel good about themselves? This question can be very revealing, so take some time to explore it!

Emotional Intelligence—EI (Emotional Quotient—EQ)

noun

Definition: Emotional intelligence can be defined as the ability to monitor one's own and other people's emotions, to discriminate between different emotions and label them appropriately, and to use emotional information to guide thinking and behavior.

Most winners happen to have a high emotional intelligence (EI). Historically, this has not been a concept that has been well understood. Therefore, very few people have had the insight to work at consciously developing a greater emotional intelligence. But make no mistake about the fact that this is a skill area that can be cultivated and trained to be more robust. The individual who lacks emotional intelligence tends to be highly reactive and find themselves in compromised circumstances in various areas of their life.

The idea of emotional intelligence and how to develop it is new to many well-educated people who have put enormous amounts of time and effort into other areas of personal development. I strongly suggest that if you wish to be a highly successful individual that you investigate and study this highly rewarding area of growth and maturation. I certainly recommend that you begin with the works of Dr. Daniel Goleman, who has proven himself to be a thought leader in this fascinating and immensely valuable aspect of character expansion and improvement. I recommend you begin with his books *Emotional Intelligence* and *Focus*. You may also enjoy his presentation on emotional intelligence in *Big Think* via YouTube.

Feelings/emotions—yours and those of others—are just as powerful as thoughts. They influence perception and perspective, and, consequently, behavior and decision making, shaping your world and the world of others. Therefore, emotions should be noted and examined. How do you want your behavior to affect your workplace or home environment? How far do you allow the emotions of others to control your environment? How do you react to others' emotional responses? Reading emotions, learning the art of being tuned in to your feelings and those of others will aid in your choice of response. How you react will be up to you. Your actions, your decisions, can

16

make a huge difference regarding your life journey. How you understand and react to emotions is key to good clear decision making and a successful outcome.

> *"What really matters for success, character, happiness, and lifelong achievements is a definite set of emotional skills —your EQ—not just purely cognitive abilities that are measured by conventional IQ tests."*

—Daniel Goleman, Ph. D. (1946-), Author, psychologist, and science journalist

In your story, how would you like your character to react to certain emotional triggers?

What steps would they take to get to a place where they were more in tune with their emotions?

How can you learn to think before you react? Do you see this is an issue that can be improved upon in your own life? How do you think a lack of emotional intelligence holds you back?

Do you have a quick temper? Are you easily offended or hurt by criticism? Write out your thoughts and feelings about this below.

Enjoy

verb
Definition: to take pleasure in (something).

Successful people enjoy life. It's that simple. The game of life is not about who dies with the most chips, but who has had the most meaningful, enjoyable ride. This means spending time with those you love and who love you. If you don't have relationships like that in your life, perhaps your idea of success is solely monetary. You may find that a short-lived joy.

It is essential to travel, see different parts of our country and the world, enjoy great foods, participate in sports and other leisure activities. This is why you work so hard, so you can thoroughly enjoy all the magnificent experiences life has to offer. Life is so beautiful. Experience it to its fullest. Share these moments with your friends and family. A good meal always tastes best when it is enjoyed with others. Don't fall into the trap that we are here only to work, only to study, only to earn and to save. There must be a balance to life. The motivation to work hard should be in the desire to afford wonderful happenings and events. Dream big dreams. Set lofty goals for yourself in terms of the pleasurable activities you would like to take part in. Do exceptional things.

Exercise what Brian Tracy calls "blue sky thinking," and don't live on a place called "Someday Isle." In other words, don't be a person who goes from saying, "Someday I'll do this," or, "Someday I'll do that," to a person who regretfully admits, "I wish I had done this," or, "I wish I had done that."

I wonder what enjoyable experiences you would share in if you would unlock your inner desires. Would you fly in a hot air balloon? Would you get your pilot's license? Would you go to Paris in the springtime? Would you take a cruise around the world? Would you buy a ticket on Virgin Galactic for a space flight?

Would you plan a simple picnic in the park with your significant other for the first time in years – or maybe for the first time ever? Do you even own a proper picnic basket and blanket? These pleasures need not be costly or extravagant to hold an immeasurable degree of value. Be focused on planning and then living such events. This is your life. As they say, "This is not a dress rehearsal." You will never have these days, weeks, months, and years back. Use them wisely, and get from them all you can. Again, life can be an unimaginably remarkable journey, but it won't play out that way by chance.

You need to be fixated on the realization of a lifetime of enjoyment and pleasurable occasions. Sit down and think hard about what you want to have, do, and see. Make a list, and on that list put dates alongside each of these desires. Make sure each one happens for you. No one else is going to see to it that they actually materialize for you. Life is for living and enjoying. Don't miss the whole point of what we're doing here.

"We are at our very best, and we are happiest, when we are fully engaged in work we enjoy on the journey toward the goal we've established for ourselves. It gives meaning to our time off and comfort to our sleep. It makes everything else in life so wonderful, so worthwhile."

—Earl Nightingale (1921-1989),
American radio personality, writer, speaker, and author

Where, in your story, do your dreams and aspirations take you? What does this new and improved character enjoy doing—painting, gardening, building houses? What would you do if you could do anything? What brings you joy?

Enthusiasm

noun
Definition: strong excitement about something; a strong feeling of active interest in something that you like or enjoy.

Enthusiasm is fundamental to success. How could a track and field athlete even entertain the idea of winning a footrace if they were not enthusiastic about the sport and the concept of competition, if they did not possess an appetite for victory? The short answer is that they could not. You must have hearty enthusiasm for any challenge you elect to take on. Enthusiasm is the engine that drives desire, that drives the dream. One key to success is finding a vocation or avocation you love and are passionate about. It is difficult to be the world's greatest skier if you are afraid of heights and hate cold weather. Similarly, it is highly unlikely that you will win the world surfing championship if you can't swim and fear the ocean. When you have intrinsic enthusiasm for a given endeavor, it makes the work more pleasurable and the goals more easily attainable.

Those individuals who have been the most successful in business, for example, are often quoted as saying things like, "I honestly feel like I never worked a day in my life," or, "I sometimes find myself astonished when I realize I'm getting paid to do what I love."

This is the holy grail of success. When the participant is passionate and enthusiastic about what they do every day, that is just the perfect scenario. Unfortunately, this is not always the case. People can be highly successful in any given area but still dread going to work every day. That's no way to live, unless you have a highly rewarding life outside of work.

However, if you find yourself in the position of dreading each day because of your occupation, you owe it to yourself to change things up. Find something else to do where you will celebrate every day of your career rather than merely settling for tolerating each day.

For many of us, the reality is we must work a bit on finding and nurturing that enthusiasm for our work. I mean, let's face it—work for most of us is, well, work. But that doesn't mean it should be drudgery or oppressive. In my own professional life, although I was once a very accomplished cardiac surgeon with outstanding operative results, I found I was not enjoying my career. In fact, I grew in time to hate it. There is a lesson here: competence and happiness do not necessarily go hand in hand.

I knew many heart surgeons who would have done anything to have my skills and surgical outcomes, but they still loved doing the work every day although they were not the most gifted surgeons. That's not to say they were incompetent, it's just to say they weren't the most talented, yet they still loved what they did every day. That's the way it should be. You should love getting out of bed every day when you head to your job.

If you don't have sincere enthusiasm for what you do, either try to cultivate that feeling in yourself or change your work. My new career is purely elective, and I don't have to deal with any unexpected emergencies. This has allowed me to be fully in charge of my schedule and spend much more time at home with my family. Each of us must look seriously at our lives, analyze our levels of satisfaction, stress, reward, and fulfillment and adjust accordingly.

If you find you cannot muster up genuine enthusiasm for the career you have chosen, it is never too late to make modifications which will provide you with heightened levels of gratification and success.

"Enthusiasm spells the difference between mediocrity and accomplishment."

—Norman Vincent Peale (1898-1993),
American author, professional speaker, minister

What are you enthusiastic about? What do you love doing? What piques your interest? Writing it down may help you decide to change careers or change your major in college. It's never too late to improve upon your story!

Experiment

verb
Definition: to do a scientific test in which you perform a series of actions and carefully observe their effects: to try a new activity or a new way of doing or thinking about something.

Winners and successful people are always experimenting. They are changing things to see what works best. It takes a curious person to do well with experimentation. They are setting new goals and trying to achieve new heights. Seeing how far or how high you can go is an experiment in itself. If you are satisfied with the status quo, there is no need for experimentation.

Examples of experiments a successful person might undertake are: dietary changes, changes in exercise routines, changes in investment strategies, changes in approach to a personal relationship, starting new streams of incomes in his or her business, etc. It is essential to understand that an experiment is just that, an experiment. No one knows the result of an experiment. Sometimes the outcome will be positive, at other times negative. But the successful person learns from these experiences and moves forward, more knowledgeable, nimble, and more effective than ever before. Don't be afraid to experiment, makes changes, take risks.

This is a good character trait to have. This does not mean being haphazard, chaotic, or self-destructive. Experimentation should have a logical design with limits to downside potentials.

21

Nevertheless, there will always be some calculated risk involved. Don't let this deter you from growth and the realization of your personal full potential!

> *"All life is an experiment. The more experiments you make, the better."*

—Ralph Waldo Emerson (1803-1882), American essayist, lecturer, and poet

In your dream or your success story, what would you take on that you never did before? What would you like to try doing a different way that you have never tried before? What if you joined a social club? How about trying to read a book a month? What are you not confident in, but would like to try out?

Fulfillment

noun

Definition: the act of succeeding in achieving (something): to make something (such as a dream) true or real.

Success is all about a profound sense of fulfillment. The feeling of being fulfilled in every way is the ultimate test of success. Fulfilling your economic dreams and obligations, your personal needs and desires, your spiritual goals, your obligations to yourself and your fellow man including community, friends, and family is what being a real success means. The opposite of fulfillment is emptiness. No one yearns for a life of emptiness.

Empty bank accounts, empty promises, an empty house, an empty mind, or an empty heart are all disastrous outcomes for the ambitious and healthy human being. Look at every conceivable aspect of your life and category by category ask yourself, "Is my cup empty, half-full, or brimming with richness?" This may be the most important question of all that you can pose to yourself. Take measure regularly of where you stand and where you want to be in the future regarding the wonderful feeling of sincere fulfillment in your life. Keep striving every day to get a little better in each area to do away with emptiness and replace that hollow state with abundance and wealth of every kind.

"We wander for distraction, but we travel for fulfillment."

—Hilaire Belloc (1870-1953),
Anglo-French writer, historian, and member of Parliament

What you think will fulfill now you may not, in the end, be satisfying at all. Take your time and revisit this concept of fulfillment several times a year, and see if your needs and wants change over time. It's perfectly natural if they do; it's perfectly okay if they do not. What do you consider fulfillment?

In your story, what does fulfillment look like? What are your dreams of fulfillment?

Imagination

noun
Definition: the ability to form a picture in your mind of something you have not seen or experienced: the ability to think of new things; the ability of the mind to be creative or resourceful.

Successful people tend to have great imaginations. I think that a very common way our imagination is expressed is through daydreaming. Interestingly, this is a word that is often associated with a negative connotation. Children are often reprimanded for daydreaming. Children are repeatedly told daydreaming is a waste of time. I couldn't disagree more. I was always a daydreamer. Like many children, I can remember vividly the wonderful and exciting thoughts I would have as a child in school, looking out the classroom window with a glazed look in my eyes. It may have appeared that I was "completely spaced out" during those moments when in fact it would be more accurate to describe me as being "totally spaced in." In a way, I was really focused during those periods of time. I was watching an incredible movie in my mind's eye that had been written and produced by my youthful, powerful, and seemingly endless imagination.

23

I would see myself being an important man and giving press conferences surrounded by journalists. I would see a beautiful home with a swimming pool and a tennis court. I envisioned myself owning and riding horses and boating on a private yacht in the Caribbean. I saw myself being in great physical condition and being attractive to beautiful women. I saw myself driving a Ferrari just like Magnum P.I. from the television series about a private investigator who lived on an estate in Hawaii. The scenarios I created in my mind were endless and exciting and thrilling.

The fascinating part is that no one encouraged me to want those things or see myself in that way. It came so naturally to me. I loved drifting off into my own fantasy world and watching the movie play in my head. It was so real to me. It seemed well within my reach. No one had put these thoughts in my mind; in fact, the truth was to the contrary. I believe that many children, maybe every child, has innate desires for an extraordinary life, just the way I did.

But what we heard from the outside world is: don't be a daydreamer, don't waste your life wishing for things that can never come true. Don't set yourself up for disappointment.

So, at some point, just about every single one of us somewhere along the line is convinced that we should give up this imaginary lifestyle and settle for the mundane, ordinary, and mediocre lifestyle everyone around us seems to be living. It's so tragic. The child's mind is genetically wired correctly, and the adults around him or her are hard at work screwing the whole thing up.

It is never too late to reawaken your imagination and believe in the visions it brings forth. You can live any way you like, but first you must believe in the power of your imagination. If you have children, please encourage them to listen to the inner voice and watch with anticipation those incredible cinematic masterpieces their beautiful young minds create. Those films are the blueprint for an exceptional style of living which will make them one of the rare few who truly live their life to the fullest potential.

At some point in your childhood, your imagination is like a raging inferno. Over time, because no one is willing to fuel this fire, the flames begin to die down. Sadly, for most people, at some point that once roaring blaze has cooled to a single glowing ember, until one day it simply goes out altogether. That moment is the end of all hope to achieve great things.

I implore you: search deep within yourself for any hint of that tiny ember and gently fan it and rekindle it. Add bits of dry grass and then sticks. When it sparks a flame again, slowly but surely nurture it to the point you can throw mighty logs on it and watch it burn again. The warmth and glow from this fire of imagination will put you back on the path of greatness, winning, and success.

"Imagination is everything.
It is the preview of life's coming attractions."

—Albert Einstein (1879-1955), German-born theoretical physicist

In keeping with the previous imagery, write down the ideas in your mind that act as fuel to the fire of your imagination. What rekindles your passion? What do you enjoy enough that it inspires you to dream? Write it all down and use it as a reference when that fire gets a little dim. You want to keep your imagination burning bright. Use it to fuel your success!

Impression

noun

Definition: the effect or influence that something or someone has on a person's thoughts or feelings.

Successful people make it their business to leave a good impression on those around them. When you leave a good impression, you have a positive impact on the overall energy of any situation. When you leave a poor impression of yourself on others, you have added to the overall negativity of the environment and our world in general. True success can never come out of a negative energy force field. The overall energy of success is positive.

The impression you leave is based largely on how you make others feel about themselves. If you make someone feel small, stupid, inferior, or unimportant, they will likely have strongly negative feelings toward and about you. If, on the other hand, you walk away from an interaction with another human being having made them feel great about themselves, the likelihood is they will have warm, positive, and complimentary feelings about you.

How you behave in front of and toward others is what will forge in their minds their impression of you. Your behavior is made up largely of the words you speak and the actions you carry out. What impression would you leave on a group if you elected to wear a bathing suit and a Hawaiian shirt to a formal black-tie affair? What impression do you leave if you are unkempt looking in a business environment? How will people judge you? What will they think of you? Do you think they will judge you for who you really are, more than what you are, or less than what you are if you come underdressed to a professional meeting? I'll leave it up to you to answer that question. My advice: always put your best foot forward. Work hard on your grammar and vocabulary. Work hard on your physical fitness and appearance. Work hard at your sense of fashion, and insist on being well groomed and well dressed. Make it your business to be a positive force in a room.

Be complementary to others and not well known for your hyper-critical personality and disposition. Develop a warm, firm handshake, and teach yourself to look everyone straight in the eye. Learn to be a good listener so you can be a great conversationalist. A great conversation is never dominated by one of the parties involved. Highly successful individuals learn at some point along the way that people's impression of you is who you actually are. We exist in the world only in the minds of others. If there is an overwhelmingly negative opinion of who you are and what you represent, you need to radically change the image you impress upon other people.

This is an essential concept. Work hard on being the best you can be. Start today and make this a lifelong journey. You can never be more than what people perceive you to be.

*"I have never experienced another human being.
I have experienced my impressions of them."*

—Robert Anton Wilson (1932-2007),
American author, playwright, futurist, psychologist, and agnostic mystic

26

In your success story, construct your character to possess the characteristics that give a good impression. Let's get personal; what attributes would you give this character in order to fulfill their dreams? Would they have your qualities, or would they have qualities you wish to possess?

Individuality

noun
Definition: the quality that makes one person or thing different from all others.

Successes very often are titans of individuality. By definition, if you win, you have set yourself apart from the crowd. By strict definition, the winner is the person who comes in first. Of course, for the purposes of this book and philosophically speaking, winning is much more than that. But still, successful people always stand out in some way. Winners stand out from the crowd in that they are highly successful as compared to others in their time or culture. You must possess great self-confidence to express fully your individual strengths and positive attributes. It's hard to win in a corner. It's hard to win from within someone else's shadow.

Winners are known for having exceptional skill sets, whether they are in business, law, medicine, sports, invention, the fine arts, music, etc. It is crucial the highly successful individual also works well with their peers and colleagues, but not in a way that forces them to lose their own identity amongst the group.

Think long and hard about what your strengths are. Foster these unique capabilities and allow them to make you shine in the marketplace. Where you have weaknesses, work equally as hard to strengthen those areas as well so you will be known as an individual with a robust set of talents and few, if any, chinks in your armor. This is a wonderfully fulfilling process. Let people see your greatness, and it will take you farther than you believe you can go.

"The American experience influenced my understanding of individuality, basic human rights, freedom of expression, and the rights and responsibilities of citizens."

—Ai Weiwei (1957-), Chinese artist and activist

What makes you, as a character in your success story, stand out? What distinguishes you from others in your field or area of interest?

Integrity

noun
Definition: the quality of being honest and fair.

Winners have integrity. They are honest and fair in their dealings with others, but this in no way should be confused with weakness. Being fair does not mean you should be a pushover.

People with integrity stand their ground and expect others to deal with them in the same manner they themselves behave.

When it comes to success, the individual who conducts themselves with integrity stands by any agreement they make and insists that anyone with whom he associates does the same. A track record of broken promises can only lead to failure. Overcommitting, even with the best of intentions, always ends poorly when you are incapable of holding up your end of a bargain. You are better served to "under-promise and over-deliver," as the adage goes. This will help to bolster your reputation and leave no one walking away feeling short-changed after having dealt with you.

"Integrity has no need of rules."

—Albert Camus (1913-1960),
French author, journalist, philosopher, and Nobel Prize winner

In your success story, how do you conduct yourself? Write down how integrity can be a positive attribute in your journey towards success. How does integrity improve your personal and professional relationships?

Invention

noun
Definition: the act or process of creating or producing (something useful) for the first time.

Not every winner is an inventor as we would typically think of such a label. Not every super-achiever need be like Thomas Edison or Alexander Graham Bell. The image of the brilliant tinkerer with tussled hair, a wild look in their eyes, and a white laboratory coat standing at a laboratory bench with Bunsen burners throwing flames is not necessary to be an inventor. Invention takes on many meanings, many guises.

The act of being creative and coming up with new ideas or solutions to problems is inventive. Typically, the greatest invention of any highly productive person is themselves. They see a vision of who they would like to be in their mind's eye and then bring that individual into being through hard work, practice, training, and determination. The little boy invents a picture of himself as a great statesman, standing at a lectern delivering a great oration, or he sees himself as the starting pitcher for the World Champion Chicago Cubs. A little girl stands before the mirror in knee socks and short-sleeve dress at age nine but sees in her reflection a thirty-five-year-old highly decorated submarine commander. These inventions of the mind are what guide us. These inventions are the blueprints by which we will design and build our realities.

Inventing a self-image is a critical first step if you are to be a pharmacological research scientist. You must first believe that you are intellectually and academically capable of such a calling prior to doing the bench research that will ultimately lead to a cure for cancer.

Successful people are always inventing new things in their heads before they exist in the real world. They invent who they will be, where they will go to school, what degrees they will earn, how much money they will make, where they will live, what car they will drive, what type of spouse they will marry, what kind of business they will be in. These inventions of the human imagination are the most powerful and valuable known to mankind. You must first invent the *idea* of landing on the moon before inventing the lunar lander.

Let your inventive capacity run wild. Never curtail what your mind tells you it wants or is capable of. Invent yourself and your life first in your magnificent brain, and the rest will follow with persistence and industriousness.

29

❝Necessity... the mother of invention.❞

—Plato (c. 428-c. 348 BC), Greek philosopher and mathematician

Your assignment here is simple: Start inventing, right here, right now!

Kindness

noun

Definition: the quality or state of having or showing a gentle nature and desire to help others: the quality or state of wanting to do good things and to bring happiness to others.

True successes are kind. Kindness is essential to super-achievement. Kindness is the bedrock of success. Anyone who believes they are going to strong-arm the world into submitting to their way has a lot to learn. Always keep in mind the adage, "You can catch more flies with honey than you can with vinegar."

Kindness must be sincere and heartfelt. Kindness takes many forms. Kindness and generosity go hand in hand. Kindness helps create the classic "win-win" paradigm of success, whereby my kindness toward you promotes a feeling of good will between the two of us. This becomes a self-fulfilling prophecy. When I am kind to you today, you will likely be kind toward me or some other individual in very near future. This is human nature.

When you are treated with friendship, generosity, warmth, and sincerity, your mind is then recalibrated into a state of joyfulness, happiness, and positive emotion. You then brim with this feeling, and it spills over onto others around you.

This philosophy holds true in the workplace as well as the home. A paradigm of animosity and mean-spirited competition puts up walls that serve as impenetrable barriers to everyone's success, not just that of your adversaries or competitors. Be kind in your thoughts, your words, and your deeds. Be generous with your time, your resources, your knowledge, and your advice.

Building a reputation of being a kind individual will help to elevate you to new levels of success that would be unattainable to a cruel person. Remember: kindness, like integrity, is not a weakness. The lift you will experience is like that of an enormous 747 jetliner, wings outstretched and thunderous engines roaring. The beauty of it is, if you will adopt this way of thinking and behaving, just like that incredible passenger jet, you will bring along throngs of people on an amazing journey. What better way to spend a life than surrounded by an army of amazingly kind, compassionate, and generous people?

"Carry out a random act of kindness, with no expectation of reward, safe in the knowledge that one day someone might do the same for you."

—Princess Diana (1961-1997), British Princess of Wales

Develop your character to possess kindness. Write here how you engage in kindness in your daily life—at home, at school, in public, or in your professional life. How does kindness improve your life?

Manners

noun
Definition: the way that a person normally behaves, especially while with other people.

No one likes a blowhard. No one likes an individual who displays boorish behavior. Possessing, and demonstrating, good manners is a manifestation of behaving with class. Truly accomplished individuals make it their business to avoid making others feel inferior, insecure, awkward, or uncomfortable in any way under any circumstances. To do this would be in bad taste and demonstrate ignorance on the part of that person.

Manners are skills. Like any skill set, they can be studied, practiced, and continually improved. How you speak, eat, dress, and behave are all based

31

upon your understanding of and respect for proper manners. Those who believe that such a position is somehow not hip, old-fashioned, stodgy, or in some way affected have no idea what they are talking about. A professor of mine in cardiac surgery put it very simply: "It's nice to be nice." If this means holding a door for a lady or allowing a stranger to enter or exit an elevator first, then so be it. No deed is too small, no opportunity too fleeting to sincerely act in a good natured, well-mannered style.

If you were not raised in an environment that promoted proper etiquette, you're certainly not alone. This is no excuse, however, for you to conduct yourself in a churlish, coarse, impolite, rude, tasteless, ugly, uncivilized, or vulgar way. There are innumerable books, courses, audio programs, and online resources at your disposal, and practice makes perfect. I strongly encourage you to avail yourself of these aids in behavioral enhancement should you feel there is even the slightest chance you may still have room for improvement in this critically important area of self-development.

Being known as wealthy, powerful, or academically successful is fine, but make no mistake about it: having a reputation of being uncouth by definition precludes you from being a true success.

"Manners are a sensitive awareness of the feelings of others. If you have that awareness, you have good manners, no matter what fork you use."

—Emily Post (1872-1960), American author

Write down where and when you believe good manners are important to success.

Maturity

adjective

Definition: the quality or state of having or showing the mental and emotional qualities of an adult: having reached a final or desired state.

Champions must be mature. Maturity has little to do with age and everything to do with attitude and behavior. Mature behavior is based on mature thinking. At the crux of this issue is decision making. The high achiever is analytical and careful in their decision making. Although spontaneity is attractive on its face, in reality, it rarely leads to good judgment.

Maturity implies wisdom. Wisdom implies experience, intelligence, and making good choices. Historically, those who were seen as most wise in the tribe, village, or community were the elders. If in the past you were lucky enough to live long enough, you would have seen and experienced a lot. This extended exposure to life's ups and downs is invaluable. You would learn how to deal with long winters, short summers, bumper crops, and lost seasons of planting. You would learn how to manage illness, birth, death, marriage, children, parents, siblings, relationship problems, wealth, poverty, and more.

Even today, you would be well advised to go to your senior family members, coworkers, or friends for guidance when confronted with good and bad times alike. There is no substitute for experience.

There is, however, a phenomenon that is often referred to as having "an old soul." Customarily, this title is reserved for those who appear to be wise beyond their years. You may ask, "How does this happen?" Often, it is seen as a gift of nature or God. But is there any other way to explain this extraordinary personality trait? I believe there is. I believe maturity is a skill like any other, and it can be learned and honed. First, as with the acquisition of all skills, you must possess a desire to learn. Once this hurdle has been overcome, you must then pursue the understanding of maturity. This is largely done by emulating the behavioral patterns of those that you recognize as being wise. This requires analytical thinking. Certainly, being older is not a sufficient criterion to earn the distinction of being mature. If you look around, you will see many people of advanced age who are still behaving in an immature and under-developed manner. To determine maturity in your character, you must evaluate the lives, achievements, and status of those around you who could potentially serve as role models and mentors. Ask yourself, "What is my impression of this person?" Ask yourself, "What is this person's employment status, financial status, and social status?" Ask yourself, "What kind of personal relationships does this individual maintain?" Ask yourself, "Do I respect this man or woman?" Ask yourself, "Would I like to trade places with them if I could?"

Ask yourself, "Am I impressed by how they behave in social situations? Do I like the way they behave in professional situations?" Ask yourself, "Does this individual appear to have their life in order?" Ask yourself, "Am I impressed with this person's knowledge regarding work related issues?"

Ask yourself, "Does this person appear well-groomed, well-mannered, and knowledgeable about current events and the world in which we live?" Ask yourself, "Does this person appear to be taking good care of their health?" Ask yourself, "Is this individual eating too much, drinking too much, using illicit drugs, or smoking too much?" Ask yourself, "Is this individual engaged in indiscriminate sexual activity?" Ask yourself, "Is this person exercising regularly, eating a nutritious diet, and seeing a primary care physician with regularity?"

I encourage you to think of as many of these questions as you can and use them as a kind of litmus test of maturity. You may be surprised how many people you would like to emulate based on how you answer each of these questions. Also, consider how your friends, acquaintances, colleagues, co-workers, and family members might answer these questions if they were asking them of you.

I think these are useful exercises which can shed a lot of light on an individual's level of personal development and maturity. Try it and see how it helps you assess your own current position in personal growth as well as how it may help you to identify role models and mentors in your life. Picking the wrong mentor is potentially more detrimental than not having one at all.

"*Some age, others mature.*"

—Sean Connery (1930-),
Scottish Academy Award winning actor, and producer

To get a measure of your own level of maturity, you may also ask these same questions of yourself in the next writing exercise.

Observant

adjective
Definition: good at watching and listening: good at noticing what is going on around you

Successful people are always carefully looking at the world around them. All of science, for example, is based on observation. Through observation, you can learn a lot about cause-and- effect relationships that exist in our microcosmic environments and glean more about the human condition and experience at large. Being observant takes many forms. You may simply sit and watch the behavior of those around you, for starters. Beyond that, you may read books, magazines, and newspapers, watch television, surf the internet, visit museums, get involved in community events, etc. The opportunity to be observant is never ceasing, even in sleep. In sleep, we can watch carefully what is happening in our dreams and ask ourselves what those mental images may mean in a broader sense in the conscious world.

Successful people observe fads and trends. Winners observe what is happening in politics, business, and popular culture. Winners tune in and observe what is happening in the arts. They look at the lessons of history. Perhaps the most valuable asset the winner has is the keen ability to observe the behavioral patterns of other winners—and losers as well.

I'm reluctant to use this term *loser* very often because I would never want to give anyone the impression that anyone who is not super-successful is a loser. Nothing could be further from the truth. I believe the great majority of people in society are winners in one way or another, often in a big way. But that is not to say that there aren't any losers in the world either. There most definitely are. And it behooves the individual who wishes to achieve success to look carefully at the behavior, habits, and actions of those people as well. This may, in fact, serve the winner best, the concept of how to avoid the path trodden by the footsteps of the real loser. Stay off that path at all costs. Don't travel a road paved by negative habits and destructive behavior; it will lead you down a dead-end street or off the edge of a very high cliff.

35

❝You can observe a lot just by watching.❞

—Yogi Berra (1925-2015),
American Major League baseball player, manager, and coach

Write down what appealing behavior and habits you see in other people. Write down what kind of repellant behavior and habits you observe in people. Which behaviors fit your goals and your success story?

Open-minded

adjective
Definition: willing to consider different ideas or opinions.

Most successful people are open-minded. Most are free thinkers and receptive to new ideas. Being open-minded is the only way you will experience personal growth and change. Remember this essential fact: without change, there is no growth.

If you cannot accept and internalize new novel concepts, philosophies, and beliefs, then you are forever stuck in neutral.

Many would argue that in the real world, neutral is actually a euphemism for reverse, because if you are standing still and the highly motivated crowd is passing you, then, relatively speaking, you are traveling backwards at all times.

It is particularly important in contemporary society to take an open-minded attitude toward things. Our culture is so fast-paced that you need to be considering every new trend in thinking, business philosophy, social customs, political attitudes, etc. This is certainly not to imply that you must adopt as your own the latest fad in any of these areas, but certainly you should be aware to remain capable of making informed decisions about your personal stance. Ignorance of what is happening or patent rejection of any new idea will not be helpful to sustain relevance in a fast-moving society. Welcome views, thoughts, and theories that may be foreign to you so you can analyze, decipher, and digest them in your own way and in your own time. This is an informed position and, therefore, an empowered one.

> *People are very open-minded about new things – as long as they're exactly like the old ones.*
>
> —Charles Kettering (1876-1958),
> American inventor, engineer, and businessman

In what areas do you feel you can improve and be more open-minded?

Pioneer

noun
Definition: a person who helps create or develop new ideas, methods, etc.

Many successful people are pioneers. Many pioneers find success either while alive or, when their idea finally catches on, when they have passed away. This doesn't mean every winner must devise a new and better mousetrap or invent the microprocessor, wheel, telephone, or light bulb; winners are willing to explore uncharted territory, however.

This is about courage and desire. Pioneers will push beyond their personal comfort zone and often the comfort zone within which they were raised. If you are the first college graduate in your family, you're a pioneer and a winner. If you're the first person in your family to be self-employed or own your own business, then you're a winner and a pioneer. If you find yourself learning skills that are new to you, then you are a pioneer. If you find yourself learning nothing, going nowhere, and playing what Earl Nightingale once called, "The world's most unrewarding game: follow the follower," then you are not a pioneer.

See yourself as a pioneer, and then behave as one. Chart a new course for success. Be the captain of your own ship, and don't be shackled by the fear of losing sight of the shore. Push yourself as hard as you can, and go as far and high as you can. Don't let preconceived notions of who you are and what you are expected to achieve hinder your continuous progress.

This life you have been given is the most valuable gift any person can be given. Don't waste it. See every moment as precious, and find a way to make the most of every single day. Learn a new language, meet new people, read a new book, read magazine and journal articles which will spark your interests and desires. Be an explorer, a pioneer in your own right. Blaze a unique trail, and leave a mark in this fleeting, yet magnificent, lifetime.

> “*If you're a pioneer and you come up with something that can change the world and you turn around and say, 'I'm not going to share this idea with anyone,' then you only impact the few and not the many.*”
>
> —Cameron Sinclair (1973-), English architect

Where or how have you been a pioneer in your own life? What about the You in your success story? What are they doing that is fresh and new? Don't hold back—dream big!

Reliability

noun
Definition: the quality or state of being able to be trusted to do or provide what is needed: able to be believed.

People who succeed are reliable and demand reliability from others. Reliability and professionalism go hand in hand, as do reliability and friendship. Whether you are referring to professional or personal relationships, people always think highest of others upon whom they can always depend. Reliability is not something you can be when it is convenient; reliability is an all-or-nothing-type behavior. You are either reliable, or you are not. It's really that simple.

I cannot overstate the value intrinsic to the idea of being truly reliable. For example, why do many of us sign up for the AAA card? Because the Automobile Association of America has proven over decades that if you have the bad fortune of getting a flat tire, you can depend on them to send someone out to assist you, no matter what time of the day or night, no matter if you are in a dangerous inner-city neighborhood or far out in the countryside. AAA has built their reputation, their brand, and their success on being a reliable resource when we get into trouble.

This theme carries across many areas of life. When a woman goes into labor—day or night, weekend or holiday—she knows her obstetrician will come to the hospital to deliver her baby. That is how a professional behaves. In the rare instance where that doctor may be caught in the operating room doing surgery or out of town on vacation, he or she sees to it that someone is there in place to cover for them. This is the standard all good physicians uphold every single day of their lives.

Reliability is a powerful resource. It is difficult to achieve any significant level of real success if you demonstrate deficiency in these areas—and more. Fixing this problem is easy. Simply wake up one morning and make the decision that you will be a person everyone can depend on, and then behave accordingly.

66*When Henry Ford made cheap, reliable cars, people said, 'Nah, what's wrong with a horse?' That was a huge bet he made, and it worked.*99

—Elon Musk (1971-),
South African-born, Canadian-American entrepreneur, inventor, engineer, and businessman

Look at yourself and ask yourself how reliable you are in every facet of your life. Can your spouse count on you? Can your parents and your kids rely on you? How about your boss, co-workers, colleagues, and employees; do they see you as reliable? What about your clients; do they see you as someone they know will be there to help them sort through difficulties should they arise? If the answer to any of these questions is no, then I strongly suggest you work hard to rectify those areas in your life.

Repetition

noun

Definition: the act of saying or doing something again and again. The occurrence of an action or event.

Repetition is fundamental to achieving excellence in any given area of life. This speaks to the importance of practice. Every great musician, athlete, surgeon, pilot, dancer, singer, teacher, student, and anything else you could possibly think of understands that their greatness comes from exhaustive repetition. These are just the facts. The most accomplished concert pianist did not possess the innate talent to sit at a piano for the first time and play Rachmaninoff's *Piano Concerto #3*. Every individual must begin at the beginning and from the most basic principles in order to eventually achieve mastery. The more hours you put into practice and repetition, the more expertise you will develop and, ultimately, possess.

Some notable celebrities have built their reputations on almost Herculean efforts regarding repetition. The professional basketball playing legend Larry Bird is famous for his many hours of shooting practice. It has been said that Bird would take 500 free throws a day. His appetite for repetition was seemingly insatiable. In Malcom Gladwell's wonderful book *Outliers*, he talks about the "10,000-hour rule." Gladwell explains that numerous studies have revealed that, to get really good at something, it takes roughly ten years of dedicated work, or approximately 10,000 hours.

If I look back at my own experience in surgical training, I think it's fair to say we worked about 100 hours a week. Thankfully, laws have since been passed to limit surgical residents' work-week to eighty hours. But in those days in the late 1990s and early 2000s, it was common to work as many as 120 hours a week. But for arguments sake, let's take 100 hours since it's such a nice round number. We had three weeks of vacation each year, so assume we worked 4,900 hours each year. Since I did seven years of residency between general and cardiovascular surgery, that means I worked about 35,000 hours during the entire period of training. If we assume about a third of the day was spent in the operating room, then you can see I indeed spent more than 10,000 hours learning to perform the surgeries necessary to graduate and go out into practice. Imagine that, 10,000 hours of practice just to officially become a practitioner.

I would say most experienced surgeons would say that the first ten post-graduate years were another very important formative phase of their career. This is the time where, early in one's career, they really establish themselves as an expert and no longer a "rookie."

So, there you have it. It takes a heck of a lot of repetition to get somewhere of real stature. Success cannot be handed to you on a silver platter. Money can be handed to you. Objects can be handed to you. Many things can be handed to you, but not real success. Success is something you must earn by putting in the time. There are no shortcuts; if there are, write them down, because I'd be the first one to read that book!

> "*I tell a student that the most important class you can take is technique. A great chef is first a great technician. If you are a jeweler, or a surgeon or a cook, you must know the trade in your hand. You must learn the process. You learn it through endless repetition until it belongs to you.*"
>
> —Jacques Pépin (1935-),
> French-born American chef, television personality, and author

What will you have to do repeatedly in order for you to achieve your dream?

Reputation

noun
Definition: the common opinion people have about someone or something: the way in which people think of someone or something.

Every contact we have with the world around us is an opportunity to foster a positive or negative image about us in the eyes of those who are close to us and the public at large. Nothing good can come of having a bad reputation. Don't buy into the philosophy that says there is no such thing as bad publicity; only an idiot would live by that sort of thinking. As the old expression says, "Your reputation precedes you."

If people hear generally bad things about you in your community prior to meeting you personally, it will be more difficult to get them to think of you in a favorable light. Do all that you can to avoid this problem. Recognize that everyone you meet, from your clients to your mailman, is a potential ambassador of your brand in the world. People talk about other people; that's just the way it is. That's human nature. I'm not here to judge that behavior and label it as good or bad. I'm just here to tell you that that is reality. Knowing that, constantly remind yourself that how you behave and interact with others will be the major determining factor in how you are perceived and what your reputation will ultimately become.

Remember, it is best to have an excellent personality. Adjectives like *agreeable, benevolent, charming, cheerful, considerate, polite, reliable,* and *smart* should come to mind when people describe you to their friends and professional associates. These words of praise will get people wondering how they might get to meet you, befriend you, do business with you, and so on. No one wants to engage with someone who is unpleasant, unprofessional, incompetent, or dishonest. Those are the kinds of words you want to distance yourself from when building a reputation. Be aware of this and have it in the front of your mind each time you have a personal or professional interaction with another human being.

"You can't build your reputation on what you are going to do."

—Henry Ford (1863-1947), American industrialist and business magnate

Think about how you present to other people—classmates, business associates, friends, and family. What kind of reputation do you have? If you reflect and find flaws, write those down. Then write about how you can work on these less-than-perfect idiosyncrasies and improve upon your reputation.

Respect

---

noun
Definition: a feeling of admiring someone or something that is good, valuable, important, etc.: a feeling or understanding that someone or something is important, serious, etc., and should be treated in an appropriate way.

Successful people understand the power of respect and are respectful. You must have respect for oneself, for starters. This means becoming the best you can be. This is a process. This is an endless journey. The highest achievers are on a constant path toward enlightenment and self-improvement. You must truly believe that you are a person of great value and you deserve just as much as anyone also on this planet to be outstanding in every conceivable way. In showing respect for yourself, you can be driven to nurture and nourish your mind, body, and soul in every way possible.

Successful people are in pursuit of physical well-being, emotional stability, psychological health, academic and intellectual prowess, and financial wealth each day of their lives. They work hard at developing and sustaining fulfilling and productive personal relationships with friends, family, and business associates.

To foster these enriching relationships, you must have respect for others. You must be open to listening to differing points of view, exploring new experiences, and traveling to new places. You must have respect for different cultures, different age groups, and both sexes. Real winners rid themselves of any preconceived notions about other people, any prejudices, and any bigotry you may have adopted as a result of upbringing, exposure, and any negative previous influences. You will discover it will be very difficult to reach your maximal potential if you are handicapped with such pathological patterns of thoughts and beliefs.

Take good care of yourself. Respect yourself. Take good care of everyone around you to the best of your ability. Respect them for who they are, and, wherever possible, be open to considering conflicting and contrarian opinions and positions. This will make you stronger, richer, and more capable in general.

Respect your elders, your peers, and those who are junior to you. Respect your occupation. Respect your education. Respect your body and your health.

Respect your planet. Respect your culture and the cultures of those around you. I think respect is one area that you can't overdo. The more respect you incorporate into your personal philosophy, the more respect you will garner from others. This will give you power which you should be cautious never to abuse.

> 66*Respect your efforts, respect yourself. Self-respect leads to self-discipline. When you have both firmly under your belt, that's real power.*99
>
> —Clint Eastwood (1930-),
> American actor, director, producer, musician, and politician

Think a bit about this. Think about how you treat yourself and everyone you encounter as you go through life. What kind of respect are you looking for from people? For what do you respect people? How do you show respect?

Self-belief

noun
Definition: confidence in oneself and one's ability.

In this section, I want to be very candid with you, but only because I believe strongly in what I am going to share. The message may seem a bit tough, and it may be very different from much of what you have been told before. Here it goes: *In the best-case scenario, just about no one really cares about you.* There…I said it. Almost no one cares about you. Here's what is even worse: *In the worst-case scenario, many people you will meet actually wish to see you fail.* They wish to see you fall short of fulfilling your dreams and living up to your extraordinary true potential. Now, I may be a skeptic, but that impression is based on a lifetime's worth of real experience competing in an extremely cutthroat profession and marketplace. This doesn't mean most people are bad, and I also mean that with total sincerity. Most people are good, but all of us possess a sense of jealousy and are prone to seeing other people's success in comparison to our own performance.

This is what is generally understood to be the zero-sum game perspective. This philosophy says that if my neighbor is doing well and succeeding, he or she is not doing that in a vacuum; they are succeeding in the same environment I live in, and, therefore, if they are doing well—or, even worse, better than I am—then I must be losing. And that makes me a loser, and I can't cope with that mentally, so in the end I want them to fail so I can avoid the pain associated with my own inability to live up to my own true potential. I think most experienced individuals reading this know exactly what I'm talking about and can relate to it. Even if they can't admit they feel this way about others, most would admit people they know behave this way.

"So, what is the point of all this?" you may be asking yourself. The point is, if you are currently in a position where you feel you aren't living the dreams you have laid out for yourself, no one is coming to the rescue. The government doesn't care, and your neighbor doesn't care. Your co-workers, employees, and boss don't care either. They have their own problems and are putting all their efforts into living their own best lives. You can't blame them for that.

Therefore, all you have is *you*. You have yourself to depend on. You have yourself to believe in you. You have yourself to push you to the limit of what you can achieve. No one else is going to do it for you. So, let me be clear, if you don't have a profound concept of self-belief, you haven't got a shot in hell of becoming anything more than average. You will be doomed to an eternity of mediocrity unless you can look in the mirror and say with conviction, "I don't give a damn what anybody else thinks! I can do it! I can do absolutely anything I put my mind to if I try hard enough and stick with it long enough."

Now, we need to be reasonable. We understand that doesn't mean you can fly by jumping out of a window if you believe strongly enough in your own innate abilities. But it does mean you can successfully build a machine that flies like a couple of bicycle mechanics from Dayton, Ohio, named Orville and Wilbur Wright did in 1903. Believe strongly in *you*. If others join the cause, all the better. But always maintain an undying belief that you are as capable and as smart as anyone else. You must never allow anyone to convince you to think otherwise.

45

*"If you believe in yourself and have dedication and pride—
and never quit, you'll be a winner. The price of victory
is high but so are the rewards."*

—Paul Bryant (1913-1983), American football coach

What are your current beliefs about yourself? How do they help or hinder your journey in life?

State of mind

noun
Definition: a person's mood and the effect that mood has on the person's thinking and behavior.

People who experience success recognize the importance of working hard at controlling their state of mind. Typically, this means staying positive and optimistic. Many of the greatest teachers and motivators now and over the course of history have stressed the importance of maintaining a state of mind which is largely focused on the present. Allowing the mind to reminisce in the wonderment or suffer in the regrets of the past are not living up to their full potential in the here and now.

Conversely, although it is essential that you have goals, it is imperative that you not become consumed with fantasizing about a perfect future which has yet to reveal itself.

Our state of mind in many ways drives our reality. It is the most powerful force regarding doing what is required now in order to go where we are going. By living in the present, which is all any of us actually have, we can truly experience our lives to the fullest possible extent. Remaining upbeat, engaged, enthusiastic, and inspired are all aspects of developing and maintaining a healthy and rewarding state of mind. For many of us, this practice is a lifelong pursuit. It is a seductive and elusive ideal. It is not possible for any of us to always function at our best. Emotional dynamics are a normal part of human behavior and nature. This said, you should study and work toward mastery of these variations. If you can nurture and sustain a confident and sanguine state of mind, you can conquer any ambition within reason.

> ❝*Success is a state of mind. If you want success, start thinking of yourself as a success.*❞
>
> —Dr. Joyce Brothers (1927-2013), American psychologist and author

To fulfill your dreams, what state of mind do you believe you should be in? What practices do you put into place to help you focus?

Testimonial

noun
Definition: a written or spoken statement in which you say that you used a product or service and liked it: a written or spoken statement that praises someone's work, skill, character, etc.

Successful people are typically the subject of wonderful testimonials. These testimonials don't need to be in writing, in the newspaper, on television, or on the radio, by the way. All a testimonial really means is that someone is out there somewhere speaking well of you. This is all about building a good reputation in your personal professional and social circles.

Also, remember to give testimonials whenever you can for others whom you respect and appreciate. This is the right thing to do. The more good vibrations you put out into the universe, the more likely they are to reverberate back to you. As a friend of mine likes to say, "There's a reason the world is round." Be complimentary whenever and wherever you can. Everyone appreciates sincere praise.

Ask yourself, after you interact with someone, "I wonder how he will speak of me when I'm not around, based upon the interpersonal exchange we just shared." If your answer is, "Probably not too well," then you want to look at how you can handle things differently if you are ever put in a similar situation again in the future.

The more testimonials there are circulating out there on your behalf, the more fulfilling and abundant lifestyle you are bound to enjoy.

> "*Becoming part of someone's testimonial is the highest honor.*"
> —Jim Rohn (1930-2009),
> American entrepreneur, author, and motivational speaker

What kind of impression do you want to leave with people you have encountered? While you develop your dreams, think about how you wish to be seen and known among your peers. What kind of character do you want to be? Charming? Educated? Knowledgeable? Generous, kind? Powerful, clever? Serious?

Training

noun

Definition: a process by which someone is taught the skills needed for an art, profession, or job.

Here, I feel it's useful to take a thoroughbred racehorse as an example. I would say most people in the United States, even if they are not sports fans or horse racing fans, have heard of the legendary Secretariat. This magnificently talented animal won the Triple Crown in 1973. For those who are not familiar with this illustrious title, it had been twenty-five years since another horse had accomplished this daunting feat. It goes without saying that Secretariat was an extraordinary physical specimen and the offspring of an illustrious pedigree. That said, this champion underwent extraordinary training to reach the pinnacle of his sport. He was trained by Lucien Laurin, a Hall of Fame thoroughbred horse trainer.

I have come to learn that top trainers, like many highly successful individuals, tend to keep their cards close to their vest. What Secretariat's particular training regimen was, I'm not sure any of us will ever know. That secret may have died with Mr. Laurin in Key West in 2000. What is certain is that, despite his physical gifts, Secretariat did train. The group of individuals charged with his care were surely extremely cautious about every aspect of his daily routine.

A horse of that caliber will have a very specific diet designed to maintain and optimize characteristics such as energy, endurance, muscular strength, explosiveness, gastrointestinal health, temper, etc. This equine athlete will be ensured proper rest and recovery as a part of his training program. There will be a prudent amount of exercise involved, to be sure. I would venture to guess that some of these workouts would be more strenuous than others. Appropriate warming up of such a creature must be an essential component of exercise, as I know cooling down also is. Generous amounts of massage to keep the large muscles supple is a routine part of any great racehorse's lifestyle. Also important is being exposed to the correct environment, with coats and blankets employed as necessary to keep the animal's core temperature at an optimal level.

The point is that even for someone like myself, who knows literally nothing about training such a competitor, I can only imagine the combination of art and science that goes into bringing even the most gifted specimen to perform at his best.

In my reading to prepare this section, I came to learn that Secretariat, although the Triple Crown winner, was not undefeated. One of his losses came prior to the Triple Crown, when it was discovered he had an abscess in his mouth. Perhaps for this reason he was not on his best on race day and was unsuccessful that day.

Each of us who expects to achieve great things must train in a way commensurate with victory. To lie on the couch and hope for success to knock at our front door is not only improbable but more likely impossible. Get the exercise you need to be at your best physically. Take a nutritious diet that will give you the strength and stamina required of a busy and competitive individual. Get the education you need by doing the reading and study necessary to afford you the skills needed in your particular area of expertise.

And remember that your training must include a healthy dose of rest, relaxation, and recuperation if you plan to go the long distance in this life. My best advice is that the most successful people I have ever known have been the best trained on top of whatever natural ability they were born with. I suggest you behave the same way to realize your full potential.

>   ❝*I hated every minute of training, but I said, 'Don't quit. Suffer now and live the rest of your life as a champion.'*❞
>
>   —Muhammad Ali (1942-2016), American professional boxer

It's your success story. What training do you need to engage in to realize your dreams of success? It's perfectly fine to dream, but there is more to it than that.

Vision

noun
Definition: something that you imagine; a picture you see in your mind

Successful people have a clear vision of their dreams, goals, and desires. You must have vision for anything to become a truth.

In Napoleon Hill's classic best seller, *Think and Grow Rich*, he teaches that, "Thoughts are things." These thoughts typically come to us in our mind's eye as a picture. This image is the vision which all the great successes possess. Walt Disney, one of the great visionaries of the twentieth century, was quoted as saying, "If you can dream it, you can do it." The dream he refers to is the vision. Just imagine, Walt Disney had to see Disneyland and Disney World in his mind before he could build them. The idea, the concept must have first begun as an ethereal vision in this extraordinary man's mind.

The astounding part about this notion of having a vision is that all new things begin this way. Just think about that for a second. Someone had to envision and conceive of the wheel before its initial manufacture and application. Someone had to conceive of the abacus in their mind before anyone had ever held one in their hand. Someone had to imagine an airplane in flight carrying passengers before it could be so. And the same could be said for radio, television, automobile, personal computers, and the internet.

I love thinking about this. I just can't get over what a powerful tool we have been given: the human mind, so full of imagination and creativity. Just think, you have the extraordinary ability to see something in your mind which has never before existed in the universe. Doesn't that inspire you to start thinking and see what you can come up with? The answer to everything is out there, it's just that no one has seen it yet in their mind's eye. Who knows what you might contribute to the world if you would just take the time to sit somewhere and quietly think! Just take the time to sit and look inside and see what image appears on that wonderful movie screen inside your magnificent brain. Currently, I'm in the process of working on something I saw: this book. I still can't get over the fact that I'm hundreds of pages and more than 125,000 words into seeing it come to life at the moment I type this sentence. Amazing!

Have courage. Use your imagination and open yourself up to the beauty and wonder of your own marvelous vision. Then make the decision to follow the vision through to completion. Don't be fearful of judgment or even how you are going to achieve what you set out to do. Just get started and follow the path. You'll be astonished by what you are capable of if you just believe in yourself and follow the vision. Disney also said, "All our dreams can come true, if we have the courage to pursue them."

> ❝ *Your vision will become clear only when you can look into your own heart. Who looks outside, dreams; who looks inside, awakes.* ❞
>
> —Carl Jung (1875-1961), Swiss psychiatrist and psychotherapist

What visions have you seen lately? Which vision inspires you? What have you dreamed up for yourself? What does your success story look like? In what field, in what capacity, do you see yourself fulfilling your vision? It all starts here. Write it out.

Vocabulary

noun

Definition: the words that make up a language; all the words known and used by a person; words that are related to a particular subject.

You must develop a vocabulary that facilitates success in your given vocation and avocation. You must be able to communicate properly with the community around you to optimize personal effectiveness in achieving goals.

Take a politician, for example. A politician may have a brilliant mind, excellent ideas, and the noblest of intentions, but if he or she does not possess a vocabulary which will both express their ideals and intentions, it is unlikely that they will ever be elected and, therefore, will be rendered ineffective in their ability to put their plans into action. It is essential that this vocabulary is accessible to the people to whom you are speaking. This is again particularly true in the case of politicians.

Another area where vocabulary is essential is near and dear to my heart. In the world of medicine, physicians build and develop a cast vocabulary specific to our profession. Our job is to care for people, the vast majority of whom are laypeople as it relates to medical jargon.

Therefore, you must possess two vocabularies to be an excellent clinical physician. The first is the vocabulary of a properly educated and informed doctor, and the second is the language of the people. Too often, doctors, lawyers, accountants, mechanics, electricians, etc. make the mistake of speaking to their clientele in their professional vocabulary. The truly effective communicator can translate his or her specialized vocabulary into a language the listener can easily recognize and understand. This skill is too frequently under-appreciated. It is a great gift to be able to present a subject in such a way that the intended message is getting across completely.

The easiest ways of building a strong vocabulary are by reading and spending time with those people who speak that language. Whether you intend to learn a foreign language or a specific set of terms related to a favorite hobby, read up on the subject extensively and avail yourself to individuals who are already fluent in that language. This process is a never-ending gift. No person can know too many words.

Perhaps the easiest way to acquire more and better words is to read as much as you can. The inimitable Earl Nightingale said, "The man who does not read is no better off than the man who cannot read." Ah, what a wonderful statement. So concise, yet so effective. Now there was a man who possessed a superior vocabulary and had a rare gift in communicating with and connecting to people. Nightingale produced a wildly popular spoken word recording of "The Strangest Secret" and connected with people as a beloved radio personality. He was a writer and a speaker, mainly addressing subjects of human character development, motivation, excellence, and a meaningful existence. He is known as the "Dean of Personal Development."

We should all make people like Mr. Nightingale our role models.

"Communication skills are very important in climbing the pyramid of life. Your skill with and use of language are things you can't hide...vocabulary correlates with income and success. A person's knowledge and language go together."

—Earl Nightingale (1921-1989),
Motivational speaker, radio personality, and author

What do you think about your vocabulary? Does it need improvement?

Wealth

noun

Definition: a large amount of money and possessions; the value of all the property, possessions, and money that someone or something has, a large amount or number.

Many of us desire and accumulate wealth. In a country like the United States, many things come at a financial cost, and it is therefore most helpful to have a plentitude of money at one's disposal to avail oneself to these products, services, and experiences.

Historically, the necessities were foremost in the mind of the human being. These fundamental requirements include food, water, clothing, and shelter. Other highly valuable, if not essential, aspects include fire and relationships with others. Over the last several millennia, civilizations around the globe developed various systems of monetary exchange and relative value. This now global system establishes a price for just about anything you can imagine.

In contemporary America, a successful individual may be motivated to provide his children with the best available education. Customarily, this would mean living in a municipality with the highest quality public schools or taking advantage of a private school education of some sort. The best municipalities tend to have high taxes, and the best private secondary institutions tend to be quite costly. Therefore, if this is something that resonates as an important consideration to you, ample sums of money will be required. Furthermore, a nice home, automobile, and clothing will require additional dollars to acquire. Beyond this, health care—including medical, dental, and eye care—would be a very nice addition to what you could expect to provide for yourself. These, too, require funds. Beyond this, you will need to eat. Food comes at a cost as well.

Then there are so many other wonderful things that life offers that we may want to partake in. Things like sports, recreational activities, hobbies, travel, vacations, excursions, advanced education, entertaining, and being entertained, just to name a few, are certainly part of what I like to enjoy in my life. How about you? Do any of those things sound appealing to you? I bet they do. If not, that's fine too. You'll need less money to get along. There is wealth in knowledge, family, friends, and a myriad of experiences that do not cost much at all but can be very rewarding, like a ride out to the country to see a blanket of stars overhead. But the rest of us are going to need some serious dough. Therefore, please be cautious of anyone who tells you money is not important.

To some, that may be true. It simply may not be a life goal to attain wealth, but to live simply and simply live. Typically, however, some people who think money is not important either have no money and are trying to cope with their relative ineffectiveness in that area, or they have so much money they have lost sight of its true value in the marketplace and in society as a whole.

My personal experience has been that life, especially when lived to the fullest based on my personal needs, can indeed be quite expensive. You may wish to live a modest existence with only the essentials. If that makes you happy, then wonderful. There is much to be said for enjoying the simple things in life, which often help create a sense of contentment and peace. But for those of us who seek more adventure in the world, to experience life for all it may have to offer, more money will be needed.

> *Money cannot be sought directly. Like happiness, money is an effect. It is the result of a cause, and the cause is valuable service.*
>
> —Earl Nightingale (1921-1989),
> motivational speaker, radio personality, and author

In your success story, how do you see yourself attaining wealth? Sit down and begin to devise a plan of action whereby you may accumulate some wealth. This will enable you to take full advantage of all the marvelous objects and experiences out there and being enjoyed by so many. You may have thought to yourself, "If they can have access to such a wonderful odyssey, then why not me? And, as importantly, why not now?"

Good questions. Start there!

Wisdom

noun

Definition: knowledge that is gained by having many experiences in life; knowledge of what is proper or reasonable; good sense or judgment; the soundness of an action or decision with regard to the application of experience, knowledge, and good judgment.

Successful people are always seeking the wisdom of others and hope to one day become wise. Wisdom is one of those things that can only come over the course of time. Wisdom and experience come hand in hand. Perhaps the only way to accelerate the process of becoming wise is by nurturing relationships with other individuals whom we respect for their wisdom. This is the process of mentorships, and it comes in all forms. A parent or other relative may be a mentor. A friend of any age may be a mentor. Your mentor need not be older than you to impart wisdom; they simply need to have more experience and knowledge in a given area than you so the learning process can take place.

Wisdom is largely related to judgment. You can be knowledgeable about a particular subject but still demonstrate poor decision making. That is not wisdom. It is what you do with the knowledge you have come to possess which will determine whether you are wise. Some people, no matter how old they grow, never get wise. Some people demonstrate wisdom that seems to be well developed for their tender years. This is a skill and a gift. The gift of wisdom is not bestowed upon each of us. Work hard at developing this characteristic, though. Look to the people you respect and emulate their behavior. This may be the best way to cultivate the nature of the wise person. If you can achieve this lofty goal, it will help you enormously to successfully navigate the oft-times troubled waters that make up the sea of life.

&&*Wisdom cannot be imparted. Wisdom that a wise man attempts to impart always sounds like foolishness to someone else... knowledge can be communicated, but not wisdom. One can find it, live it, do wonders through it, but one cannot communicate and teach it.*&&

—Hermann Hesse (excerpt from "Siddhartha") (1877-1962)
German-born Swiss poet, novelist, and painter

In your success story, does the main character in your story possess wisdom? If so, how is it manifested? How does a wise person act? How does this wisdom help them with their goals and aspirations? How will wisdom enhance your life? Write down some ideas below.

Yes

adverb

Definition: used to give a positive answer or reply to a question; used to express agreement with an earlier statement or to say that statement is true.

To be a success, you must have the courage to say: yes! Without the word yes, nothing happens. No is a conversation ender. No is a deal breaker. No is a momentum killer. No is safe. No is fearful. No is cautious. No, as pointed out elsewhere in this book, is sometimes the correct answer, but no cannot be the only answer in the armamentarium of the winning personality.

Yes is daring. Yes is accommodating. Yes is fun. Yes is happy. Yes opens the door to opportunity and possibility. Yes is adventurous. Yes is sexy. Yes is the beginning of every great journey. Yes is exciting. Yes is risky. Yes is the only possible pathway to success.

Learn to say yes. More importantly, learn to say yes when yes is the right answer. If you can master this one skill, the world is your oyster. Two very simple answers to so many of life's most important questions: yes and no. Knowing just when to use each of these words, intermingled with the occasional *maybe*, and you're on your way to a lifetime of abundance, wonder, fulfillment, fantasy, and intrigue. But how do you know when to use each of these critically important terms? Well, that is really the crux of the matter, isn't it? The best advice I can offer is: let an abundance of experience be your teacher.

Just as a great hitter in baseball must stand in the batter's box thousands of times and see many thousands of pitches before they become an expert at selecting which pitch to swing at, with only a fraction of a second to decide, you too must participate robustly in the game of life. You need to see many opportunities come and go. Watch what happens to those around you as they make certain decisions, and let this guide you.

Make your own choices and see where they lead. Remember: a calm sea never made a skilled sailor. There is no perfect formula on when to say yes or when to use no.

Just be certain that if you expect to produce extraordinary results, you'll have to use yes quite generously. It's impossible to play it safe all the time and achieve much of anything.

The guy sitting on the bench in the dugout will never strike out, but then again no one knows who the hell he is or why he's even there. I suggest you do everything you can to avoid being that guy.

> *"The big question is whether you are going to be able to say yes to your adventure."*
>
> —Joseph Campbell (1904-1987),
> American mythologist, professor, writer, and lecturer

Okay, this is YOUR success story; will you say yes to the adventure? Where will you begin? What is the most important thing to say yes to in your life? What is the "yes!" that will start you off on your new adventure?

Section Two:

Setting Goals to Determine the Setting of Your Story

In storytelling, where and when your story takes place are as important as the characters living in that setting (the main character in your success story being, of course, *you*). Describing the physical characteristics of the location or background of your story is important, but that is not enough; there are other elements that must also be considered. *Setting* has to do with you living in that setting as well. Where do you see yourself living when going for this dream of yours?

For instance, I love the way Alaska looks, but I don't see myself living there—ever. Some elements to consider when you are creating the setting of your success story are physical location, time-period, and lifestyle. While you think of the *where* and the *when* of your story, you will also think about how to go about setting your goals. You'll want to create a time frame, perhaps, to give yourself a deadline to reach.

As Napoleon Hill said, *"A goal is a dream with a deadline."*

The rule, simply put, is: *Set your goals where your heart tells you.* Ask of life exactly what you want. As far as we know, we only get one chance at living our best life. Don't sell yourself short, and don't be afraid to work your ass off to get what you want.

When you can create a clear plan of what you want, and then match that with unwavering industriousness, there is absolutely no limit to what you can accomplish in this wonderful world of ours. Don't be afraid to ask for a lot, and never fear doing the work required to earn it. And remember to avoid the catastrophic miscalculation of working like a dog with no particular ambitions, desires, or goals in mind. This will leave you with a broken back, a broken heart, and probably financially broke as well.

Decision

noun
Definition: a choice that you make after thinking about something

Successful people are decision makers. Decision making takes many shapes and forms. Whether you must decide to take the final shot at the final buzzer or to invest $50,000,000 in a new cargo ship as a freighting company considers expansion, decisions are a mandatory part of doing business and succeeding.

Deferring decisions, especially important decisions, to a higher-ranking individual is a hallmark of the individual who lacks what it takes to really rise to the top. Anyone can make simple decisions, but those aren't really decisions at all, are they? Ordering more envelopes for the company when we are out of envelopes doesn't require any real decisiveness.

This sort of activity is mechanical, and so many of us who believe we are making significant decisions every day really aren't.

True decisions require difficult deliberation and weighing of pros and cons. Decisions are made when you are setting goals, and tough decisions that consider risk/reward relationships are invariably left to the real leaders. It should be pointed out that this does not mean all the decisions will be correct or, furthermore, the result will be what was intended even if the logic were correct. In other words, the fact that Michael Jordan elects to take the game-winning shot at the buzzer doesn't mean the ball is going to go into the basket. Missing the shot does not necessarily mean he should have passed to someone else, nor does it mean he will not make the same decision in a similar situation in the future.

Decision making is tough. When the ramifications of decisions fall on your shoulders, the weight can be oppressive at times. Winners get stronger from carrying this burden; they do not collapse beneath the pressure of being the decision maker. Winners live and die by the decisions they make, and they ultimately need to stand by, and learn from, those choices. The truth of the matter is, successful individuals are constantly moving forward and, therefore, cannot be indecisive in their approach to their professional or personal lives. They must decide whether it is better to buy a home or rent forever, whether to move to a new city to follow the money and the promotion or stay where they are because it is comfortable and they are closer to their family, etc. These are not always easy or obvious choices, but successful people are willing to make them and take responsibility for the outcome in the long run.

Decision making is a learnable skill like any other, and aptitude comes with experience. The sooner you elect to make the tough decisions and take ownership of the consequences, good or bad, the sooner you will see yourself growing and advancing in every imaginable way.

> ❝*Truly successful decision-making relies on a balance between deliberate and instinctive thinking.*❞
>
> —Malcolm Gladwell (1963-),
> British-born Canadian journalist, author, and speaker

Decisions must be made when you are setting your goals. What schools are you applying to? Which profession are you going into? As far as your setting, where do you see yourself working or raising a family? How many years are you giving yourself to achieve your set goals?

Eager

---

adjective
Definition: very excited and interested: feeling a strong and impatient desire to do something or for something.

Successful people are eager to learn, to grow, to change, to expand, to try. They are eager about just about everything. In my experience with ultra-high achievers over the years, I have noticed they almost all have a hungry, thirsty, almost impatient sort of yearning to do more and move to the next level.

At each level of success, the barriers seem to get more challenging to overcome. I think of this again in terms of my experience in medicine. There needs to be an inner fire burning to take the individual from high school, through college, medical school, general surgical residency, and then on to super-advanced fields like cardiovascular and neurosurgery, for example. Another good analogy would be that of the race car driver, perhaps beginning as a child in a soap box derby, then go-carts, then Formula 4, Formula 3, Formula 2, and finally, for the truly elite athlete, Formula 1. And then, at that ultimate level, the field begins once again to declare itself from the annual world champion to the last place finisher in terms of points for the season.

You cannot assume such positions without an inner eagerness to get out of bed in the morning and give it absolutely everything you've got. This may be in the professional kitchen, the research laboratory, on the floor of the stock exchange. It doesn't matter what the arena is. The sense of competition and effort that go hand in hand with eagerness is irrefutable. You must want it deep down in your gut, in your soul if you want to be a success. No one is going to have the desire or energy to push you to the loftiest of goals in life. That requires inner drive and desire. That may be "God-given" or it may develop with time; but if you're not eager to be the best in your pursuit, in my opinion, you haven't got a chance of getting past mediocrity.

> *"I arise full of eagerness and energy, knowing well what achievement lies ahead of me."*
>
> —Zane Grey (1872-1939), American novelist and dentist

What are you eager about? What passions drive you on? What motivates your eagerness?

Effective

adjective

Definition: producing a result that is wanted.

It is essential to be effective in order to succeed. They go hand in hand. Otherwise, without an effective outcome, no matter how much work or effort is put into a project, you are only generating heat. Heat is lost energy, and that is never good. The desired result must ultimately be achieved if effectiveness is to be realized.

To be effective, you must be goal-oriented and you must set goals for yourself. Understand clearly where the finish line is. Coming up six inches short in a marathon is not adequate, unfortunately. We have seen this so many times. Think of the people you have known who took a year or two of college and then dropped out, the friend who had a fantastic idea for a business that never opened its doors or sold a single product, the associate with a genius idea for an invention but never went through with the patent application and approval process. These are the common acts of ineffective individuals.

This again has to do with completion and follow-through. Good ideas and good starts are worthless, no matter how lofty your goals. It may sound harsh, but the only thing that ultimately counts in this world is where things finish. That is why it is important to set goals you are eager about, feel passionate about. And more, you must figure out how to attain these goals and how to do it most effectively.

There is no point to a smooth airplane flight that comes up 100 yards short of the runway and puts you in the harbor. This is not an effective job of piloting. No one cares about who leads in the first 499 miles of the Indianapolis 500 or who wins the first two stages of the Triple Crown thoroughbred racing series. Effective individuals are finishers. They get the job done. This is an imperative facet of the high achieving personality, the ability to demonstrate effectiveness again and again over the course of a lifetime.

<blockquote>

"The most effective way to do it, is to do it."

—Amelia Earhart (1897-1937), American aviation pioneer and author
</blockquote>

Have you figured out what you want to do and how to go about doing it? Write down your ideas as to what are the most effective ways to go about achieving your goals you have set.

Remember: *most effective* does not necessarily mean *easiest.*

Enjoy

verb
Definition: to take pleasure in (something).

A legitimate winner enjoys life. It's that simple. The game of life is not about who dies with the most chips, but who has had the most meaningful, enjoyable ride. This means spending time with those you love and who love you.

If you don't have people like that in your life, get some.

It is essential to travel, see different parts of our country and the world, savor great foods, participate in sports and other leisure activities. This is why you work so hard, so you can thoroughly experience all the magnificence life has to offer. Life is so beautiful—experience it to its fullest. Share these moments with your friends and family. A good meal always tastes best when it is experienced with others.

Don't fall into the trap that we are here only to work, only to study, only to earn and to save. There must be a balance to life. The motivation to work hard should be in the desire to afford wonderful happenings and events. Dream big dreams. Set lofty goals for yourself in terms of the pleasurable activities you would like to take part in. Do exceptional things. Exercise what Brian Tracy calls "blue sky thinking" and don't live on a place called "Someday Isle." In other words, don't be a person who goes from saying, "Someday I'll do this," or "Someday I'll do that," to a person who regretfully admits, "I wish I had done this," or "I wish I had done that."

I wonder what enjoyable experiences you would share in if you would unlock your inner desires. Would you fly in a hot air balloon? Would you get your pilot's license? Would you go to Paris in the springtime? Would you cruise around the world? Would you buy a ticket on Virgin Galactic for a space flight? Would you plan a simple picnic in the park with your significant other for the first time in years—or maybe for the first time ever? Do you even own a proper picnic basket and blanket? These pleasures need not be costly or extravagant to hold an immeasurable degree of value.

64

Be focused on planning and then living such events. This is your life. As they say, "This is not a dress rehearsal." You will never have these days, weeks, months, and years back. Use them wisely and get from them all you can.

Again, life can be an unimaginably remarkable journey, but it won't play out that way by chance. You need to be fixated on the realization of a lifetime of enjoyment and pleasurable occasions. Life is for living and enjoying. Don't miss the whole point of what we're doing here.

❝We are at our very best, and we are happiest, when we are fully engaged in work we enjoy on the journey toward the goal we've established for ourselves. It gives meaning to our time off and comfort to our sleep. It makes everything else in life so wonderful, so worthwhile.❞

—Earl Nightingale (1921-1989),
American radio personality, writer, speaker, and author

Sit down and think hard about what you want to have, do, and see. Make a list, and on that list put dates alongside each of these desires. Make sure that each one happens for you. No one else is going to see to it that they actually materialize for you.

Evaluate

verb
Definition: to judge the value or condition of (someone or something) in a careful and thoughtful way.

Those who succeed learn to evaluate opportunities and situations carefully.

There is a tendency, particularly early on, for ambitious individuals to jump right in and make "snap" decisions. Although decision making and decisiveness are key elements to high achievement, careful consideration is essential and can take a significant amount of time.

This kind of serious evaluation falls under the category of "slow thinking." This is, in and of itself, a vast and complex topic which has been the subject of much scholarly activity and debate. Here I would direct you to the fascinating books *Blink* by Malcolm Gladwell and *Thinking, Fast and Slow* by Nobel laureate Daniel Kahneman. Here you will learn much more about the power, strengths, weaknesses, and pitfalls of making quick, intuitive decisions or taking longer to deeply ponder decisions you are making.

> ❝*True genius resides in the capacity for evaluation of uncertain, hazardous, and conflicting information.*❞
>
> —Winston Churchill (1874-1965),
> English Prime Minster of the United Kingdom

In the area of evaluating opportunities, recognize there is fast and slow thinking. Before making a decision and committing time, money, or other resources to it, simply ask yourself if this is an appropriate place to exercise fast thinking or slow thinking. Take the time to slow yourself down at least enough to consider and evaluate this question. This tool will pay enormous dividends in building your best future.

Experiment

verb

Definition: to do a scientific test in which you perform a series of actions and carefully observe their effects: to try a new activity or a new way of doing or thinking about something.

Successful people are always experimenting. They are changing things to see what works best. They are setting new goals and trying to achieve new heights. Seeing how far or how high you can go is an experiment in itself. If you are satisfied with the status quo, there is no need for experimentation.

Examples of experiments a successful person might undertake are: dietary changes, changes in exercise routines, changes in investment strategies, changes in approach to a personal relationship, starting new streams of incomes in his or her business, etc. It is essential to understand that an experiment is just that: an experiment. No one knows the result of an experiment. Sometimes the outcome will be positive; at other times, it will be negative. But you will learn from these experiences and move forward, more knowledgeable, nimbler, and more effective than ever before.

Don't be afraid to experiment, makes changes, take risks. This is the behavior of successful people. This does not mean being haphazard, chaotic, or self-destructive. Experimentation should have a logical design with limits to downside potentials. Nonetheless, there will always be some calculated risk involved. Don not let this deter you from growth and the realization of your full personal potential.

> ❝*All life is an experiment. The more experiments you make, the better.*❞
>
> —Ralph Waldo Emerson (1803-1882), American essayist, lecturer, and poet

Experiment with your setting. Think about that character; what would that person do in life if they were to test things out? If you've ever wondered what it was like to live overseas, go for it. Want to lose fifty pounds before you are fifty? Try it! Set goals and experiment with those goals. What would you like to try? Write it down; think it through.

Extraordinary

adjective
Definition: very unusual: very different from what is normal: extremely good or impressive.

This word reminds us that we must understand the stark truth which makes up the foundation of success: if you are ordinary and only do ordinary things, you should expect ordinary results. It would be wonderful if we could experience extraordinary results with ordinary or "infra-ordinary" effort or skills, but this is a myth. The sooner you liberate yourself from such misconceptions, the sooner you can begin to realize the benefits of a life filled with happiness, health, professional fulfillment, and financial independence.

The world renowned motivational expert and coach Tony Robbins has become famous for teaching that if you desire massive change in your life you must take massive action immediately. I couldn't agree more with this philosophy. Now, it must be said you cannot do everything instantaneously. You cannot simply fold your arms and blink your eyes and become a huge success in whatever area you wish. But you can indeed make that massive change philosophically and intellectually in an instant. That is the key.

The fundamental basis for all the change must begin with the conscious and deliberate decision to change everything, radically and right now.

In the end, the actual process of change will be made up of innumerable tiny steps over a long period of time, but the belief component *must* be a decision which only takes a fraction of a second.

I can still recall the moment, while in college, when I made the clear and unshakable decision to become a cardiac surgeon. From that moment on, it was not *whether* I would become a heart surgeon, it was merely a question of *how* I would do it and how long it would take. I never doubted, from that instant forward, my goal would be realized. It was as real to me as my need to breathe air. I had fully internalized the goal and made it a part of my fabric as a human being.

Those decisive periods in your life lead to all future gains and successes. It is impossible to overemphasize the importance of this kind of thinking. It is fully empowering and paves the way for extraordinary achievement. After truly internalizing the idea that the goal will be accomplished as imagined in your mind's eye, you then set out and do absolutely everything necessary to make that dream a reality. You take massive action in your life to produce massive change and to yield extraordinary reward.

"Consume those 'popular' things, and you'll be part of the common, average pack. But that's ordinary. There's nothing wrong with ordinary. I just prefer to shoot for extraordinary."

—Darren Hardy (1971-),
American motivational speaker, author, and publisher

68

Ready to make your life extraordinary? Excellent. How do you go about it? Think of what extraordinary things you wish to do. In your success story, create the extraordinary setting you are in in your wildest dreams—the what, the where, the who—and write them all out here.

Family

---

noun
Definition: a group of people who are related to each other.

Successful individuals understand the incalculable value family brings to the basic richness of one's life. Loneliness and success are, in my opinion, paradoxical concepts. That's not to say most winners recognize a need for periods of solitude.

It is in the times of being alone you have an opportunity to listen to your inner voice and thoughts and often have a chance to reflect on the importance of the relationships you have with others. The relationships may be between parent and child, siblings, grandparents, cousins, friends, or lovers. But these personal interactions are the meshwork that forms the ground for all of life's most pleasurable and meaningful feelings, experiences, and emotions. Without such connections, there can only be a limited extent to happiness and contentment.

Broken or injured family relationships almost always carry with them wounds which damage the well-being of the healthy and well-adjusted individual. My suggestion is to work hard at maintaining and nurturing these invaluable members of your personal microcosm. Cherish them and treat them well. Do all you can to find forgiveness when necessary, charity, generosity, and hospitality whenever possible, and by all means, work hard to keep lines of communication open at all costs. There is nothing costlier than the loss of the love of someone close to you. This is not always easy.

Like all things of great value, this will require hard work. It's worth it. There is no object to replace a warm and mutually rewarding family dynamic.

> *"Happiness is having a large, loving, caring, close-knit family in another city."*
>
> —George Burns (1896-1996), American comedian, actor, and writer

People don't usually dream up a family, but you can set goals to improve relations with your family members. How do you think you can bring your family closer together? What is your idea of a successful relationship with family or your group of close friends? How does having family affect you?

Friendship

noun
Definition: a friendly feeling or attitude: kindness or help given to someone.

One of the most valuable things in life is friendship. If you achieve success by making numerous enemies, you haven't won the game. Attaining financial or professional success and having no one to share your good fortune with is a sign you have been doing something seriously wrong. It is fundamental to be surrounded by good people and that you enjoy the company of others as much as they enjoy being around you. It is impossible to find true fulfillment in a lonely existence. Be sure to be good to those around you as you ascend the ladder of success.

As the adage goes, it can be very lonely at the top. Be sure to bring some friends along with you for the wonderful climb. Sharing the view from that high perch is much more pleasurable than viewing it all alone.

> *"Never refuse any advance of friendship, for if nine out of ten bring you nothing, one alone may repay you."*
>
> —Hafez (1325-1390), Persian poet

In many stories, there is always a true friend or a group of friends who move the plot along and who come to the aid of the protagonist. Who are the people in your life that make up this group of friends? Who are your good friends? Are they loyal? Are they supportive? Write about your friends who are with you through thick and thin. How do they help you reach your goals? What kind of friend are you? Do you encourage your friends to be and to do their best and to live a good life?

Goals

noun
Definition: something you are trying to do or achieve.

Successful people are goal-driven. Being goal-oriented keeps you moving forward on life's path. It may even be fair to say that highly successful people are goal-obsessed. Each time one milepost in life is reached, they are looking out on the horizon for the next marker of achievement and progress.

Highly productive persons are constantly taking stock of where they stand currently and what their station is in life at any given point. Based on this information, they postulate where they can go from here and what more they can realistically achieve in a reasonable measure of time. That is one of the key elements of successful goal setting and achieving: setting *realistic* goals for where you stand currently in life. If your goal is to be 175 pounds in two weeks, that's a perfectly acceptable goal for someone who weighs 180 pounds or 182 pounds perhaps. But if the individual who would like to see the scale read 175 currently weighs 302 pounds, that's not going to happen in two weeks. Unrealistic goal setting is not only unhelpful, but it is, in fact, radically counterproductive in that it can cause significant emotional demoralization.

Set goals regularly, but make sure they are not preposterous.

You may have a long-term goal of becoming a multi-millionaire, but if you are currently overdrawn on your only bank account, first set a goal to have a balance of zero. When you get to zero, make your goal to have the discipline to save $100. Continue to work from there. It is not useful or instructive in any way to think you will go from a debt-laden circumstance to having $5,000,000 in the bank in six months. In lieu of hitting the lottery as a result of sheer luck…that ain't gonna happen.

> *Most people are not going after what they want. Even some of the most serious goal seekers and goal setters, they're going after what they think they can get. Set a goal to achieve something that is so big, so exhilarating that it excites you and scares you at the same time.*
>
> —Bob Proctor (1934-),
> Canadian-American philosopher, entrepreneur, author, and teacher

Write out your goals. What are they? Change of job? Weight loss? Weight gain? Marriage? Divorce? Travel to all continents? Big or small, having and working towards goals builds character and success.

Growth

noun

Definition: The process of developing or maturing physically, mentally, or spiritually.

Embrace and nurture growth. Growth of many types is essential to getting better, remaining competitive, being the best you can be, and keeping life interesting. Without growth, there is no change, and if you are not changing, you cannot be improving. Life is a fascinating journey and there is so much to learn. If you are learning, you are growing. If you are sharing, you are growing. If you are giving, you are growing. If you are receiving, you are growing. Growth is an absolute must in order to achieve personal development and betterment.

You may choose to grow regarding physical fitness, intellect, spiritual awareness, financial success, business achievement, personal relationships, inner peace, personal fulfillment, and satisfaction. There are no limits to how you can grow; nor is there any limit to how *much* you can grow. Growing physically is an obvious aspect of moving from childhood into adulthood. But this measurable growth should serve as a metaphor for you internally for the rest of your life.

For those of us who elected to pursue higher education, in my case fifteen years after graduating high school, academic growth was a natural part of the process of getting older. That said, whether or not you are in school, you should always be growing, expanding, maturing, and developing intellectually, emotionally, and psychologically. There is an endless stockpile of resources available to all of us in the contemporary world. There are books, magazines, blogs, websites, YouTube videos, night classes, etc. I urge you take advantage of some or all of these incredibly powerful and empowering tools to foster your own personal growth as long as you are alive. It is the most rewarding, wonderful feeling in the world.

You are not as good now as you could be a week or a month from now. There is no limit to your extraordinary potential for growth. Accept this philosophy as your own, and tap into the energy available to all of us. Let that positive energy propel you to new heights, heights you never before believed were attainable. Don't stand still. Don't stay the same. Stagnation is not the modus of super-achievers; it is the way of the ordinary crowd, and you should have no intention of being amongst them.

66*The key to growth is the introduction of higher dimensions of consciousness into our awareness.*99

—Lao Tzu (570 BC -?), Chinese poet and philosopher

How does your character in your story change for the better? What challenges help them grow? What changes the person you wish to be? Whether you are creating a character as an exercise to know yourself better, or you are writing down actual examples in your own life, writing down ways to expand your horizons is a great way to develop yourself and help you define and recognize what you want from life.

Health

noun
Definition: the condition of being well or free from disease.

Health is by far the most valuable possession you can acquire. Without health, there is nothing. Without health, there can be no happiness, no pleasure, no future. It is incumbent upon the successful individual to work hard at achieving and maintaining good health. Self-destructive behaviors must be purged from the lifestyle of the high achiever. Illicit drug use, excessive consumption of alcohol, and gluttonous eating must be avoided at all costs. Moderation and discipline must be the rule and not the exception.

As discussed elsewhere in this book, regular exercise is fundamental to the productive individual's habitual behavioral pattern. In addition to a nutritious dietary plan, regular visits to your primary care physician for an annual physical examination and analysis of blood indices is essential and should never be omitted. Other forms of health maintenance such as yoga, meditation, and stretching are highly encouraged.

A properly maintained body and mind are absolutely critical in creating a platform upon which to build a life filled with joy, contentment, and prosperity. If you are ill in any way, this sickness will, by definition, disable you from achieving anything close to your full potential.

"To keep the body in good health is a duty...otherwise we shall not be able to keep our mind strong and clear."

—Buddha (c. 563 BCE– c. 483 BCE), founder of Buddhism

In what ways are you improving your mental and physical health?

Ideas

noun

Definition: a thought, plan, or suggestion about what to do: something you imagine or picture in your mind: an opinion or belief.

Successful people tend to be "great idea people," constantly coming up with new concepts and asking the motivational questions: What if we did this? Why don't we try this? I wonder if we could produce that?

One of the biggest problems for highly prosperous individuals is finding the time and the resources to pursue all their new ideas. That's why often they will ultimately surround themselves with other talented and highly motivated individuals. Without partners, colleagues, and assistants, too many of these new innovations could never come to fruition.

I'm reminded of one of my favorite contemporary artists, Jeff Koons. Mr. Koons is a bit of a controversial figure in the art world. Not the least of the reasons for some disagreement regarding his career and credibility is the fact he himself no longer actually produces many of the works he signs and sells. For me, this isn't a problem whatsoever. His mind has been so replete with groundbreaking ideas, he would never have been able to produce the tremendous works he had if he were working alone. The most important thing for me, and I would guess him, is the ideas do get realized. It is immaterial whether they are by his own hand so long as the quality of the product meets his extremely high standards.

This could be said for other great thinkers, innovators, and creative-types such as Andy Warhol, Damien Hirst, Henry Ford, Jack Welch, Thomas Edison, etc. If we expected Mr. Ford to hand-build every automobile that came out of his manufacturing plant, the world would be a very different place today—I think, not as good.

Be an idea person. Take time to for silent solitude, and listen to your creative voice inside. It is yearning to be heard, I can assure you. We all have wonderful ideas. You just have to take the time to listen. And when our ideas and resources become so plentiful you cannot carry them out by yourself, be sure to employ others and see that they come to be realized. This will be good for you, your team, and the world. There is perhaps no greater tragedy than a wonderful idea that never sees the light of day.

"*Great minds discuss ideas; average minds discuss events; small minds discuss people.*"
—Eleanor Roosevelt (1884-1962), American politician, diplomat, activist, and First Lady of the United States of America

75

So, you have an idea or two? Write them down! The story of your success depends solely on the ideas you dream up *and* your ability to see them come to fruition.

Image

noun
Definition: the idea or impression that people have about someone or something.

It is important to make every effort to put forth a positive image. Successful people recognize that others will typically judge you based on your image. Your image is created not only by your physical impression but also your other personality traits. Are you friendly? Are you a good conversationalist? Are you good-natured? Are you rude? Are you well-spoken? Are you self-centered and arrogant? Are you a good listener? Do you have hobbies and non-work-related activities that make you interesting?

These questions and more are things you should consider of how your image may appear to others and how that may reflect on the status of your own quality of life. Work on your image. Try to stay in good physical condition. Work on maintaining a stylish, up-to-date and well-cared-for wardrobe. Understand the fashion of your time. Make an effort to dress "age appropriate." It should never be your goal to stick out in a crowd like a sore thumb because you are overwhelming or obnoxious; but you don't want to blend into the background and come across as flat or boring either.

> ❝*I believe that my clothes can give people a better image of themselves—that it can increase their feelings of happiness.*❞
>
> —Giorgio Armani (1934-), Italian fashion designer

Does the character in your success story have a style all their own? How do they dress for success? What is the image you wish to create? Write down your positive attributes. What character traits, both physical and personality, do you possess? Which do you want to possess? How do you go about possessing these traits?

Independence

noun
Definition: freedom from outside control or support.

Independence is the greatest form of success. Doing what you truly want to do with your life is the greatest form of richness man has ever known. If it is your desire to sit in the studio and paint every day, then having achieved the independence to do so is the greatest reward in the world. It is this ability to fully live our dreams and spend our days filling the hours with what makes us happy—that is how I would define true independence.

If you make a million dollars a year but feel trapped in a job, career, or profession you can't get out of, then you lack independence and true wealth. That person is poor in the most important sense of the word, because they are not doing what they love. Fight for an independent lifestyle. You deserve it. Wouldn't it be wonderful to live a life where you are not being bossed around and being told what to do by others? I cannot imagine a lifestyle more compelling than one where you are your own boss, make your own decisions, and plan your own path. The ability to make choices and follow your heart is such a wonderful concept. Put this kind of existence at the top of your goal list, and then dogmatically pursue it until it becomes a reality for you.

Being true to yourself in this way, you will open all the doors necessary to truly take you to the top of the fulfillment mountain.

"Independence is happiness."

—Susan B. Anthony (1820-1906),
American social reformer, feminist, suffragist, and abolitionist

Which steps do you take to achieve independence—from your parents, from bad habits, from your old life, from a go-nowhere job? Think of the things you can do with that freedom. You have finally broken free; what do you want to do with your time? Write it down! Then write down how you would go about obtaining that freedom.

Intention

---

noun
Definition: the thing you plan to do or achieve: an aim or purpose.

Except for hitting the Powerball lottery, nobody trips over success by accident. High levels of academic success, financial success, professional success, interpersonal success, etc. come from having a specific intent in mind. The biggest problem regarding success for most people is they are not aware of how effective a tool the power of intention is.

I became a cardiovascular surgeon for one reason: I had the intention for it to be so from the time I was around fifteen years old. I saw it clearly in my mind. I never thought about anything else. It was an idea my father had suggested, a seed he had planted.

Prior to doing anything necessary to achieve the goal, I was convinced in my mind nothing would stop me. I was in high school. I didn't know if I was smart enough, dexterous enough, responsible enough, tough enough, or anything else. But through the incredible force of intention of thought, my mind made the goal a reality. I never wavered. I never had a single setback. There were no hiccups, no extra years, no detours. The path was straight and uncomplicated.

I strongly believe, with every fiber of my being, the only reason I made such easy work of this very lofty goal was because I never allowed doubt to enter my mind and dilute the purpose of my intention.

If you can accept this philosophy as true, you can set incredible goals—goals that heretofore you would have been convinced were beyond the reach of someone like you.

If you make up your mind about where you want to go, what you want to do, and who you want to be, nothing can stand in your way. You will find the answers to every single question that arises along the way and every single obstacle that presents itself. Just remember to never lose sight of your initial intention and the road will reveal itself to you as you travel along it.

One major mistake people frequently make is to try to envision the entire path in their mind prior to setting out on their personal journey. This is an enormous and crippling error in judgment. If you make that your habit, you will invariably become overwhelmed with the sheer immensity of the task at hand and quit even before you get started.

Think of these great expeditions in life as a simple drive down a winding country road at night. There are no moon or stars in the sky, no street lamps, no light from surrounding farmhouses. Other than your car's headlights, it is pitch-black. You can only see as far as the headlights will illuminate the road in front of you. This may be thirty yards or so, as the road continuously twists and wends its way through the rolling countryside.

What would you do in such a situation? You would focus on the road you could see. It would be impossible to predict if a deer or fox were to dart across the road. It would be impossible to know if the bridge a mile down the road were out. It would impossible to know in advance if there was a fallen tree across your path somewhere ahead in the blackness of the night. But you would keep going, trusting your instincts, reflexes, judgment, and your vehicle.

Why? Because you have a clear map in your mind of where you are going. You see with perfect clarity the destination in your mind's eye. This is the power of intention, and it can take you anywhere at any time. Use this incredible ability to chart a course for a high place and begin today your remarkable journey to pursue your personal goals.

"Our intention creates our reality."

—Wayne Dyer (1940-2015), American author and motivational speaker

So…what are your intentions? Maybe you have one, maybe you have many. Write it all down. You have a success story to tell, so create intention and plant that seed!

Invest

verb
Definition: to make use of for future benefits or advantages.

Successful people invest in themselves, and it's a good idea that you do this too. Investing is like farming. You plant a tiny little seed, and something miraculous happens. One tiny little seed can grow a tomato plant, a stalk of corn, or a bean plant. One tiny little seed can also grow to become an enormous, mighty redwood tree that can live for 2,000 years! Imagine that. It's truly awesome.

Imagine what you could do with just a few seeds. I'm not talking about a handful of seeds, mind you; I'm literally talking about a few, maybe five or six. If you prepared a little plot of earth in your yard each spring and planted one tomato seed, one cucumber seed, one corn seed, one eggplant seed, one snap pea seed, and one zucchini seed, imagine what would happen.

Those tiny seeds would produce more vegetables than you could personally consume over the course of one summer. That's what six minuscule seeds can do.

This is what a good investment does—it grows nicely over time. Successful people love investments of all kinds: investment of their time, their effort, their knowledge, their money, their skills, their advice, their expertise, their sweat, etc.

One of the things a good investor loves more than anything is the concept of the power of compounding interest. All successful people relish the idea that as time passes, their investment will grow more and more, ultimately becoming a "gift that keeps on giving."

Investing in yourself and your future are the wisest investments you can make. These efforts will pay dividends like no other when wisely practiced. Investing in your education and growing your skill set steadily over time is the most intelligent place to put forth effort and energy. Whether we are talking about your financials or your personal development, make a habit of steadily putting aside a little bit of money, time, or energy each week. Over the course of years, you will harvest more abundance than you could have ever dreamed possible at the outset. Don't put off this practice until tomorrow. Like all activities of great value, please begin today.

> *I seldom read anything that is not factual in nature because I want to invest my time wisely in things that will improve my life. Don't misunderstand; there is nothing wrong with reading purely for the joy of it. Novels have their place, but biographies of famous men and women contain information that can change lives.*
>
> —Zig Ziglar (1926-2012),
> American author, salesman, and motivational speaker

It is your life, invest wisely. What do you need to concentrate on? Money? Energy? Time? Studying? What investments will bring you closer to your goals?

Knowledge

noun
Definition: information, understanding, or skill that you get from experience or education.

Success is not going to come to you by way of chance. You must acquire mastery in your field of endeavor to lead the field. Doing this is easy. Please don't fall into the trap of having someone sell you on the idea that this is a difficult process. The acquisition of knowledge has never been easier in the history of mankind.

The avenues by which to build and bolster your personal knowledge base are too numerous to list here, but let me get you started by reminding you of at least a few. Of course, you may begin with your pursuit of knowledge along the traditional academic path. Go to school whenever possible, and make scholarly pursuit of your area of interest and occupation. As far as I am concerned, the more degrees you have documenting your fund of knowledge and expertise the better. This is not to say, by any means, this is essential in a vast number of disciplines. Depending on where your personal ambitions lie, this may be a necessary venture, though. For example, you are not going to practice brain surgery in the United States of America based purely on desire. To have a career in neurosurgery, you must have formal and accredited training, of course. This is true of many of the professions such as medicine, dentistry, architecture, law, etc. So, if a highly successful career in one of these vocations is your primary ambition, begin today to put yourself in a position to begin and finish the scholastic program required.

On the other hand, many highly accomplished individuals have succeeded outside of the rubric of formal didactic education. You can own, run, and manage countless other businesses without the equivalent of a high school diploma. This does not mean you can be ignorant and succeed. Whether you intend to own gas stations, laundromats, fast food outlets, a real estate firm, a construction company, become a novelist, inventor, cartoonist, artist, musician, actor, etc., you must develop a broad and deep knowledge base upon which to build a future.

Access to such knowledge may come in the form of practical experience or on the job training, for example. There remains no good substitute for daily independent reading of books, magazines, blogs, etc. in the field of your main interest. The internet is replete with informational databases such as encyclopedias, Wikipedia, YouTube, TED talks, etc.

Never forget the incredibly powerful, and affordable, national treasure of the system of public libraries. Here you will have free access to computers, books, magazines, microfilm, microfiche, periodicals, physical objects and artifacts, professional assistance, etc. Beyond this, we have an extraordinary system of museums that hold untold bounties of information which can be transformed into personal knowledge simply by exposing yourself to it. Many communities offer adult school and night school classes in myriad subject matter, much of which is either highly affordable or free.

How you can claim that in today's age you have impaired access to knowledge is beyond a reasonable person's imagination. The information and material is there, just waiting to be had. A massive infrastructure has been created, literally begging any citizen to access it and utilize it for their own personal good and the good of humanity as a whole. Don't make excuses for your inadequate fund of knowledge in any area of interest you may have.

Acquiring the information necessary to empower yourself as an expert will take hard work, but that's just the way it goes. Get over it. Remember the adage, "Nothing hard is ever easy."

"*Knowledge without action is vanity, and action without knowledge is insanity.*"

—Al Ghazali (1058-1111), Persian theologian, philosopher, and mystic

Your success story needs action! What actions will you take to educate yourself in the field or your area of interest? Knowledge *is* power!

Language

---

noun

Definition: the system of words or signs that people use to express thoughts and feelings to each other.

Recognize the power in language. This has several meanings. The language we use to communicate with others is a strong driving force in how effective and successful we will be. Language is the essence of understanding one another. Whether this pertains to personal relationships, interactions with coworkers, employees, clients, etc., this skill's importance cannot be overstated.

Language not only pertains to having a robust vocabulary so that you can express yourself in a precise and effective manner to the others around you, but it also refers to the many languages of the world. Knowing more than one language is very powerful. Imagine being able to tap into numerous cultures through the power of the spoken word. This gift gives you the ability to understand more thoroughly the nature of the human species. This skill set allows you to engage in a dialogue with so many more of your fellow citizens of the world. This opens so many doors of enlightenment and opportunity.

Make a strong effort to know your native language as richly and thoroughly as you can, and simultaneously reach out to other cultures by learning additional languages as well. Fluency in a second or third language is an admirable goal, but even mastering common phrases in ten or twelve additional tongues will also serve you well in your life in ways that are hard to even contemplate until it happens.

"The limits of my language mean the limits of my world."

—Ludwig Wittgenstein (1889-1951), Austrian-British philosopher

No matter what you decide to do to make your mark, having a good vocabulary will help you make that mark. Do you think you have a strong vocabulary? Do you think it can be improved upon? How can expanding your vocabulary—and even learning a new language or two —help you achieve your success? Write about it.

Lifestyle

---

noun

Definition: a particular way of living: the way a person lives or a group of people live.

Living an exceptional lifestyle is a key component to personal happiness, peace, and joy. Be careful here, though; this word is more complicated than it may appear to be at first glimpse. The reason for this is when truly understood, it can mean such a wide range of things. For one individual, the lifestyle that brings sincere fulfillment means a big house on the hill, with a swimming pool, tennis court, and five-car garage. For the next individual, lifestyle may mean living in a small walk-up apartment a block or two from the beach.

The point is, it doesn't matter. It isn't a question of opulence, environment, or cost. The critical component of designing and living a wonderful lifestyle is you earn the financial freedom to do exactly as you wish.

Your favorite mode of transportation may be a Bugatti, a beach cruiser, a skateboard, or a set of cross country skis. That part is completely up to you and based solely on the vision you fantasize about in your mind's eye while you are writing your success story. The vision may also change year to year or season to season. Your concept of the perfect lifestyle is yours alone and for no one else in the world to judge. It is important you recognize this decision is totally up to you. You need not feel influenced by anyone else's idea of "the good life." What is fundamental to happiness, though, is being true to yourself and living out your own dreams.

"My definition of success is to live your life in a way that causes you to feel a ton of pleasure and very little pain—and because of your lifestyle, have the people around you feel a lot more pleasure than they do pain."

—Tony Robbins (1960-),
American motivational speaker, author, and life coach

Be clear and true to yourself regarding how and where you want to live. This is your life's setting, so use your imagination while you engage in soul-searching. Ask yourself, "Where would I vacation if I could go anywhere in the world?" Ask yourself, "If I could live in different places throughout the year, where would they be and what would my home be like?" Build that lifestyle in your mind's eye with total clarity, and then work continuously toward making that goal a reality. Without first seeing it clearly in your imagination, you will have absolutely no chance of getting there. Get creative with your life story.

Listen

---

verb

Definition: to hear what someone has said and understand that it is serious, important, or true.

Be a good listener. Without listening, your ability to learn is severely impeded. Listening, focusing, concentrating, and learning go together very harmoniously. Too often, people have not fully appreciated the value of this extraordinarily powerful skill.

Listening should not be confused with sitting quietly in a passive state of mind and not speaking. Listening is not a passive process; in fact, it is a very active process. To be a good listener requires a surprising amount of energy and effort. Listening can be exhausting, as it utilizes extremely high levels of mental resources. Anyone who has sat through a difficult academic lecture knows the feeling of sheer exhaustion at the end of only forty-five minutes of intense focus and concentration. This is different than simply being present and hearing someone speaking at the front of the lecture hall.

Also, like everything else, listening requires balance. You must also learn to speak well. Speaking is an art and a skill, just like listening. Good communication is based on a well-balanced combination of speaking and listening. These are the rudimentary elements that make up a conversation. A good conversation should involve a sincere process of sharing and exchanging ideas, whereby each participant comes away from the experience richer for it.

> ❝*I like to listen. I have learned a great deal from listening. Most people never listen.*❞
>
> —Ernest Hemingway (1899-1961), American author and journalist

Are you a good listener? How can you go about improving that trait? How do you want to go about setting this goal to improve your listening skills?

Luck

noun

Definition: the things that happen to a person because of chance: the accidental way things happen without being planned: good fortune.

This is a bit controversial in some ways, perhaps. This concept has been the subject of significant debate over the eons. I once happened upon a fascinating interview with Robert De Niro, the Academy Award winning actor, and the conversation turned to how he perceived his own extraordinary success. Interestingly, he attributed it exclusively to having had good luck. You may still be able to find this clip on YouTube, but just in case you can't or it is taken down at some point, allow me to share the salient portion of the conversation with you here. I think you may find it as intriguing as I did.

De Niro: "I was lucky."

Interviewer: "Lucky?"

De Niro: "I'm lucky that I have the…whatever I have that makes me have, um… a successful career, if you will."

Interviewer: "It's gotta be a little more than luck because the amount of work that you would put into characters."

De Niro interrupts: "Well, then, I'm lucky I have the drive to do the work. But you're always lucky."

Well, there you have one incredibly successful man's vision of his own life's work and accomplishment. Do I agree? I don't know. I don't know Mr. De Niro, and my opinion certainly doesn't matter. I'm certain he believes what he said, that's for sure. It is a very humble stance, and I can appreciate that. In fact, there is absolutely nothing wrong with this idea of how super-achievers do what they do. We could say, or assume, that Albert Einstein was lucky to be born smart and to have the drive to do the work. We could say that Usain Bolt was lucky to be born fast and to have the drive to do the work. We could say that John McEnroe was born lucky to be left-handed, with eagle-eyes and a natural touch for a tennis ball, and to have the drive to do the work. We could say that Donald Trump was born lucky to have the ability to put together fantastic real estate deals and to have the drive to do the work. Mr. Trump might disagree. Or who knows? He might not.

This is fine for the wealthy, productive, talented, driven group of people who make up the top one percent to .001 percent of the world's earners, doers, movers and shakers; but what about the rest of us? I mean, what if we are not lucky? Does that mean we're all screwed? Frankly, I guess it's possible. But I don't think it would do the reader of this book much service to leave it at that on the odd chance he or she was born unlucky.

In the case you came into this world with little or no discernible good luck, I still believe there is hope. I think this hope is found in the idea of "creating your own luck." This circles back, in a way, to Robert De Niro. He's an actor. I believe we're all actors, in a sense, in that we are playing a character—or many characters. We play different roles and behave differently depending on the situation, time, and environment. I think we should embrace this truth.

For instance, a husband doesn't "act" or behave the same way while having sex with his wife behind a locked bedroom door as he does in front of his children when he takes them to play at the park. You don't conduct yourself the same way at a funeral as you do at a wedding reception either. We all know how to "act." We play the part that works for the "scene." Not everyone who dances at a wedding reception can dance. That's often painfully obvious. But at the insistence of their date, friends, or family, they frequently dance although they are not dancers.

Keeping this philosophy in mind, I would like you to act lucky if you were one of the unfortunate many born without any particular evidence of luck in your life. If you feel unlucky, think as hard as you can about it. You may find you have a bit of luck after all.

It's likely your life isn't perfect, but where has good fortune smiled upon you? Are you attractive? Are you an American citizen? Do you have anyone who loves you in your life? Do you have a friend? Do you have your health? Do you have a job? Do you have a roof over your head? Do you have clothes on your back? Do you have any degree of education? Can you read? Do you have any money at all? Do you have access to a free public library? Ask yourself these questions and as many others as you can possibly think of that may raise your awareness of the gifts you have been given.

Almost everyone can answer yes to at least one of these questions, probably more than one. If the answer is no to some or most of these questions, ask yourself if there is anything you can do to change your luck in those areas. If you're unhealthy, have you done all you can to improve the situation? If you are poorly or minimally educated, is there anything left that you might try in order to change your level of formal education? Be honest with yourself. If you do this, I believe there is an excellent chance you may see your luck begin to change.

Then, when you become a highly successful super-achiever, you can tell people, "I was just lucky I had the kind of personality that allowed me to ask myself such questions and turn my luck around."

"*Luck is a matter of preparation meeting opportunity.*"
—Lucius Annaeus Seneca (c. 4 BC–65 AD), Roman Stoic philosopher, statesman, and dramatist

Use this space to address all the questions you were asked above, and ask yourself how things may begin to change once you decide to *act* lucky. How would a character in your shoes go about succeeding if they felt lucky enough to make it? You may find it builds your confidence.

Mentality

noun
Definition: a particular way of thinking.

In order to succeed, you must adopt a winning mentality. I cannot express to you how shocked and amazed I remain at the fact that most people never comprehend this very rudimentary notion.

If you wish to be successful and to be a winner in the game of life, you must first make a conscious decision to do so. Exceptional levels of success rarely if ever come to people through serendipity. If you make the effort to study the lives of the most prosperous individuals throughout history, you will quickly notice this was almost always their desire. To think that great wealth and accomplishment will befall you merely by chance is naïve and unrealistic.

You must assume a personal mentality which makes such goals part of your daily philosophy if you genuinely wish to live a life filled with abundance, happiness, and fulfilling interpersonal relationships.

All the success you will ever enjoy in your life begins within your extraordinary mind. You must be a visionary when it comes to your own remarkable future. Use the writing space below, and get creative! See every detail of what you want to possess, where you want to live, how you want to look, who you want to be surrounded by each day of your life. Build yourself as a character. This life is a miraculous gift. Don't waste it on leading a mundane or ordinary existence.

You have been granted an unimaginable blessing in the possession of a powerful, imaginative, resourceful brain. This organ, which greatly outperforms any other in the entire animal kingdom, is your key to unlock the vault holding all treasures of human experience. Recognize and embrace the marvelous tool you have been naturally equipped with. Use your mind to its full potential and your greatest personal advantage. Never underestimate your own intelligence, capability, and ingenuity. You are as deserving as any other person ever born to this phenomenal planet. All of this will be driven by just one thing: your personal mentality toward how you think of yourself and how you decide to live your life.

Sometimes I think I could have got some better results if I had a different mentality, if I could have pushed hard and attacked. But then I would have a good chance making a mistake.

—Alain Prost (1955-), French racing driver

What is your main character's overall mentality toward life? How does he or she look at the world and approach it? How has this mentality affected the setting of where your personal story takes place and unfolds? How could a change in your mentality improve your current living circumstances? What strengths and weaknesses do you possess in this area? Think hard about this. It's important.

Mindfulness

noun
Definition: the practice of maintaining a nonjudgmental state of heightened or complete awareness of one's thoughts, emotions, or experiences on a moment-to-moment basis.

To be mindful, in my opinion, is to be respectful. Specifically, I believe being mindful is being respectful of time. The time we have been given in this life is precious and fleeting. I find it helpful to think of sand dropping through the waist of an hourglass. The sand at the top of the glass is your life. In your mind's eye, imagine right now how quickly it slips away to the bottom of the glass. It's a powerful visual representation of our lives.

To be mindful of time makes us deeply aware of the value of time and in turn the value of our individual lives. Be alert. Set a goal to create the space for mindfulness. Be aware of the world around you and your own feelings. Be tuned in to who you would really like to be if there were no limits and no obstacles. Be turned on to what your actual potential is each day for living the life you sincerely desire. Be ever mindful of your own personal innate greatness, genius, creativity, and strength to change yourself and the world around you. Don't let time simply slip away without you taking full advantage of this unmatched resource. Use your time wisely always so you can have robust experiences filled with joy and satisfaction. Be mindful of others and their intrinsic value on this marvelous planet we call home. Be mindful of the breeze, the sun in the sky, the beautiful array of colors in the autumn leaves. Be mindful of your loved ones. Be mindful of the Earth.

Be mindful of your personal power to make an impact and leave a mark. Don't sleepwalk through life. Open your eyes wide. Open your mind's eye wide. See all you can and all you can be, and take concrete steps towards achieving the greatness you were put here to share with the world.

> ❝*Mindfulness is a quality that's always there. It's an illusion that there's a meditation and post-meditation period, which I always find amusing, because you're either mindful or you're not.*❞
>
> —Richard Gere (1949-), American actor

How can you strengthen your mindfulness? That is the easy part —just pay attention. How can being mindful help you create the life you desire? Try mindfulness as an exercise, then come back and write about how it has helped give you clarity and how it has enriched your life.

Nuance

noun
Definition: a very small difference in color, tone, meaning, etc.

Nuance is present in language, communication, negotiating, deal making, insight, understanding, and more. This is a term that definitely doesn't get enough attention, discussion, or explanation. To a degree, nuance is an innate ability, but like all other skills, it can be developed, practiced, and improved.

Being careful and deliberate is central to understanding and demonstrating mastery of nuance. Reading carefully and thoughtfully, listening carefully and thoughtfully, and speaking carefully and thoughtfully are all essential aspects of bettering your deeper understanding of this critically important concept.

Helpful questions are, "What is this passage really trying to convey?" or "What is he really saying to me?" or "Which words should I choose to express exactly what it is I want to say?" These are the kinds of things you must ask yourself to nurture a feel for the nuance of every situation.

If you do not develop expertise in this area, you will come across as a bit heavy-handed or ham-fisted in circumstances which require greater levels of understanding and delicacy in order to be effective and successful.

> " *The greatest compliment that anyone can pay me is that after I say something, they remember it. I'll go over a piece of copy until I've gotten the essence of what the writer had in mind—every nuance.* "
>
> —Casey Kasem (1932-2014), American disc jockey, music historian, and actor

Set a goal to become more aware of nuances. In this hectic and frenetic world, it may seem, firsthand, an impossibility, but nuances are everywhere. We must slow down and tune in to experience them. What nuances have you experienced or witnessed in your practice of mindfulness?

Opportunity

noun
Definition: an amount of time or a situation in which something can be done.

Recognizing opportunity is a great start. Actively searching for and seeking out fruitful opportunities is terrific also. Acting on opportunity that presents itself is essential to becoming a prosperous and productive individual. If you can do these things, you will be among the top 5% of individuals in society.

That said, opportunity isn't always in abundance. Often when you look at the playing field, it appears there isn't much offering itself up for advancement and new possibilities.

This dilemma is common and creates an environment for the true winners to shine. This is where the *mover and shaker* concept comes into play. This is where the doers of the world bypass those who are waiting for help. The truly exceptional individual creates opportunity where there is none. These are the giants of history. Consider the first person to control and utilize fire as a tool when there was none before, the first individual to build and utilize a functional wheel where there was none prior, the first man to build a printing press when the world had never seen such a thing, the first people to create a personal computer for home use with the vision that every home would have one, or the first group to conceive of an electronic information superhighway called the Internet.

From the first telephone to the cordless phone to the cellular phone, mankind has demonstrated again and again that where there is imagination, creativity, and desire, opportunity can arise seemingly out of the clear blue sky.

Be an action person. Pave your own path. Encourage your own creative juices to flow and act on them. Be fearless in your pursuit of accomplishment.

Whatever you do, don't wait for success to come along and tap you on the shoulder while you're sitting on the couch eating chips and watching TV. You're likely to wind up being gravely disappointed.

> ""*If opportunity doesn't knock, build a door.*""
> —Milton Berle (1908-2002), American comedian and actor

How will you take action and create opportunity?

Optimism

noun
Definition: a feeling or belief that good things will happen in the future: a feeling or belief that what you will hope for will happen.

You need to adopt optimism as your basic approach to life in order to succeed. Life is replete with obstacles and stumbling blocks. Difficulties and problems seem to lie in wait around every corner. This is a normal environment for the human experience. The optimist sees hope. The optimist sees the good in things.

The optimist sees the need for improvement in all things and recognizes these imperfections in the status quo as opportunities to get involved and make changes that matter. The pessimist sees only the trouble with life and none of the solutions.

Successful people are solution-oriented. Their lives are no different from anyone else's. The life of the successful person is chock full of difficulty and obstructions to forward progress. The successful personality takes this reality in stride, never allowing such nuisances to deter their desire for fortune and happiness. The winning attitude is one of undying optimism. Any setbacks you experience are merely seen as a customary part of day-to-day life.

There is an old saying that says, "*It would be impossible to climb a mountain if it were perfectly smooth. The side of the mountain needs to have lots of rough spots, cracks, and imperfections to give the climber a place to hold on and push off from.*" This is how the optimistic winner sees his or her ascent to the summit.

> "*A pessimist sees the difficulty in every opportunity; an optimist sees the opportunity in every difficulty.*"
>
> —Winston Churchill (1874-1965),
> British Prime Minster of the United Kingdom

What are you optimistic about? What steps will you take to become more of an optimist? Can you see how being positive can help you succeed?

Philosophy

noun
Definition: a set of ideas about how to do something or how to live.

Adopt a winning philosophy. This may seem obvious, but it isn't obvious to everyone.

Many people are under the misconception that most successful people are so because they are lucky, gifted, or talented, etc. In fact, they win because they are focused on succeeding. Their personal philosophy is geared toward succeeding, not simply to participation.

I believe this is particularly apropos today. We are living in a culture which now promotes the following philosophies for example: "Winning isn't everything," ; "Everyone is a winner," ;"There are no losers," ; "It's not whether you win or lose, but how you play the game that is most important," ; "What's most important is that we all have fun," and so on and so forth.

Now, let me be clear, I do think how you play the game is critically important in that you don't lie, cheat, steal, or break the rules in order to win. No one should aspire to being a dirty player under any circumstances. But I do believe it is far better to win, fair and square, than to lose by the same standards. I personally believe it sets a bad precedent to teach young people that simply by participating in an activity, "Everyone is a winner." The fact of the matter is, that simply isn't the case; that is what we refer to as reality.

Winning is important. Success and winning are heavily associated and interconnected. This is true in everything. It's true in school, business, personal relationships, your personal finances, physical health, mental health, your role as a citizen in society, etc. Let's be honest—if you had a child in school who came home with failing grades but had perfect attendance, would you tell them they were doing fine? Would you tell them what was important was they were participating? How about C or D grades? Would that suffice?

How about if they were in college and you were paying $50,000 or more per year for their tuition? Would you be satisfied with such marks? I think it's unlikely. Most of us would push for a better performance.

I recognize I use the following examples frequently, but I just feel they are so helpful in putting things in perspective. How would you like to go to a surgeon who didn't "win" every time in the operating room or a commercial pilot who didn't "win" every time he was charged with transporting a group of passengers from point A to point B on the map? Would you be satisfied with a loved one who died on the operating room table despite the fact the doctor had "given it his all" or with a pilot who came up 100 yards short of the runway because he "had tried his best"? I doubt it.

I understand as parents, friends, and spouses we often want to be kind to those whom we love at times when they don't perform as well as you might wish. It's human to demonstrate compassion and support in such situations. But is this really helping them if this scenario becomes chronic? And, more importantly, do we want to lower the bar for our own performance? I don't believe so. I think we should push to have a philosophy geared toward winning. No one wants an epitaph that read, "John also ran."

> *Your philosophy determines whether you will go for the disciplines or continue the errors.*
>
> —Jim Rohn (1930-2009),
> American entrepreneur, author, and motivational speaker

What is your attitude about success? What is your belief in your own success? Do your beliefs hold you down and discourage you? Do you possess a healthy mode of thought that keeps you positive and eager to succeed? Write it down and think on whether this philosophy helps or hinders your moving forward and accomplishing something worthwhile.

Play

---

noun
Definition: exercise or activity for amusement or recreation.

Most super-achievers I have had the good fortune to know are highly competitive and love to play. Winning matters to them. They see life as a marvelous game they adore playing. The true winners recognize there are very different rules, and they enjoy playing within them. Winning honestly is the only real way to win, and therefore playing by the rules is the only fun way to play. Being dishonest and breaking the rules is strictly for losers.

When you see the challenges of life like that of any game, it adds to the thrill of victory. Just as any great athlete only desires competing against the best, so too is this true for those who specialize in the game of life. It would be no fun to play a beginner if you were a high-level tennis player, for example. That's a bore—no challenge, no excitement, no drama, no suspense, no fun. There is something exciting about not knowing how things will turn out or who will come out on top. No one wants to tune in to watch me race Usain Bolt in a 100-meter dash, for example. Nor would Mr. Bolt be interested in taking me on in such a debacle. His sights are set on competing against, "playing" if you will, the very best in the world. Only then can his true talent, ability, and exceptional speed be put on display. Only then can his hard work, determination, and sacrifice be made worthwhile.

Rather than seeing life as a burden or a struggle or an unjust test of your ability to cope, see it as a glorious game. See yourself as a competent player, and set your goals as high as your immense imagination will allow. Only then will you be able to truly enjoy the fruits this extraordinary life and world have to offer.

Think back to childhood. All we ever wanted to do was play. Well, the same is true right now if you will take the time to look deep inside yourself. We all want to play. Playing is fun. Everybody knows that. Everyone has had the beautiful experience as a child of playing for hours. Now is your chance to see life that way again. See everything as a magnificent game, the whole world being your playground, and practice and train in your field so you can win as often as possible. It makes playing that much more pleasurable.

"You can learn more about a person in an hour of play than in a year of conversation."

—Plato (c. 428- c. 348 BC), Greek philosopher and mathematician

Put more play into your setting. Make time and carve out a place where play can occur—it is *that* important. Can you remember a time in your life when you treated work or school as play and felt the pull of competition? How did you feel? What were the results when you put your joy into doing something? Did you get more out of the experience? Write about it.

Pleasure

noun
Definition: a feeling of happiness, enjoyment, or satisfaction.

Take pleasure in life. No matter what your level of education, position of power, or degree of wealth, if you are not finding an abundance of pleasure in your life, you are not really living. If, on the other hand, you have no

97

formal education, wield no power, or have little in the way of monetary richness, you can still be a tremendous success if you find deep pleasure in your daily life.

Typically, to enjoy the great pleasures life has to offer, you must find balance. A balance between work time and private time is essential. Finding pleasure in your workday is as important as finding the same emotion in your personal life. Misery in one or the other will negate strongly, if not completely, the pleasure response you are experiencing in the other. Ask yourself if you are experiencing pleasure in the various areas of your life.

Again, introspection is so crucial to personal growth, understanding, and development. If you find you are not enjoying pleasurable moments regularly as a routine aspect of your existence, ask yourself why not. Then probe deeper. Using the space provided in this book, ask yourself what you could change to make life more pleasing, and write it all down. Also, ask yourself how and when you could begin to implement these changes.

Keep in mind change is typically difficult. Therefore, do not be surprised or discouraged if you should encounter a transitional phase which you perceive to be even less pleasurable. This is normal. This is called experiencing growing pains. Just as the long bones in children ache as they mature, so might your inner self. But remain committed to the process, for on the other side of this pain threshold lies a lifetime of pleasure.

"Each morning when I awake, I experience again a supreme pleasure—that of being Salvador Dalí."
—Salvador Dalí (1904-1989), Spanish artist

What place would give your character the most pleasure in being himself or herself? Where would they work? Where would they live? Where would they vacation? This is a fabulous setting word. Work at seeing these places in your mind's eye, and then take a little extra time here to write them down—not with broad strokes, but in vivid detail.

98

Positivity

noun

Definition: the quality or state of thinking that a good result will happen: hopeful or optimistic.

To be successful, you must be positive. A positive direction is a forward direction and uphill direction. A negative direction means going backward or descending the mountain. Which way do you want to go? If your answer is upward and onward, then you must recognize the engine that drives this progress is a positive attitude, which will bring positive results. This may take the form of better health, a more robust bank account, a more substantial investment portfolio, better personal relationships, a kinder and more generous demeanor, etc.

Tell yourself every day you are doing great, you are feeling great, you are looking great. More often than not, this is a difficult proposition, particularly in the beginning. Learn to smile. Smile at everyone with whom you make contact. If they ask you how you are doing, tell them with enthusiasm that you feel "Great!" Fake it if you must. Try it though. Don't skip this exercise, even though it seems a bit silly and superficial at first. I can assure you it's neither. When you encounter your spouse, kids, friends, employees, customers, colleagues, superiors, etc., be that individual who is always upbeat and energetic. Let this positive behavior and disposition become your calling card. I can assure you if you make the effort to be that person, you will attract energetic, enthusiastic, positive people like moths to a porch light on a pitch-black night.

If you work hard at becoming positive, it will slowly but surely take hold of your personality. You'll no longer need to make believe. It will no longer be an exercise. You will, in fact, become that positive person people love to be around. You will become that energy source others feed off. This will lead to more and deeper friendships and a vastly richer professional life. Let's face it, no one wants to do business with or give their hard-earned money to a "Debbie Downer."

Take this advice seriously and work hard at developing this highly valued mentality and attitude. You will never regret it, not only because of the results it will lead to, but, most importantly, how you will feel and how you will live your wonderfully abundant and enjoyable life.

“Like success, failure is many things to many people. With Positive Mental Attitude, failure is a learning experience, a rung on the ladder, a plateau at which to get your thoughts in order and prepare to try again.”

—W. Clement Stone (1902-2002),
American businessman, philanthropist, and self-help author

Maybe you have not been very positive lately. It's easy to get discouraged when things don't go your way. Write down times you have been discouraged, and think of how you could turn that around with the right attitude—whether it was a breakup, an argument, a failed test, a job loss, etc. What did you learn from your failings? Taking note of what you have learned is a positive move! See? Your attitude is improving already.

Possibility

noun
Definition: a chance that something might exist, happen, or be true.

Learn to hone the ability to see the possibilities in life. This is a very useful skill set to possess in a complicated world which appears so replete with obstacles, problems, troubles, stumbling blocks, and impediments. It is very easy to fall into negative thinking, focusing on the impossibility of achieving, success, happiness, good health, and fulfilling relationships with others. But that's too easy for someone like you. You desire more from life than being hung up on believing all the best things will be impossible for you to enjoy. Decide right here and now you will behave as a winner from now on, and see each day as a new set of extraordinary possibilities and opportunities.

I have had the good fortune to know personally an incredibly successful man by the name of Mehdi Fakharzadeh. If you happen to be in the life insurance business, you are likely to have heard of him, as he is now in his 90s. Mr. Mehdi, as he was affectionately called by many, was a legendary salesman from Metropolitan Life Insurance company. He has spoken and inspired people inside and outside of his profession for decades and all

100

around the world. The reason I bring him up is because I am fortunate to have in my personal library a copy of each of his very fine books. One is titled *Nothing is Impossible,* and the other is called *Everything is Possible.* If you are lucky enough to find copies of these incredible books somewhere, I certainly encourage you to do so. Frankly, their titles say it all. If you wish to be at the absolute pinnacle of your field, whatever it is, you must adopt this philosophy and live by it every day.

There is opportunity and possibility everywhere. You simply must open your eyes and ears and be receptive. Once you begin to see you are truly being inundated with possibilities, please begin to act upon them. This will be the beginning of an amazing new phase in your life. Trust me when I tell you, the opportunities available to you are boundless. Now go out and begin to act upon them immediately!

> ❝*Invincibility lies in the defense; the possibility of victory in the attack.*❞
>
> —Sun Tzu (544-496 BC), Chinese military general, strategist, and philosopher

In your success story, what do you want to achieve? What are the possibilities of happiness and success you can think up? Be generous with your response, and set the goals of endless possibilities for yourself.

Prioritize

verb

Definition: to organize (things) so that the most important thing is done or dealt with first: to make (something) the most important thing in a group.

Very successful individuals recognize prioritizing is a key element in building success. Developing an understanding of what comes first and what can wait until last is critically important. At every level of maturation, this skill set is valuable. Whether you are a student with four hours of homework or a business person with a desk full of paperwork, you must cultivate and perfect the ability to put things in a rational, feasible, and productive "pecking order."

101

All things cannot be done at once. This should be obvious to anyone. Moreover, some things are best done before others. Certain projects and responsibilities require varying degrees of urgency, whereas others do not. Being able to recognize the difference and act accordingly is a telltale sign of a highly effective personality type. Not possessing a haphazard approach to tasks and work is an absolute requirement if you are to realize your full potential. Disorganized behavior leads to inefficiency in your efforts and, ultimately, less than optimal results no matter what the endeavor might be.

> ""*The key is not to prioritize what's on your schedule, but to schedule your priorities.*""
>
> —Stephen Covey (1932-2012),
> American educator, author, businessman, and keynotespeaker

What are your priorities in your success story?

Responsibility

noun

Definition: the state of being the person who caused something to happen: a duty or task that you are required or expected to do.

You are responsible for your own life. Taking responsibility for your actions, behavior, and the results of your actions is one of the greatest forms of power you can master. This philosophy is on the opposite end of the spectrum from blame and excuses. When you live an unfulfilled life and try to justify your dissatisfaction through an indictment of outside forces, you are demonstrating perhaps the ultimate weakness and are walking the path of continued unhappiness.

Being a responsible person and living a life rooted in responsible behavior is not always easy—but it is always right. Stand on your own two feet. Forge your own path. Recognize anything you have or have not achieved is a direct result of everything you have ever done up until this moment in your life. Realize it is largely true that, except for a few core individuals, no

102

one really cares about you. No one is going to help you live your dreams. One of my favorite mantras is, "No one is coming to the rescue."

Now, this is not to say the world is pitted against you; in fact, it is not. It simply means, for the most part, no one really cares what you do. Therefore, although it's true they don't care if you lead a mediocre or even a below average life, it is also true they don't care enough about you to stand in the way of your extraordinary personal success, either.

In my most formative years, except for my parents, essentially nobody cared how well I did, how hard I worked, how much I studied, or how high I set my personal goals. On the other hand, no one took the time or put forth the energy to stand in my way. Frankly, they couldn't be bothered, just as I had no intrinsic ambition to get in the way of their dreams, goals, wishes, or desires. I was too wrapped up in my own life, as most people are.

This is the beauty of it all. This is the most wonderful thing about living in a free society. If you play by the rules and don't break any laws, you can achieve as much success in any form you like. No one cares. No one is coming to the rescue, but no one is coming to erect a roadblock on your personal highway to success either. Only you are in charge of your destiny. Take ownership of this stark reality. Own it. Accept responsibility for your life, your education, your health, your financial situation, your occupational status, your personal relationships, and anything else you can possibly think of. Don't put your life in the hands of anyone else. Truthfully speaking, they'll do a crappy job.

Don't wait for friends, family, co-workers, or the government to pave a path to happiness or prosperity. They're not coming. Most people wouldn't have the first clue how to provide that for themselves, so what in the world would lead you to believe they are inclined to do so for you?

Don't be naïve. Be a realist. Act like a responsible adult. You—and only you—can adjust the sail to direct your personal ship toward ultimate fulfillment. Be mature and responsible and take a firm grip on the rudder. Set your course to a life of richness, achievement, contentment, and gratification. The sea is open to you without obstruction. Don't imagine impediments where they don't exist. Stop making excuses and start making progress—today.

"The price of greatness is responsibility."

—Winston Churchill (1874-1965), Prime Minister of the United Kingdom

This is your story. Do not put it in the hands, or in the control, of anyone else. Are there places in your life where you have given up power and control? Write them down, and write down your plans—set your goals—on how you will go about changing those situations to improve your life.

Sacrifice

noun

Definition: the act of giving up something that you want to keep, especially to get or do something else or to help someone.

Sacrifice is a cornerstone of excellence. Everyone whom I know personally that has achieved an uncommon measure of success has made sacrifices in one area of their life or another.

Typically, these sacrifices mean depriving yourself of some pleasurable experience you would very much like to experience. Examples would be: missing social gatherings; working on weekends, nights, and holidays; or waking very early in the morning or staying up late. Top athletes might deprive themselves of certain foods they might like to eat if they were not in training to be the best in their field. Top investors might sacrifice certain material things for the sake of putting money away at regular intervals so their financial wealth will grow steadily over time. The number of illustrations is seemingly endless. But the common thread in all of them is: high achievers recognize, at some point in their personal development, that to gain something they wish to have, they must always give something up which is equally dear to them.

The trick here is to train yourself to replace the painful, negative emotion that tends to come naturally with the sacrifice with a feeling of pleasure. This is a key concept. This may seem counterintuitive at first, but this is a very powerful mental and emotional tool. To successfully associate pleasure with sacrifice, you must not focus on the irritation that comes with the sacrifice, but instead focus on the joy and gratification that will come because of this loss in the long run.

For example, you must not focus on the pain associated with lifting weights in the gym. Pumping iron is hard work and requires a tremendous amount of effort and labor. This is not particularly pleasant. Paying for the gym membership or the exercise equipment is a financial sacrifice. The time required to go to and from the gym and the time spent at the gym is time you might otherwise spend with friends and family, relaxing or watching television. There are all kinds of hardships and sacrifices associated with exercise if you elect to look at it in that light. But what I strongly suggest you train yourself to do is to flood your mind with images of a stronger, fitter, healthier, and more appealing physique instead. Associate pleasurable ideas and emotions with the hard work rather than the prerequisite pain and discomfort. This is a difficult mental exercise but an incredibly valuable one.

Try applying this liberating technique to all the areas of your life you can think of, whether it's studying for a test, putting money in your 401K accounts, doing push-ups, or passing on dessert. See the eventual immense pleasure you will derive from such choices and actions, rather than agonizing in the immediate discomfort that may be experienced at the time of such sacrificial decisions. This philosophy will take you a long way toward building an exceptional lifestyle.

> ❝*I think the good and the great are only separated by the willingness to sacrifice.*❞
>
> —Kareem Abdul-Jabbar (1947-),
> American professional basketball player and NBA champion

This is a hard question, but it will yield some beneficial answers. Where do you need to make sacrifices to achieve your goals?

Service

---

noun

Definition: the work performed by one that serves: contribution to the welfare of others.

Our success is directly related to the service we provide to the community. The more service you provide, the more success you will enjoy. You can't cheat your way to the top. You can't steal your way to the pinnacle of your field. In the end, each one of us who desires extreme prosperity must earn it through service.

The higher the quality of the service you provide and the greater the quantity of the service you provide, the more abundant the rewards shall be. Do all you can to provide the absolute best products and services you can to the public, no matter what field you are in. Imagine how you can extend and expand the services you offer.

A personal example of how I have applied this in my own career relates to how I have developed and grown my own private medical practice. As a surgeon with training in cardiovascular surgery, I found I was unhappy doing open heart surgery. This was for a combination of reasons. First and foremost, the fee reimbursement schedule had been drastically reduced over the years, and I felt I was being underpaid and undervalued for the extraordinary quality of work I was providing to my community and the many years of training I had to endure to provide such service. The second reason I ceased to perform cardiac surgery was the grueling lifestyle and never-ending responsibility associated with the field. As one of my old professors used to say, "The juice to squeeze ratio was completely out of balance."

Therefore, I elected to develop an office-based, outpatient, elective surgical practice focusing on a wide age-range of patients. Many of the younger patients had private insurance where the payments for services rendered were much more realistic, appropriate, and respectful of my expertise. So this is rule number one: provide service that gives you satisfaction and you find personally and financially rewarding. Don't stay in a job you hate. After creating my private vein center, I began to treat patients with spider veins for cosmetic purposes in addition to the people who had varicose veins, which were of a medically necessary nature.

106

My foray into cosmetic injections led to cosmetic injections for other problems like wrinkles. Neuromodulators and filler injections came next. Ultimately, we added a medical weight loss program, a vascular ultrasonography laboratory, a plastic surgical program, and a hair transplantation program. We added more and more services. I began public speaking and writing books, sharing my knowledge. I also began producing audio tapes. Later, we created a vascular ultrasound screening company for people interested in knowing if they were at increased risk for vascular disease.

As you can see, I kept growing and expanding the practice in logical directions and in so doing provided more and more service to the community at large. There is no way to become more prosperous by doing and offering less to your fellow citizen. You must find ways to give more and do more if you wish to receive more. Look at Walmart for example; if you go into that store you can eat lunch, have your hair cut, get your tires rotated, buy a new bathing suit, and buy logs for your fireplace. They obviously understand the concept of providing lots and lots of services at a good price. Is it any wonder that each of the Walton siblings is currently worth more than $40 billion dollars? I think not. The other thing they have done to provide extreme quantities of service is to open stores in essentially every community around the country. This is obviously an extreme example, but this is how it's done. This is how Henry Ford did it, how Bill Gates, Andrew Carnegie, and Steve Jobs did it. They provided tremendous service to an enormous number of people. They didn't do it by sitting on their backsides.

"A business absolutely devoted to service will have only one worry about profits. They will be embarrassingly large."

—Henry Ford (1863-1947),
American industrialist and founder of Ford Motor Company

In your success story, how do you plan to serve your community or the world at large?

Skill

noun

Definition: the ability to use one's knowledge effectively and readily in execution or performance: a learned power of doing something competently: a developed aptitude or ability.

Strive to possess success-oriented skills. There is no substitute for having and exercising skills that have value in the marketplace. There are all kinds of skills you can attain and even master. Not all skills are going to be translatable into success, especially from a monetary point of view in the marketplace. Even rare skills are not always useful regarding earning money. For example, there aren't too many people who can touch their eyebrows with their tongue or play the *Hardingfele*, but the rarity in and of itself does not equate to financial worth.

The individual who desires economic success should research and study talents which are noted to be associated with profitability. The college student who studies neurosurgery is more likely to live a life of prosperity than he who studies underwater basket weaving. Those are called the facts. That's just the way it is in the world which we call reality. Now, there are exceptions to every rule, and I am not here to profess that you may not be the exception. On the contrary, I am here to tell you that you are exceptional. You may become the Pablo Picasso of subaquatic basket manufacturing; there is no way for me to know that you won't be. That said, I am also a realist and believe in mathematics and probability and would advise someone that they are more likely to be an outlier in excellence in neurosurgery before they create a multimillion dollar industry around basket weaving. The choice is yours in the end.

My only advice here is you take the time to do your homework and evaluate the playing field. Make informed decisions. Don't shoot from the hip. Don't make the common mistake of believing falsely that everything will take care of itself. It won't. You must have a plan based on truths. This plan is bound to change as you travel the path toward an abundant lifestyle, but you do yourself a disservice by starting so far afield it will take more than a lifetime to become highly productive.

"*Don't wish it were easier; wish you were better. Don't wish for fewer problems; wish for more skills. Don't wish for less challenges; wish for more wisdom.*"

—John Earl Schoaf (1916-1965),
American entrepreneur and motivational speaker

So…what is your plan? Even if it changes a few times—or a few dozen times—it's good to write down a plan.

Talent

noun
Definition: a special ability that allows someone to do something well.

You must ultimately develop a great talent to do something that sets you apart from the rest. By far, my favorite definition of talent comes from the author of a must-read book (amongst other great ones) called *Outliers*. The author, Malcolm Gladwell, concludes after much research and writing that, "Talent is the desire to practice." Now, in my opinion, that's not only good, it's correct.

I had mentioned earlier Gladwell's idea of the so-called 10,000-hour rule, where researchers have generally agreed it takes 10,000 hours of practice to become expert at something.

Again, when I look at my own professional path, it's easy to calculate rough hours applied to becoming a competent and certified cardiovascular surgeon. If we leave out all the thousands of hours of prerequisite work—including everything learned in twelve years of secondary school, four years of college (including biology, chemistry, physics, calculus, and organic chemistry), and four years of medical school (including such trivial subjects as gross anatomy, physiology, biochemistry, physiology, pathology, histology, microbiology, and neuroscience)—we still have a hell of a lot of hours to consider. In the remaining seven years of my education, there was a lot of practice put forth before performing my first open-heart procedure as practicing cardiac surgeon in 2002.

109

These seven years were made up of five years of general surgery residency and two years of cardiothoracic surgical residency. It is fair to say that in those years we residents put in 100 hours per week. We were given three weeks of vacation each year. Therefore, the math becomes simple: 49 weeks X 100 hours = 4,900 hours per year. This represents the number of hours we were in the hospital operating, making rounds, taking care of patients.

There were some periods of sleep while on call, but not many. If I take away twenty hours per week for sleep while on call in the hospital (a gross overestimate), this leaves eighty hours. Let's recalculate to be conservative: 49 weeks X 80 hours = 3,920 hours of work (practice) per year.

Multiply that number times seven years and we get: 27,740 hours of practice to become a board eligible cardiovascular surgeon. If you assume that only one-third of that time was spent in the operating room, that is still more than 9,000 hours. And that was before we even earned a diploma and went into actual practice.

It takes a hell of a lot of work, practice, commitment, and persistence to achieve great things. Don't let anybody fool you that anything else resembles reality. If you expect to get much done in a four-hour work week, well, all I can say is good luck. But one thing is for sure, I don't want that person operating on *my* heart.

"Talent is cheaper than table salt. What separates the talented individual from the successful one is a lot of hard work."
—Stephen King (1947-), American author

Where do your talents lie? What skills do you desire to improve?

When

adverb
Definition: at what time: at or during which time.

Develop a keen sense of when to act. This is a very important skill. Often the best answer to *when* is now. This is not always the case, but it often is.

110

This philosophy speaks once again to the importance of timing. My personal experience has taught me to trust your instincts. Rarely will you regret this if you believe in what you are doing and make decisions you will stand by.

When I have opened new companies or added new services or products within any of my companies, I have almost never regretted that decision. What I have regretted from time to time is I had not acted sooner. I often wish I had made the move when I first thought of a particular idea and had the inclination to act. Too often in my own life, I listened to the voices around me. These voices often like to masquerade as the voice of reason. Unfortunately, this voice is really negativism and fear speaking. People feel they will shield you from failure by pointing out all the things that could possibly go wrong.

Please be cautious of this. Don't completely disregard the advice of those around you. Take their thoughts, ideas, and opinions into careful consideration. But don't ever assume someone else knows more than you do. If I had listened to those around me who really and truly care about me, I wouldn't be the medical director at John A. Chuback, M.D., LLC. In fact, Chuback Medical Group and Contemporary Hair Transplant would not exist. Ultra Life Scan, LLC would never have been created. I would still be an employee of another physician doing something I really disliked and going through my life miserable. I must tell you, just to make you aware of how real this problem is, my father, the person in the world who possibly loves me more than anyone, initially advised me against going out on my own and starting my own company. He felt it would be safer for someone else to take care of me. He didn't want to see me get hurt. He didn't want to see me lose my life savings. The fact of the matter is, he had the best intentions but the absolute worst advice.

When you feel the time is right to make a major change in your life, trust yourself. You are smarter than you may think. You are stronger than you may feel. You are more resourceful than you may believe. You are more capable than you may understand. If you feel now is the time, then now is the time. This is your *when*. Go for it. You will deal with any obstacles when they arise. I can assure you there will be plenty of obstacles. You can't allow that to be a good reason to stop you.

❝I remember, I still remember when the first time I pointed the telescope at the sky and I saw Saturn with the rings. It was a beautiful image.❞

—Umberto Guidoni (1954-),
Italian astrophysicist, science writer, and astronaut

In the setting of your success story, *when* is an important element. Use this space to reflect on your time frame.

Where

adverb
Definition: at or in what place.

Successful people succeed where they are. There is often little choice in this. They will also move to where the action and opportunities are when necessary.

What do the following companies have in common?

1. Amazon (Jeff Bezos, Bellevue, Washington)
2. Apple (Steve Jobs and Steve Wozniak, Cupertino, California)
3. Disney (Walt and Roy Disney, Los Angeles, California)
4. Google (Larry Page and Sergey Brin, Menlo Park, California)
5. Harley Davidson (William S. Harley and Arthur Davidson, Milwaukee, Wisconsin)
6. Hewlett-Packard (Bill Hewlett and Dave Packard, Palo Alto, California)
7. Lotus Cars (Anthony Colin Bruce Chapman, Hornsey, North London)
8. Maglite (Tony Maglica, Los Angeles, California)
9. Mattel (Harold "Matt" Matson an Elliot Handler, Southern California)
10. Yankee Candle Company (Michael Kittredge, South Hadley, Massachusetts)

They all began in a garage (or shed or stable, to be precise). These brilliant innovators started where they were. What was special in each of these examples was the people involved, not the location of the people.

I suggest you make it your business to avoid excuses. If you think you may be in a suboptimal area to be creative, successful, and prosperous, you're mistaken. You're in an amazing spot to do amazing things because, as they said in the 1980s cult classic movie *Buckaroo Banzai*, "Wherever you go, there you are." As long as you're there, I have no doubt extraordinary things can happen if, and only if, you truly believe in yourself.

"Start where you are. Use what you have. Do what you can."

—Arthur Ashe (1943-1993), American professional tennis player

Where are you now? Where do you want to be? This is the most obvious setting word of them all.

Section Three:

Making a Plan to Succeed and Overcome Obstacles

This section is focused on your plan and the obstacles and conflicts you may face when implementing your plan into action. Do not be discouraged. To achieve your goals, you must overcome the conflicts and obstacles that come your way, just like any strong character in a novel. Facing trouble head-on is one of the best ways to vanquish your foes—be they negative opinions, doubts, criticism that has no basis, and other negative things that seem to rear their heads just when you embark on your life adventure.

In your success story, you will meet adversaries and antagonists—and maybe that voice in your head becomes adversarial as well. In this section, you will work through those difficult issues by writing about them. This will help you overcome any unforeseen difficulties as you move onwards along your path to success. A plan works as a guide to help you navigate your way around possible pitfalls. Getting to know yourself will better equip you to face life's dragons. Let's begin to build your plan!

Abundance

noun
Definition: a large amount of something .

Attaining abundance should be part of your plan. Abundance, of course, can refer to anything, not just money, objects, possessions, and material things. Things that are best when found in abundance are: freedom, free will, independence, beauty, free time, friends, family, art, music, peace, choice, happiness, pleasure, generosity, love, knowledge, wisdom, empathy, and kindness.

I believe everyone should see the virtue in trying to achieve a truly abundant life. This requires you to constantly try to be your personal best. The very best part of having a lot of these things is sharing them with as many others as you can.

"According to this law (the law of Dharma), you have a unique talent and a unique way of expressing it. There is something that you can do better than anyone else in the whole world—and for every unique talent and unique expression of that talent, there are also unique needs. When these needs are matched with the creative expressions of your talent, that is the spark that creates affluence. Expressing your talents to fulfill needs creates unlimited wealth and abundance."

—Deepak Chopra (1947-),
Indian-born American author, public speaker, and physician

Write down in your plan what you want a lot of. It can be money—there is nothing wrong with that. Some wish for an abundance of contentment, energy, adventure. In your success story, what is your plan for abundance, and what do you want a lot of?

Action

noun

Definition: a thing done: the accomplishment of a thing usually over a period of time, in stages, or with the possibility of repetition.

116

Perhaps you do not know how to create a plan. This next segment can help. I have long felt there is probably no more important term than action when it comes to how to live your life.

One of the most basic algorithms for success is as follows:

1) Think
2) Set a goal
3) Develop and design a plan of action to achieve the goal
4) Act on the plan
5) Work at the plan through completion

This five-step process may seem unrealistically simple, but in fact it is how you become a cardiovascular surgeon, it is how a nation puts a man safely on the moon, it is how a team locates the sunken Titanic ocean liner, it is how you get an A in algebra or become a millionaire.

Like a chain, this process is only as weak as its weakest link. Therefore, if any one of these steps is not carried out, there will be no successful realization of the goal. In my experience, though, the most common area for a person to fail is the area of action. By nature, people are full of wonderful ideas. People are bursting with hopes and dreams of starting their own business, making more money, or earning their degree, but too often they never get started. I know this sounds overly simplistic, but you can't succeed if you don't act.

Winners are action people. Super-achievers are doers. Ideas themselves are valueless and useless; only a good idea that is acted on can bear any fruit. A jar of apple seeds on the shelf in the basement will not yield a single tree. The seed needs to be planted, fertilized, watered, exposed to sunshine, and eventually pruned to become a fruitful occupant of your personal victory garden. Become an action person. Adopt this behavior immediately, and you will see greater results almost as quickly as you begin.

"Action may not always bring happiness, but there is no happiness without action."

—William James (1842-1910),
American philosopher, psychologist, and physician

117

Let's get this all on paper. Create a sound plan, using the algorithm from above:

1) Think
2) Set a goal
3) Develop and design a plan of action to achieve the goal
4) Take action on the plan
5) Work at the plan through completion

Advertise

verb
Definition: to make the public aware of something that is being sold.

Successful people recognize that no matter what their primary vocation appears to be, we are all salesman in the end. I'm well aware this concept may raise eyebrows in certain circles. In my primary profession of medicine, it was long believed traditional forms of advertising were considered to be in poor taste. Well, those days are long gone. Today, the biggest and most reputable health care systems in the country spend millions on advertising to attract business (A.K.A. patients).

Clearly there is nothing wrong with this if the services being offered are of high quality and ethically applied in every case. In fact, you might argue if you had the highest standard of medical care to offer and did not make every effort, no matter how much it cost you to get the word out, it would be unethical and irresponsible. Advertising only becomes an ugly or unsavory word when you are attempting to cheat someone by selling an inferior product at an inflated price. This type of behavior is inappropriate and unacceptable.

But make no mistake, we all have something to sell, whether professionally or personally. Advertising takes many forms. An advertisement may take the form of a billboard on the highway, a TV commercial, or a website. Just as importantly, an advertisement might be in the shape of a confident handshake, a warm smile, or a reassuring look in the eye. Good advertisements always instill trust in the consumer. Whether you make a living by selling used cars, preparing tax returns, dancing and singing, or performing triple bypasses, it is essential the consumer knows you exist.

> ❝*Many a small thing has been made large by the right kind of advertising.*❞
>
> —Mark Twain (1835-1910), American author and humorist

Advertising is part of the plan. Think of ways to get the word out about your skills and expertise.

Attitude

noun
Definition: a feeling or way of thinking that affects a person's behavior.

Having a good or positive attitude is essential to success. Nothing can guarantee success, but an optimistic, hopeful, upbeat attitude is essential to having any chance at achieving great things. On the other hand, there are things that can ensure failure, or at least greatly limited levels of success. One element which will certainly curtail your degree of economic and personal growth and development is a bad attitude.

Pessimism, an unfriendly or negative demeanor, and excessive skepticism are all characteristics of a personality which certainly lead to poor results in every potential arena. The surgeon who goes into the operating room feeling the patient has no hope of survival, the golfer who addresses the tee-shot convinced he will not drive the ball well, or the tennis player who is consumed by thoughts of double-faulting rather than serving aces has greatly diminished the chance of a good outcome.

Always work hard to build and maintain a positive mental attitude. This is a powerful tool which will serve you well. This is a far from being easy in a world that presents many challenges, obstacles, and difficulties, but if you are focused, you can achieve this very helpful and productive state of mind.

"An attitude of positive expectancy is the mark of the superior personality."

—Brian Tracy (1944-),
Canadian-American motivational speaker, consultant, and author

Do you have a good attitude? Think on how having a negative attitude can mar your chances of success. If you do possess doubts and the specter of failure looms over you, do your best to turn that attitude around; it will only deter you from doing what you love, what you want. And you deserve to live the best life, the life you desire. Here, write, in a positive way, thoughts and feelings about your talents, skills, and interests. When you are feeling discouraged, you can come back to this part of the workbook and feel inspired!

Can

transitive verb

Definition: to be able to do, make, or accomplish.

Remember: words make up thoughts, and thoughts influence action. The words you use in your thoughts influence how you act. Begin using the word can often. If you are going to believe anything, believe you *can*. Avoid thinking there is anything you cannot do. The first step in any great undertaking is believing it can be done. After that, the next and most important step is acting and getting things done. *I can* and *I will* go hand in as motivation in overcoming obstacles. There is nothing better than *I could* and *I have*. This means the dream has become a reality.

Always remember the Little Engine That Could. *As the train makes his way up the steep incline, he encourages himself with the mantra, "I know I can. I know I can." After he reaches the summit and enjoys the sweet sensation of coasting down the other side of the mountain, he sings, "I knew I could! I knew I could!" The sooner you start climbing, the sooner you'll be coasting joyfully along on the other side of all that hard work.*

—Walt Disney (1901-1966),
American entrepreneur, cartoonist, animator, voice actor, and film producer

How do you remain positive when the going gets tough? List the ways you dig yourself out of negative thinking.

Commitment

noun
Definition: a promise to do or give something: a promise to be loyal to someone or something: the attitude of someone who works very hard to do or support something.

To succeed, you must understand and live by the concept of commitment. Nothing of significant worth is achieved by chance or in a short period of time. Commitment implies a sustained effort over a prolonged period. Commitment means not quitting before the desired result has been achieved.

Be committed to good health, a proper diet, an exercise regimen, education, professional development, personal relationships, and financial success. Success is not about quick fixes and giving up when things become difficult. A great runner doesn't slow down or stop because she finds herself behind in a foot race. Instead, she works as hard as she can to catch up and remains focused on doing her level best all the way through the finish line. A winner never wishes for another competitor to stumble and fall, because she wants to win fair and square. But a winner is also aware of the fact that by remaining committed to the race, these unforeseen events do sometimes occur, and the leader may weaken for any number of reasons, opening an opportunity to prevail when all the odds seemed to be against that possibility at the sound of the starter's pistol.

If you wish to be an outlier, one who is unusually successful in whatever vocation or avocation you choose, remain committed. Staying committed may not guarantee a first-place finish in life, but a lack of commitment will ensure a poor result no matter what the goal.

Kenneth Blanchard said, "There's a difference between interest and commitment. When you're interested in doing something, you do it only when it is convenient. When you're committed to something, you accept no excuses—only results."

> ❝*Unless commitment is made, there are only promises and hopes; but no plans.*❞
>
> —Peter Drucker (1909-2005),
> Austrian-born American management consultant, educator, and author

What are you committed to doing? Commit to your success plan. Do you have any examples in your life where commitment has led to success? Perhaps you have applied yourself before in school, in sports, in studying, in relationships, in work, in a vocation, in spiritual devotion, etc. Do you have examples of your commitment? If you don't already, you will.

Comprehensive

adjective

Definition: covering completely or broadly.

Be comprehensive in your approach to any undertaking. The highly successful set are not known for being superficial or flippant in their attitude toward getting a job done. This is true of the expert automobile mechanic, who evaluates and repairs your vehicle as if it were his own, knowing your safety and the safety of your family may hang in the balance. His is a serious job and one which is not to be taken lightly.

An expert in any field is thorough and comprehensive in their work. As they say, a good writer, attorney, or accountant should cross every *T* and dot every *I*. The brilliant men and women who work at NASA are known for their comprehensive attention to detail as they design, build, and develop spacecraft which are meant to carry out highly challenging missions extended far into deep space.

See yourself in this light always. You may not be a neurosurgeon, nor an astrophysicist, but be comprehensive about your work. Be the best journalist you can be by doing the background research on your subject, the best butcher you can by knowing your craft thoroughly, knowing where your beef comes from, how it is raised, what is fed, whether it is humanely slaughtered, etc. There is no profession where this rule of comprehensiveness does not apply if you truly want to be at the top of your field. Be serious and disciplined so you will stand out from the crowd and be recognized as a leader in your area of interest. This will lead to winning results and unparalleled success.

❝The last rule was to make enumerations so complete, and reviews so comprehensive, that I should be certain of omitting nothing.❞

—René Descartes (1596-1650),
French philosopher, mathematician, and writer

Your success story is contingent upon this. In your plan in creating your success story, you need to apply yourself one hundred percent. What is the use of doing something if you will not do it one hundred percent? Be thorough in your planning, be thorough in your learning your skills. What are your thoughts on this?

Concentration

---

noun

Definition: the act or process of concentration: the state of being concentrated; especially: direction of attention to a single object.

To excel, you must find a way to create an environment and state of mind which is conducive to deep thought and focus. This can be hard work for the novice. The human brain is a highly metabolic organ, burning through glucose like 747 burns through jet fuel. Although the human brain only weighs approximately three pounds, it utilizes twenty percent of the total oxygen and receives twenty percent of the total blood flow in your body. The brain consumes roughly 120 grams of glucose per day, which is about sixty percent of what the body consumes at rest. In other word, your brain is an incredible supercomputer that requires tremendous energy to keep running. Distraction can be eliminated; it just takes a little work and a little practice.

Just as lifting heavy weights requires the concentrated force of muscular contraction, deep thinking and difficult problem solving require concentrated neurological function. It is imperative that successful individuals learn to concentrate for long periods of time on challenging issues, ideas, and concerns. It is only through this that new ideas will be added to the complex fabric of your consciousness.

Do not expect answers to life's most troublesome dilemmas to effortlessly reveal themselves to you. Make time to think hard about the various issues facing you in your life. Consider them deeply and routinely if you expect to be a true super-achiever.

> *"Concentration comes out of a combination of confidence and hunger."*
>
> —Arnold Palmer (1929-2016),
> American professional golfer, businessman, and entrepreneur

Lack of concentration can foul up your attempts at success. Write your thoughts down here or in a work notebook so you have your plan in order.

Dedication

noun
Definition: a feeling of very strong support for or loyalty to someone or something.

Dedication means getting started at something and sticking with it forever. It's about not quitting. It's about seeing each task and project through to the end. When you are truly dedicated, you never give up, even when things become difficult.

Keep marching forward when others sit down to rest. Look to inspiring men like Mehdi Fakharzadeh (whom I have mentioned earlier in this book) and hear their motivating life stories. We are fortunate we can find video interviews of such outstanding individuals on the internet and turn to them whenever we feel like quitting. Perhaps there is no skill more important to success than "stick-to-it-iveness," also known as dedication.

> "*If I were to look back on my work, I think I accomplished probably seventy to seventy-five percent of what I could have. Maybe sixty percent. Somewhere in that area; two-thirds of what I could have accomplished. If I had been a really dedicated person, and worked hard, I think I could have accomplished more.*"
>
> —Jack Nicklaus (1940-),
> American professional golfer, entrepreneur, and author

Do you feel totally dedicated to your goals? Are you doing your very best? Where have you come up short in the past, and where are you committed to doing better in the future? Use this opportunity to think about those important questions deeply. Work it out on paper.

Defeat

noun
Definition: failure to succeed or win.

125

We all know defeat. To be successful, however, learn to not get defeated by it. There are so many wonderful examples of this all around us. All great athletes have been defeated at some point or another. All great salespeople have been rejected and denied. Most business people will tell you about bad deals they've made, poor investments they made, poor decisions they've made. But the real winners don't let these experiences stop them from continuously getting up off the ground, brushing themselves off, and moving forward.

As the great inspirational speaker and educator Brian Tracy says, people with the winner's attitude are "unstoppable." The unstoppable nature is the fabric that leads to a successful private and business life. This approach to the obstacles, situations, and stumbling blocks of the real world is what ultimately culminates in victory and living the good life.

Winners don't win all the time. If you know a "winner" who never loses, he or she is probably not pushing themselves to their true personal limit and haven't yet realized their full potential. Fear of failure will often lead modestly or moderately successful people to believe they have achieved all they can.

If a batter in baseball hits a home run every time at plate, they are probably a grown man playing in little league. The "big leaguers" go to bat against world-class pitchers, so a batting average of .300 (or three out of ten) is considered incredibly good.

Find a way to push yourself to the limit so you know you are really doing the best you can. If you don't get beaten occasionally, I can assure you aren't testing the limits of your own capability. Find out what you are really made of. Don't play golf or tennis only with people you can beat handily; make sure you go out occasionally and get your tail whipped by the best player in your community so you recognize you can still do better. That may mean more lessons, new equipment, more practice, strength training, or stretching, but I can assure you, if you're the kind of winner who never loses, you may not be as great as you think.

> 66*While one may encounter many defeats, one must not be defeated.*99

—Maya Angelou (1928-2014),
American author, poet, playwright, civil rights activist,producer, composer, dancer, actress, and singer

Here is where your story gains a dramatic foothold. Disappointment, defeat, or failure have come into the story to vex our protagonist. How to handle these setbacks? What kind of attitude do you think will help overcome these obstacles?

Delegate

verb
Definition: to give (control, responsibility, authority, etc.) to someone: to trust someone with (a job, duty, etc.).

If you wish to win big, you had better learn to delegate—and I mean fast. Successful people only do what is essentially important and only take on jobs and carry out tasks they can do better than anyone else. If someone else can do a job better, I suggest you have that person do it. Imagine for a moment I told you I had a very successful friend who owned a national trucking company. What image would come to mind? Would you envision a scenario whereby my friend had one truck and drove it? Of course not. Would you imagine he had a fleet of 1,000 trucks and drove them all? Of course not. That would be not only absurd, but also impossible.

If I told you I had a friend like that, I bet I know what you would see in your imagination. To begin with, you probably would not conjure up the image of a man who dressed casually like a truck driver. Furthermore, you would probably assume he didn't drive a truck—at this point in his career at least. You might see a man behind a desk. You would likely picture a man who attended meetings, spoke on the telephone, and made plans. I would assume a man who ran such a company would not take out the garbage, sweep floors, clean bathrooms, change motor oil, check tire pressures, load and unload cargo, answer the telephone, transcribe letters, file paperwork, or change lightbulbs in the central office. It is likely he didn't prepare his own tax return, balance his own books, or prepare the defense of any legal matters the company might have.

I would suppose such an individual would have people in place to carry out just about every task one could imagine other than what was essential he do. This is how winners win big. One cannot get the contract for a delivery, load the truck, drive the truck, unload the delivery, go home, check the oil, fill the tank with gas, replace the windshield wiper fluid and antifreeze, and then start doing billing for services. That said, many very fine, small outfits start that way. But, if you desire growth and prosperity, at some point you must delegate these services to someone else. The old saying, "If you want something done properly, you have to do it yourself," is a charming quip, but it is a recipe for minimal achievement. If you wish to be a super achiever, start delegating immediately. It can be scary at first, but it is a must. No man is an island.

> *“If you want to do a few small things right, do them yourself. If you want to do great things and make a big impact, learn to delegate.”*
>
> —John C. Maxwell (1947-), American author, speaker, and pastor

Delegating is a huge part of your plan. At first, you'll have to do most of the work as you start out on your journey. However, we can do some dreaming here and think about what kinds of people you want on your team. Who would you delegate to do which task? Why?

Direction

noun
Definition: the course or path on which something is moving or pointing.

By definition, everyone, not just winners, is moving in some direction. The caveat here is winners are constantly taking of stock of what direction they are moving in, and they are working tirelessly to keep the bow of their personal ship headed in a positive, productive direction. A powerful metaphor that has helped me immensely in my own life is shared by Jim Rohn, who was famous for saying, "You can't control the wind, but you can trim your own sail."

In other words, we can't change the tax code. Furthermore, we can't change the market price of flour, yeast, or salt if we are opening a pizzeria. We can't necessarily affect the terms of a lease for the retail space which we wish to open. But there are factors we can affect, and it will be those elements which will have the greatest impact on what magnitude of success we will enjoy and what quality of life we will engineer. This is by setting the direction of our own personal sail.

For example, how delicious is the pizza you sell? How consistent is the product? How excellent is your customer service? How clean is your establishment? How prompt are your delivery people? How polite is your staff? How professional is the dress code in your restaurant? Has every lightbulb been changed in the fixtures? Is the restroom immaculate, and are there always toilet tissue, hand soap, and paper towels available? How comprehensive is the training for the young people who answer the telephone and take to-go orders? The answers to each of these questions will determine the set of your personal entrepreneurial and financial sail. If you have the sail in the wrong position, it will never be filled with wind. In fact, if you answer too many of these questions incorrectly, your ship may be bobbing dead in the water, or worse...it may capsize.

Be the captain of your own destiny. Don't let gusting winds blow you to and fro on the expansive sea of life. Take hold of the ropes and the wheel of your personal, financial, emotional, and psychological cutter. You must oversee the direction your life takes. Don't blame the boat, the wind and the waves, the salt air, and the sunshine. In the end, they're all you've got to navigate your way through this challenge we call life. Learn to master the seas by charting a course and working hard to get there, recognizing it will not always be easy. As the old saying goes, "A ship in port is safe, but that's not what ships are built for."

> ‶*Lack of direction, not lack of time, is the problem. We all have twenty-four hour days.*″
>
> —Zig Ziglar (1926-2012),
> American author, salesman, and motivational speaker

When writing out your plan, the direction of your dreams is very important. Where do you see yourself in five years? Ten years? When you combine action and attitude with commitment, you are going to do well regarding the direction you wish to take your dreams. Write it out now so you have an idea of where you want your life to be headed. Onwards and upwards, slow and steadily upwards, full steam ahead…

Disappointment

---

noun
Definition: the state of feeling sad, unhappy, or displeased because something was not as good as expected or because something you hoped for or expected did not happen.

Everyone must contend with disappointment in their lives. The question is how are you going to let disappointment impact you in the long term. Winners take disappointing experiences in stride, and, in fact, try not to see them as such. Rather, the high achiever recognizes all things in nature ultimately can be charted in terms of peaks and valleys. This is true for the stock market, a blood pressure tracing, an EKG tracing, a pulse wave, the seasonal temperature, seasonal rainfall, etc.

The individual with the successful approach to life recognizes at the outset of any undertaking that there will be times when profits are not what are expected or projected, illness of various severities will strike, losses both small and great will occur. No one enjoys the down times, but the winners never quit when the going gets tough. In fact, it is in these moments that the true greatness of the expert is most glaringly demonstrated.

Again, because of my background as a cardiovascular surgeon, it is always easy for me to draw analogies between life and the operating room. What makes a great surgeon great? Have you ever considered that? Well, I think for the most part we look at results to judge surgeons. In the profession, we call these results morbidity and mortality statistics. This metric is a measure of how frequently patients operated on by a given surgeon get sick or die after surgery. This is obviously an incredibly valuable and important barometer of quality. What makes the best surgeons is the ability to deal with complications, difficult cases, unexpected developments, etc.

In fact, one of the major steps in the process of becoming board certified in a surgical specialty in the United Sates is the ability to pass a written qualifying examination followed by a live, in person, oral certifying examination. This oral examination is felt by many to be the most difficult step in a very grueling process of training and testing for surgeons. Typically, the examinee will be questioned for several hours by as many as six different examiners in two-on-one encounters. To clarify, one examinee will be tested, questioned, and quizzed by two board certified surgeons simultaneously, and he or she must pass through three such rooms successfully to be considered safe and competent.

Invariably, the clinical scenarios put forth by the examiners culminate in the young surgeon being tested suggesting that the fictitious patient be taken to the operating room to undergo surgery. Typically, what happens is that the professors giving the exam ask what the surgeon would like to do, and despite giving the appropriate response, he is told the patient is getting sicker. This can be a very stress-provoking experience. The individuals remain straight-faced throughout the process and give no feedback other than the patient's condition to indicate how well the examinee is doing. Again, this can create a tremendous amount of stress for a recent graduate. Ultimately, he or she is pressed for what else they might do to improve the patient's condition so that they begin to improve clinically and ultimately make a full recovery.

The purpose of this exercise is not only to test the surgeon's knowledge base and judgement but also to see how they will react under intense pressure. Anyone can remain calm and collected when things are going well; the diagnoses are obvious, the treatment options are clear, and the patient responds positively to all the therapies prescribed. The question is how will the inexperienced physician react to a patient who gets more ill despite doing everything right? That is where the rubber meets the road, as they say, in the field of surgery. How will you react when unexpected bleeding occurs? What if the stitches you place make the hole in the blood vessel larger rather than smaller?

The point here is that the real world is rife with disappointments, problems, troubles, and hitches. Again, anyone can captain a ship on calm seas. The real test of being a winner is how you weather the storms. Don't let disappointing results or moments stop you from proceeding forward and working hard to solve problems and create new and exciting opportunities.

❝A pier is a disappointed bridge.❞

—Julian Barnes (1946-), English writer

This section of the book is all about obstacles and overcoming them. How do you deal with disappointment? Think about the last time something or someone disappointed you or you were disappointed in yourself. How did you feel? How did you get over it? What steps can you take to accept that disappointments happen and make them work for you in the present and future?

Education

noun

Definition: the act or process of imparting or acquiring general knowledge, developing the powers of reasoning and judgment, and generally of preparing oneself or others intellectually for mature life: the result produced by instruction, training, or study.

Not every successful person is formally educated, but every successful person knows the value of an education. Education takes many forms from on the job learning, mentorship, apprenticeship, to university and graduate school. No education is a wasted experience. Whether formal or informal, there is no substitute for feeding and expanding the mind and its capacity for understanding and problem solving.

One key component of living an educated life is to never assume you know it all. Those who are "know-it-alls" are doomed to an existence of mediocrity, if not inferiority.

Education is really nothing more than the sharing of ideas. This requires being generous with what they know and keeping an open mind to what others are willing to share. Receiving an education can be an active or passive process. In other words, the student can decide to read or study a well-defined course of material or simply be conscious about watching and listening to the people and events that surround them every day. The process can be structured and rigorous, but it can also be more ethereal and relaxed. Perhaps you learn the most when the mind is most relaxed and prepared to absorb new information without the stress of judgement and testing.

In any event, the essence of the matter is to keep nourishing your wonderful brain with novel material and, as you do, you will find that assimilation of future wisdom will only become easier. This philosophy will set you on a trajectory for inconceivable success.

> **"*I have never let my schooling get in the way of my education.*"**
>
> —Mark Twain (1835-1910), American author and humorist

Whether formal or informal, name some ways you have gained an education. Has what you learned helped you reach your goals? How? How can education improve your personal success story? What must you learn to succeed? Is furthering your education part of your plan? Write down some real-life characters who have been a part of your education, people who have taught you something beneficial or have guided you in some way. These people are an important part of your success story.

Excuse

noun
Definition: a reason you give to explain a mistake, bad behavior, etc.

Simply put, successful people don't make excuses. Losers make excuses. Whether you are striving for a new position at work, pushing to get better grades, planning to lose a certain amount of weight through a healthy eating and exercise plan, nothing breaks your stride quite like explaining a failure away or, rather, making an excuse. An excuse works differently than an explanation; an excuse bears weight that will hold you back.

It is what we tell ourselves and others when we do not want to be honest. We failed a class because the teacher hates us. We ate the entire pie because traffic was bad on the way home. You mistreated a friend because you were in a bad mood. You didn't get that report done because...

Perhaps you did not want to get it done because you dislike your job. Perhaps you ate an entire pie because you really wanted pie. Stress eating is an explanation; bad traffic is an excuse. If you can tell the difference between the two, you are on your way to becoming more honest with yourself. And once you achieve that, you will have greater confidence in yourself and maybe, just maybe, do better next time.

Obstacles and conflict are great learning tools because they shake things up in our lives. They make up the drama of a good story, mainly because the audience wants to see how our protagonist gets out of a jam. How will you get out of your jam? How will you face an obstacle like wanting the whole pie, having strained relationships because of your bad temper, or facing a difficult task at work or a difficult paper or test at school? Successful people shed their excuses and get to work at bettering themselves and moving through conflict, not allowing excuses to get in their way of happiness and success.

"Ninety-nine percent of the failures come from people who have the habit of making excuses."
—George Washington Carver (c.1860-1943), American botanist and inventor

So…you have come up against an obstacle. What excuse would you normally use for it regarding why it successfully defeated you? Now think of a way you can overcome that obstacle.

Failure

noun
Definition: lack of success.

All winners fail. All people fail. That's normal. How often you fail and how badly you fail is another story altogether. Just like a student or an athlete, you don't want to make failure your calling card, but some setbacks and disappointments are to be expected in the course of life, particularly when you set lofty goals for yourself.

Great hitters in baseball strike out frequently. Great shooters in the NBA like Michael Jordan have missed thousands of shots. You can look at these

134

experiences as failures or simply as a part of "the game of life." Again, when you set ambitious goals, the chances of facing problems, obstacles, and losses from time to time must be anticipated. If you find you never fail at anything you set out to do, this most definitely means, in my opinion, you are setting the bar too low for yourself. There is no risk in that, sure, but are you really pushing yourself?

Think about the stories you have read. What fun is reading about someone who floats through life, always getting what they want, always succeeding in everything they do, barely breaking a sweat, never having doubts, always winning? Gets kind of boring after a while, doesn't it? Where is the drama in that? What do you learn from always succeeding? Not much, except it can get boring.

As the Hall of Fame football coach Vince Lombardi was famous for saying, "It's not whether you got knocked down which is important. What's important is whether you get back up." Remember: winners never quit, and quitters never win. This adage will serve you well in your life. Fight the good fight. Expect to take some licks along the way. Don't assume you will be successful in every endeavor you undertake. Take failure in stride and make every effort to take instructive lessons from every experience where things don't go your way. Ask yourself how you could do things differently next time and what mistakes you made. This is how we learn.

As always, remember the old saying, "Good judgement comes from experience, and experience comes from poor judgement." Failing doesn't make you a failure. Overcoming failure and trying again and again to get to where you are going will make you a true success at the end of the day.

"I haven't failed. I've just found 10,000 ways that won't work."

—Thomas A. Edison (1847-1931), American inventor and businessman

This may not be a pleasant exercise, but it is enlightening and important. Name the times you have gloriously failed. What did you learn? Failure is always worth something if you got a life lesson out of it.

Fear

---

noun
Definition: an unpleasant emotion caused by being aware of danger.

Everyone feels fear. Fear is a natural response to certain stimuli in the surrounding environment. We are hardwired to react to fear. In physiology, this is known as the *fight or flight* mechanism. When we come under any sort of attack or outside threat, a trigger between the brain and the adrenal glands causes a sudden release of adrenaline. This chemical stimulates the body's organ systems to either run as fast and hard as you can away from danger or to thrust forward into battle.

The purpose of the adrenal surge is to assist in survival of the species. How to react to fear depends on the situation. Sometimes it is best to run and avoid a fight; other times it is best to stand and go toe to toe with the adversarial situation at hand. This is a subtle balance. This decision must consider an infinite number of variables. Successful people seem to have a knack for knowing not only which battles are worth fighting but also whether they have a real chance of winning.

Taking on every opponent in life may be heroic, but this is not always a harbinger of victory. You must consider the absolute value in the contest in the first place. Fighting for the sake of fighting is an idiotic endeavor. There must be some fruit to be won in any given contest, and that fruit must outweigh whatever pain and injury you endure because of the conflict.

At times, like it or not, the stakes are too high, the opposition is too strong, and the resulting defeat may set you back too far in your effort to achieve success. Walking away from such fights, although hurtful to the ego, may indeed be the best option.

Running from every fight will ensure that you never achieve any notable height on the ladder of achievement. You must be able to manage fear. You must be able to look fear square in the eye and decide whether you should run so you can return to fight another day when better prepared or to stand and rumble right now.

These decisions are made on a person-to-person and case-by-case basis. It is impossible for me to teach which fights are worthwhile and which are simply an exercise in futility. The point of this passage is to make the reader aware that fear is normal and coping with fear is the key to having a winning record in the end. Look at each situation and ask yourself: Do I run, or do I stay and fight? What are my odds of winning, and what do I get as a reward should I win?

Also, what do I lose buy running this time, and is there anything I might win by avoiding this hostile interaction?

Successful people don't take on every fight, and they don't win every fight, but the scorecard should reflect more wins than losses and more trophies than broken bones.

> **F-E-A-R has two meanings: 'Forget Everything And Run' or 'Face Everything And Rise.' The choice is yours.**
>
> —Zig Ziglar (1926-2012),
> American author, salesman, and motivational speaker

Fear can be a great obstacle and a great learning tool, both in fiction and in real life. When has feared stopped you? What did you do about overcoming it? How has it been a learning tool? Do you have a plan? Or maybe a few ideas about how to overcome fear of failing? Write them down.

Flow

verb
Definition: to move in a continuous way and smooth way.

See the natural beauty in flow. Who doesn't appreciate the sounds of a babbling brook or the rush of a mighty waterfall? Who doesn't feel the exhilaration of the power produced by the flow of air through a jet engine?

Flow is so essential to life and all living things. As a cardiovascular surgeon and a biologist, I recognize the pure necessity of flow. Blood flow is, of course, what keeps us alive, along with the rhythmic flow of air in and out of our miraculous lungs. The flow of oxygen into our tissues to keep them healthy and thriving is a must to maintain our existence. The flow of words in a good conversation, the happy flow of tears during a wedding ceremony, the flow of secretory fluids while making love and creating new life, these are all the basis for a complete and rich life. The flow of sap in a maple tree, or the flow of the waves the ocean—the examples are endless.

There is no flow more fulfilling or enjoyable than the kind of flow I am in right now as I write this book. This is the flow of concentration, pleasure, focus, creativity, productivity, and accomplishment. We've all experienced this feeling. It is the sensation we get when we are lost in thought or in physical activity, the feeling we have when time loses all meaning and we feel we could continue whatever it is we are doing forever and ever. This is the flow state.

Highly successful people almost become addicted to this feeling. This is the place you want to be every day of your life if you are lucky enough, particularly as it pertains to your work. If you can get into flow when you are working, you will become super productive and creative. By doing the work, new ideas will flow though you, from you, and out of you. These ideas and creative images that are often realized in the mind's eye will propel you to new heights of reward, fulfillment, happiness, success, and wealth.

"Competition is an easy way to get into flow."

—Mihaly Csikszentmihalyi (1934-),
Hungarian-American psychologist, professor, author, and speaker

Getting into the flow is a magical feeling. Part of your plan is getting to a place in your life that enables you to experience this magic as often and as thoroughly as possible. If you are in a relationship or a job where you do not feel this flow, where time drags on and you wish you were somewhere else, then it is time to make some life changes. Perhaps you experience this flow on your own time, working on a hobby you find fulfilling and enjoyable.

When have you been in the flow? Write about it. No doubt it is inspiring and will help you prepare your life to experience more flow!

Focus

noun

Definition: a main purpose or interest: a subject that is being discussed or studied.

Learn to master focus. Focus and flow tend to go together. When the mind is focused, things flow spontaneously and beautifully. We are productive when we are focused. We are at peace when we are focused. When our goals come clearly into focus we are much more likely to achieve them. Focus gives us clarity of thought and vision. Think of a master surgeon, musician, or marksman: focus is absolutely *everything*.

Consider for a moment how irritating and utterly annoying it is to listen to a radio station that is not perfectly tuned in. Imagine watching a TV program, or an old movie from a projector, or a low definition video on YouTube. When things are only slightly out of focus, it can be miserably distracting to watch. Sharpness is everything, whether one is looking under a microscope at organisms on a glass slide or a telescope aimed far into the heavens. If one loses focus, even minimally, the result is often frustration and a lack of progress.

Successful individuals know exactly what they wish to achieve. They create a plan. Their goals are in focus; it is their main preoccupation. How to get to their desired destination is in focus. The work they do in pursuing their personal desires is focused and disciplined. It requires hard work. Just like focusing intensely on something with your eyes can be strenuous, focusing on your work or goals can also be remarkably tiring. With training and practice, your endurance for focus improves dramatically. When you can take focus to the state of "flow," then the journey becomes a joy to be a part of. Time passes effortlessly, and your productivity multiplies many times over.

Attaining and sustaining focus—whether it is on homework, reading a brief, or preparing a document for an important presentation—is a skill that requires practice like any other. The more time spent on focusing, the sooner the results will be realized.

For most individuals, the ideal environment to foster focus is one that is quiet and provides solitude. It is in this type of surrounding where one can best "hear themselves think." Make every effort to gain comfort in silent solitude. This is the milieu that will lend itself best to creativity, imagination, effectiveness, efficiency, productivity, and inner calm. Do all you can to eliminate unnecessary noise of any kind, keeping in mind not all noise is audible. Visual distractions like a television, other people, a computer screen, passing traffic, etc. can all be significantly destructive to the focused environment. This type of environment can bring on varying levels of anxiety and apprehension at first, as few of us in contemporary society are accustomed to silent solitude.

Classically, another place to find focus is in nature. Some of history's greatest thinkers and achievers did their best work in nature. Perhaps at the seashore, in a park, in the woods, or alongside a flowing river, you might find a kind of comfort that is new to you.

Thinking, planning, setting goals, reading, and writing in such atmospheres may bring out a creative force in you the likes of which you have never known before. Experiment with different settings. See what works for you. For some people, music is an absolute must to be alone and to work. For me, although I love music, I find it a distraction when I want to do my best and most focused work. Again, find what brings out the most intense level focus in you and then stick with it.

> ❝*The key to success is to focus our conscious mind on what we desire, not things we fear.*❞
>
> —Brian Tracy (1944-),
> Canadian-American author, motivational speaker, and consultant

Flow and focus do go hand in hand. For flow to occur, you must focus. What raises your level of concentration? What do you do that can hold your attention for long periods of time? Write about it, and perhaps make a plan about making this a larger part of your life.

Impact

noun

Definition: a powerful or major influence or effect.

140

Impact comes from acting on ideas. As I have said before, ideas are worthless. Shakespeare's famous Dane, Hamlet's greatest flaw was his inaction. Sure, he had lofty musings and tons of interesting plans and ideas he dreamed up, but when it came to acting upon them, he tragically, fatally, fell short. Not having an impact is not usually how one writes a protagonist, either. You want your main character to influence people, to make a difference, to stand out from the crowd.

Hopefully, you want to make a positive influence on your community and in your relationships, both personal and professional. Unless you are willing to act on your ideas, the ideas have no value whatsoever. In sports, they talk about the great athletes as being "impact players." These are the individuals who positively affect the outcome of the game. Find your greatest areas of strength and see how you can make an impact on your finances, your personal life, your company, your friends, your community, and your world.

Why not become an impact-oriented type of person? What is the alternative, to live a life that leaves no positive mark at all? You are better than that, and you know it. You want more from this life than that, and you know it. The only reason you might deny that is out of fear. Are you afraid to try because you worry that even your best effort won't be enough to achieve something great in this world? Leave those insecurities behind you. If you try hard enough, long enough, you will make a difference not only in your life but in the lives of those around you.

> 66*The only limit to your impact is your imagination and commitment.*99
>
> —Tony Robbins (1960-),
> American motivational speaker, life coach, and author

What kind of impact do you want to make with your life? No matter how big or how small your idea, it is important, so write it down. Explore the idea of leaving a lasting impression upon those around you. How will you do it? Will you leave the world a better place? How?

It's good to have a plan!

Influence

noun

Definition: a person or thing that affects someone or something in an important way: the power to cause changes without directly forcing them to happen: the power to change or affect someone or something.

People have the power to influence situations. To be successful means to not wait for others to roll out the red carpet for your success because you understand the reality is, that isn't going to happen. As I stated previously, one of my philosophical mentors, Mr. Jim Rohn, became famous for saying, "You can't change the direction of the wind, but you can change the set of your own sail." These are some of the simplest yet most powerful words you will ever hear. If you can internalize and truly digest the meaning of these words, you will be forever empowered. This is all about influencing your environment rather than allowing the environment to blow you around like a piece of torn newsprint swirling meaninglessly in the wind. Focus and planning play a part in this.

Use your influence in a positive way. You may not even think you have any influence but we all do. You may not be a leader of industry, a politician, a clergyman, etc., but make no mistake, we all have the power of influence. It can be used as a hindrance as well as an aid to success. The key is knowing how you want to live your life. The most marvelous thing is that influence begins within. The most important person each of us can ever influence in a positive and productive way is ourselves.

Influence begins within. Talk to yourself about being the best you can be. Talk to yourself about your nutrition. Talk to yourself about your exercise program. Talk to yourself about your educational status. Talk to yourself about your appearance. Talk to yourself about your bank account balance. Talk to yourself about your personal relationships. The more you look deep into who you are and how your inner winds are blowing about, the more you can take control of your own personal sail and chart a new course where necessary. The plan for success includes taking to heart the positive influences in your life and creating a life that will be a positive influence on others.

When others around you see the changes you are making in yourself, they will be intrigued. They will want to know more about what is guiding and influencing this new and improved you. That will be your opportunity to influence someone else by sharing what you know and what you have learned. This is a terrific feeling. Sharing and being generous with your time and knowledge is one of the great experiences of life. You can influence members of your family, members of your community, co-workers, colleagues, and employees just by "walking the walk." It's a fabulous experience.

Be a person of influence. Be an individual who influences change for the better in themselves and those around them. This is the kind of person that makes an excellent protagonist of a success story! This can happen in little ways and in big ways, but the sooner you get started, the sooner you'll see what I mean. Don't live your life as a piece of paper being thrown around by whatever wind decides to blow your way. Live a life or purpose. You direct your person where only you decide it should go, and each adventure will be more glorious than the last.

> *The key to successful leadership today is influence, not authority.*
>
> —Ken Blanchard (1939-),
> American author, professional speaker, consultant, and management expert

Can you list some negative as well as positive influences on your life? Talk about how effective they have been to you. How do you go about releasing yourself from the negative influences, and how do you allow positive influences to change your life?

Innovation

noun
Definition: a new idea, device, or method: the act or process of introducing new ideas, devices, or methods.

Most successful people are innovators. Keep in mind, this doesn't necessarily mean you must "re-invent the wheel" to succeed. The innovator asks themselves, "How can I make things a little bit better?" and, "How can we do things just a little bit smarter?" The innovator is always looking to add a little more value. This may be done in giant leaps on rare occasions, but in general, innovation is much subtler than that. Innovations commonly come to fruition through small, manageable modifications to the status quo.

The Japanese refer to this style of innovation as *kaizen*. Kaizen in Chinese and Japanese literally means *improvement*. Japanese businesses used this concept to mean getting a little bit better every day. This applied to workers on the line, managers, and executives. This is the kind of innovation that applies to most of us, like compounding interest can have dramatic effects on our quality of life if applied faithfully and over a long period of time.

To be innovative, you do not need to invent the combustion engine, the assembly line, Facebook, or the personal computer. If you can look at every aspect of your life—whether it is your health, your finances, your knowledge base, or your personal relationships—and be innovative, you will see tremendous change in the fruit the tree of life will provide for you. If a big idea comes along occasionally as well, then so much the better.

By the way, I believe strongly that the best fuel for innovation is being involved in the work. Through being involved and doing whatever it is you do every day, thoughts will come to you seemingly out of thin air. Your incredible brain will spontaneously ask itself, *How can I do this better, more efficiently, and with better outcomes?* It's a wonderful experience to be innovative. We all have the capacity to be innovators. Be sure not to dismiss your ideas as inconsequential or silly. Try them out in an applied way, and be sure to share your ideas for improvement with friends, family, and colleagues before deciding to label them as worthless. The feedback you get may surprise you.

❝*Innovation distinguishes between a leader and a follower.*❞

—Steve Jobs (1955-2011), American entrepreneur and inventor

List some of your innovations, no matter if you think they are silly.

144

Judgment

noun
Definition: the ability to make good decisions about what should be done.

Exercise exceptional judgment. To be clear, not every decision highly successful individuals make is spot on, but their overall scorecard must be excellent to have a winning record over the course of a lifetime. This is a fundamental principle of extraordinary performance in any vocation.

Whether you are faced with the challenge of deciding which ninety-miles-per-hour Major League curve ball to swing at, which blood vessel can be safely divided in the operating room, or which wire should be snipped to defuse an incendiary device on the battlefield, successful people make tough decision-making look easy.

The first thing that is mandatory in becoming an exceptional decision maker is recognizing the importance of, and value in, this skill. Many people have no idea how important their daily decisions are. Simple questions like, "What should I eat for breakfast?" are so basic, yet so important to forging a healthy and properly fueled day. "Where should I invest my surplus income?" is another one that too many people don't put enough thought into. Questions regarding health, exercise, personal relationships, money, work, family, education, etc. face each of us all the time. Making the right choices comes from recognizing the importance of such judgements and working hard to accrue the proper information so we can make a wise choice. Don't take this role lightly. It may very well be the most important determinant of where you are now and where you are going.

"Good judgment comes from experience, and a lot of that comes from bad judgment."

—Will Rogers (1879-1935),
American stage and motion picture actor, cowboy, humorist, newspaper columnist, and social commentator

Write about yourself as how you want to see yourself. Do you see yourself making wise decisions? Do you learn from your mistakes? What were the last few important judgment calls you made that changed the course of your life?

145

Leverage

noun

Definition: influence or power used to achieve a desired result: the increase in force gained by using a lever.

Understand the value of leverage. Archimedes, the Greek mathematician said, "Give me a lever long enough and a fulcrum on which to place it, and I shall move the world." This is a wonderful image and a very strong philosophical concept. However, it does contain some nuance that should be dissected. Although there is no question in the power of a lever and a fulcrum, look at what the statement really says: "Give me." Ah, if only it were that simple. "Here you go, John, here's a really long lever and a fulcrum upon which to place it, now go kick some ass."

Sadly, this is not the way of the real world. In the real world, first you must understand and appreciate the function and potential of a good lever. But, perhaps more importantly, the second aspect of utilizing leverage lies in the process of obtaining the actual lever and fulcrum. Rarely are you going to be gifted such devices. The successful person goes out into the world and obtains various levers and fulcrums upon which to place them. This is the real trick. This is the hard part. This is where you must roll up your sleeves and do the "dirty work." By definition, implementing a lever makes work a hell of a lot easier. But life isn't that simple. Again, the difficult phase in the process is the acquisition of the levers.

So, how is this done? The answer is: in many ways. Almost anything can be used as a lever if you are constantly on the lookout for them. Otherwise, you may be fortunate enough to find a wonderful lever lying at your feet, step over it, and just keep on walking. Levers take all forms. A good friend is a lever, money is a lever, knowledge is a lever, education is a lever, various skills act as levers. The list goes on and on.

Certainly, one of the greatest levers of the last three decades or so that has been put in the hands of the average citizen is the technology lever. Not long ago, it would have been inconceivable—if not for the vision of individuals like Bill Gates and Steve Jobs—that essentially everyone would either own or have access to a powerful computer. The so-called "world wide web" and the internet have opened a world of resources, knowledge, and services that had been for millennia even beyond the realm of fantasy. But are you truly utilizing this incredible lever to your greatest personal advantage? My guess is: probably not.

> **❝I believe it is in the world's best interest to develop environments that fully engage women and leverage their natural talents.❞**
>
> —Weili Dai (1961-), Chinese-born American businesswoman

Name some of your levers, and write out how they influence your life.

Lose

verb
Definition: to fail to win (a game, contest, etc.).

Successful people lose, but they are not losers. Losing simply means you are in the game of life. There are endless analogies to illustrate this point. Take some time to search online for how many times our greatest sports legends lost or suffered setbacks and defeats. The numbers are staggering. The following quote has been ascribed to Michael Jordan: "*I've missed more than 9,000 shots in my career. I've lost almost 300 games. Twenty-six times I've been trusted to take the game winning shot and missed. I've failed repeatedly in my life. And that is why I succeed.*"

Larry Bird, Roger Federer, Muhammad Ali, Magic Johnson, and many other all-time great athletes in their respective sports have lost major championship contests. That is one thing they all have in common. Another thing they have in common is they never quit. They have within them the steely determination of the winner.

What fun would be to win all the time be anyway? Most likely, if all you do is win, you aren't facing stiff enough competition. Then you are likely setting the bar way too low. When winners do lose, when they do face defeat, they want to know they were beaten by the best, not just some run-of-the-mill, mediocre local talent.

This is true of super-achievers in every facet of life. The greatest heart surgeons ever known to mankind have lost patients in the operating room or in the post-operative period. This occurs not because of some egregious error in judgment or technical performance, but because they were willing to take on the sickest patients, at the highest risk for complications, who had no other chance at survival except surgery. The world-class surgeon takes on these patients because he or she knows that although a very small fraction won't make it through, the vast majority will, and they will therefore be given a new lease on life. No guarantees can be made at the outset, although winners take every precaution to help avoid undesirable problems and poor outcomes.

This is true in every endeavor. Winners take chances and push the limits of what others feel is possible. This can apply to business deals, creating new and exciting works of art, composing and performing music, acting or singing on a stage in front of hundreds or even thousands of spectators. Winners must always be willing to lose, otherwise they are not even in the arena competing in the game. On that note, I direct you to Theodore Roosevelt's now famous "Citizenship in a Republic" speech from the Sorbonne in Paris, on April 23, 1910. This is often referred to as the "Man in the Arena" speech. I urge you to look it up and read it through entirely, whether you are familiar with it or not. For the purpose of this section on losing, I will leave you to ponder the following key excerpt:

"It is not the critic who counts; not the man who points out how the strong man stumbles, or where the doer of deeds could have done them better. The credit belongs to the man who is actually in the arena, whose face is marred by dust and sweat and blood; who strives valiantly; who errs, who comes short again and again, because there is no effort without error and shortcoming; but who does actually strive to do the deeds; who knows great enthusiasms, the great devotions; who spends himself in a worthy cause; who at the best knows in the end the triumph of high achievement, and who at the worst, if he fails, he fails while daring greatly, so that his place shall never be with those cold and timid souls who neither know victory nor defeat."

❝I treat winning and losing exactly the same. I see them both as necessary steps to get us where we are going. Big failures, big lessons; little failures, little lessons.❞

—Bob Proctor (1934-),
Canadian-American philosopher, entrepreneur, author, and teacher

Although some losses are truly heart breaking, many losses are the conflicts that make a novel intriguing and exciting—although, in the real world, most of our losses can be seen as heroic successes only in hindsight. However, I am sure you have suffered a loss, and you are alive and well to tell the tale. List a loss or two that greatly influenced you. How a person overcomes derision and loss is the stuff of life—and the stuff of success stories. Did it deter you or spur you to move forward towards your goals?

Mediocrity

noun

Definition: the quality of something that is not very good: the quality of a person who does not have the special ability to do something well.

Learn to loathe mediocrity. Being somewhere in the middle of a huge pack typically implies that you've "played it too safe." I think back to watching the famous Iron Man triathlon competition on television when I was a child. They would show the leaders all day long as the grueling event unfolded. At some point, they would show the winners of each class cross the finish line first. The top male athlete, the top female athlete, perhaps the oldest athlete, and a disabled athlete would be highlighted on television for coming in first in their respective category. As I recall, the programming for the station would come to an end and other sporting events would be shown throughout the day. Ultimately, later that evening, the coverage would return to Hawaii, where the producers would be sure to show the accomplishment of the person who finished dead last. Coming in last was, in its own way, a major accomplishment. It demonstrated the resolve of this particular individual. It proved they were committed to never quitting, no matter how long it took to complete the challenge. I get it. That's great. It was indeed quite inspirational.

What occurs to me all these years later, though, is they cut away for hours as all the contestants who made up the "middle of the pack" crossed the finish line. Basically, what the program's producers were saying was, "Nobody cares about the mediocre group." In fact, if you wanted national attention and recognition, you were better served to come in last. I think that really says something. "The system" is built to reward to best and the worst, not the great majority of people who fall somewhere in the middle.

Now, let me be clear, I'm certainly not encouraging you to be the worst at what you do. On the contrary, I am urging you to be the best. I am also trying to bring to light what so many of you already know: there is no valor or value in being mediocre in this culture—or any other, for that matter. Look at how middle management is treated as compared to upper management. If I can be political for a moment, look at how the middle class is treated versus the upper class or the lower class. The middle class complains, and perhaps rightly so, that the rich keep getting richer and the poor keep getting all the perks of the numerous social programs our country offers—all while the middle class gets shafted.

Don't be satisfied with mediocrity. Don't make being an "also ran" your ambition. Aim high. Shoot for the moon. You are as valuable and capable as anybody else. If you make the crippling error of fooling yourself into believing being average is adequate, you will be incapable of doing any better than that.

Keep in mind that, by almost every measurable standard, the overwhelming majority of all the people you will ever meet in your life will be somewhere in the middle of the pack. Don't look to these people for inspiration, motivation, or advice when it comes to being exceptionally successful. This is not to say these people can't be terrific friends, relatives, neighbors, and coworkers; it just means they are not equipped to advise you on what is required to become a super-achiever.

> *"Excellence is a better teacher than mediocrity. The lessons of the ordinary are everywhere. Truly profound and original insights are to be found only in studying the exemplary."*
>
> —Warren Bennis (1925-2014), American scholar, consultant, and author

Millions of people are comfortable in the middle—they are content, and that is not a bad thing. If, however, you desire more, don't hold yourself back. If you have the drive and the desire to excel, then do it. Reach high.

How high do you want to go? How far do you wish to take your talents or your goals? Make a plan. Dream big.

Modify

verb
Definition: to change some parts of (something) while not changing other parts.

To be successful, you must be willing to make modifications. This is all about being dynamic. Dynamism is one of the great strengths we have as human beings. We are not purely working from midbrain and hind brain function. We have an exceptionally well-developed forebrain which allows us to have the freedom of choice and of change.

There is a very simple example of this put forth by one of my favorite motivational speakers and business philosophers of the twentieth and twenty-first centuries, Mr. Jim Rohn, who pointed out that, "You are not like a goose." He explained that a goose always flies south in the winter. But he asked, "What if south doesn't look so good?" Then what? Well, for the goose, he still flies south. But we aren't geese. We can modify the plan. We can change things if we don't like the way they look or the way they are going. Mr. Rohn pointed out that as a human being, you can fly east or west or north if south doesn't appeal to you for whatever reason.

Learn to be willing to modify your plan. I had spent many long hard years flying hard into the wind to become an open-heart surgeon. And although I landed at that destination quite successfully, I was terribly unhappy and unsatisfied. So, unlike the goose, I took to the air in a new direction and found fulfillment, success, and tranquility in a different field. This is the beauty of being a human being and, quite frankly, about being an American. You have the opportunity and ability to modify your personal course, no matter how far down the road of life you appear to be. There is always a chance to make a fresh start, a new and better beginning. I did this, and I can assure you that no matter how daunting the prospect seems, you can too.

Don't act like a goose if you're not one. You are so much better than that. You don't possess a bird brain. You have been gifted a biological and physiological super computer nestled right between your ears. Make full use of it and take full advantage of its unimaginable power and ability. You will never regret this decision. Always be willing to modify your positions, big and small.

Being intellectually, emotionally, physically, economically, academically, politically, and socially entrenched is never a good thing. Just be certain to make modifications in a positive direction and take care not to turn backward or downhill in your personal journey.

“One thing is sure. We must do something. We must do the best we know how at the moment…If it doesn't turn out right, we can modify it as we go along.”

—Franklin D. Roosevelt (1882-1945),
thirty-second President of the United States of America

Just like the protagonist in your success story, you can change the story and drive in a completely different direction. What in your life have you modified for the better? What is it you wish to change? As you create your plan, leave room for modification.

Negotiate

verb
Definition: to discuss something formally to make an agreement: to get over, through, or around (something) successfully.

Negotiating is an essential skill, whether you are talking about a business partnership, a contract agreement, a purchase of any kind, or maintaining healthy and rewarding personal relationships.

There are droves of books, articles, seminars, courses, blogs, etc. devoted to the art of honing your negotiating skills. Typically, you should resolve never (with very rare exceptions) to accept the first offer in any potential deal.

152

Whether you are purchasing a home, an automobile, a piece of jewelry, fine art, or a new suit, the initial price is almost certainly too high. Be prepared to always make a counter-offer. Don't be timid in such situations. Your job is to get a fair price, not to gouge the other entity.

Remember that in negotiating, you're also building your reputation. Making situations impossible or untenable for the other party will be more destructive to your ability to come to reasonable terms in the future. Always aim to reach an agreement between two or more representatives at the negotiating table where everyone walks away having won something and has been able to save face in the community and in the eyes of their colleagues.

"Beating" people should never be an objective. Not being taken advantage of should be. No one likes to feel they have been had. Making equitable deals and negotiating from a position of fair play will open the door to many more mutually beneficial opportunities down the road. Your word and your reputation are still as invaluable in contemporary society as they were fifty, one hundred, or a thousand years ago. *Never* underestimate the value in this asset.

Being known as an individual who can take advantage of others or cheat them in some way, besides being ethically improper, will also be a very self-destructive distinction. You should make it one of your primary goals to create notoriety for being one who believes in the time-honored concept of fair play. This is possibly more important to understand than ever, as this era of social media and endless online review platforms can disseminate a bad reputation across the internet faster than the Black Plague spread across Europe in the Late Middle Ages.

Accomplished negotiators go into a negotiation not only knowing what they insist on "winning" in the deal but, more importantly, what thing, which is important to them, they are willing to lose. If you are engaged with capable individuals on the other side of the bargaining table and you expect to win everything, you will be sorely disappointed and invariable waste a lot of time, energy, and perhaps money on a negotiation which will never come to agreeable terms.

A failed deal is often the result of poor negotiating skills on the part of one or more parties involved. Think hard about this critical important asset and how it affects your day to day life. Negotiating is a great way to circumnavigate obstacles. This may be as simple as what television program to watch in the evening with your partner or spouse. This may also be as simple as coming to a mutually beneficial term when negotiating homework versus internet time with a teenage son or daughter. The art of negotiating is needed everywhere if your eyes are open to it. Whether you are going to your boss for a raise or an employee is coming to you for one, you best be well schooled in this vitally important concept if you wish to grow and prosper over the course of your lifetime.

This book is not the forum to go into specific techniques, tactics, and approaches with regards to negotiation as it is too vast a subject, and I am not qualified to call myself an expert. That said, there are many excellent books on this important subject. I strongly recommend you find one or two that suit you and study them carefully so that you become competent in negotiation when such skills are needed.

> ❝*You don't get what you want. You get what you negotiate.*❞
> —Harvey Mackay (1932-),
> American businessman, author, and syndicated columnist

Write about negotiations you have been involved in. How do you think you did in the art of negotiation to overcome obstacles? Where can you improve your skills for the future?

No

adverb

Definition: used to give a negative answer or reply to a question, request, or offer.

Learn to say no. No is a tiny little two-letter word with enormous power. Saying *no* can change your life, save your life, or make your life exactly what you dream it to be.

The Greek philosopher and mathematician Pythagoras said, "The oldest, shortest words—'yes' and 'no'—are those which require the most thought." He made that statement roughly 2,500 years ago. Don't you find that

154

astonishing? I do. The impact of such a seemingly inconsequential word was recognized by the world's greatest thinkers going all the way back to ancient history. I just think that's incredible.

I think that teaches us a very important lesson about this word: it is to be used wisely and with great care. This is not a word that should be thrown around indiscriminately, nor is it one that should be withheld when it needs to be uttered. No is simple and strong. As they say, "No means no." No means anything and everything except yes. No is clear and to the point. No has no caveats. No has no exceptions. No never implies maybe, or perhaps later. No has only one meaning.

I remember as a child growing up here in the United States hearing the First Lady of our great nation, Nancy Reagan, teaching the country's youth to "Just say no to drugs." This statement was so clear, even a child could understand it. "Just say no" became a mantra. Later, Nike picked up on the simplicity of this phraseology with their undeniably effective campaign of "Just do it." So simple. So clear. So straightforward.

Saying no seems easy. I mean, it's one syllable and so easy to pronounce. But somehow, even though we know that it's the right answer in so many difficult situations, it somehow has the tendency of getting stuck in our throats when we need to express it the most. No can be taken as an insult. No one likes to hurt another person's feelings. No can mean rejection. No indicates disagreement, and no one wants to seem disagreeable.

I've spoken earlier in this book about being well-mannered. Being polite and saying no seem to be incongruous at first glance, but I assure you they are not. There is nothing more impolite than being insincere or giving another individual the impression that you agree when in fact you do not. Few things can lead to more trouble than saying yes to someone initially, no matter what the question is, and later have to recant and replace that position with no."

The only thing more painful than hearing no is hearing yes followed by no at some point later in time. This is a sure setup for grave disappointment and potential animosity.

Again, take the word no seriously. For that matter, yes should be seen with equal respect. Few of us have really taken the time to consider the weight these little words carry. When deciding whether to answer yes or no to a question, be deliberate, thoughtful, and unrushed. The consequence of your word choice may be felt for as much as a lifetime, depending on the seriousness of the given scenario or situation.

> ❝ *The art of leadership is saying no, not saying yes.*
> *It is very easy to say yes.* ❞
>
> —Tony Blair (1953-),
> Prime Minister of the United Kingdom from 1997-2007

Give examples when saying no was the best choice.

Obstacle

noun
Definition: something that impedes progress or achievement

Obstacles are a part of life. In fact, they are not only essential, but, when approached with the proper attitude, they can be enjoyable. They certainly foster growth and strength. There is very little more entertaining than watching ultra-fit athletes work their way through a challenging obstacle course. And how do you think they became ultra-fit? That's right—by working at traversing walls, jumping water hazards, and leaping over hurdles. Nothing gives one a sense of accomplishment like coming through such as set of physical barriers. If you have ever known anyone who has prepared for and competed in a "tough mudder" race, you'll know exactly what I'm talking about.

But this kind of challenge is not limited to sport. Look at how Navy SEALs train to get their bodies and minds honed for service and for battle. The obstacle course is a mainstay of their regimen. Climbing ropes and crawling beneath barbed wire in the mud are just two vivid images we can all conjure with little effort. We tend to have great respect for such people. We admire them for their courage, tenacity, and physical and mental strength. Obstacles are good. They make us strong.

That said, the greatest obstacles we face live inside of us. They are ever present in our psyches. These are our fears, our phobias, and our worries.

These are the invisible fences which stand in the way of personal greatness. We see them clearly despite being invisible to those around us. These barriers take the form of self-doubt, anxiety, and inferiority complexes. Somehow, we can easily envision others scaling mighty walls, but not ourselves. Why not? Perhaps this is an unintentional byproduct of how so many of us were raised—that is, to avoid failure, injury, or harm.

As children, we are constantly being admonished to "be careful" and "not to touch" for fear of falling or being scalded. Let's face it, no one likes to fall on their face or get burned. This is especially true if other people are watching. Our subconscious mind is programmed to believe that it is better to avoid failure than to test our limits. This paradigm is self-defeating. In fact, it is better to fail than to avoid an obstacle in an attempt to avert embarrassment.

In my many years of surgical training, there were many obstacles which I had to surmount. Some were physical, like working without sleep for seventy-two hours or tying one-handed knots with the non-dominant hand using suture material finer than human hair. Some challengers were psychological and emotional, like taking full responsibility for another human being's life, knowing that if things did not turn out well, one had to answer directly to the patient's family. These are just a couple of examples of what was required in training as a general and cardiovascular surgeon. I'm sure you can imagine that the list of such internal and external challenges was daunting. That said, such training was mandatory to develop strength, expertise, and courage. Those of us who completed this difficult educational process would not trade the experience for anything. I speak for myself when I say I would not be the same person had I not pushed myself to the limit. This process unveiled my true potential.

> ❝It's always appealing to play a character that has to overcome himself as well as an obstacle. It makes the drama so much deeper.❞
>
> —Clint Eastwood (1930-), American actor, filmmaker, and musician

What obstacles exist in your life that you would like to overcome? How would your protagonist deal with the issues you face? Would he or she be brave, or would you like them to act like a coward? Would they approach obstacles head on, or would they take a tangential approach? Use this time to write about how you want to respond to the impediments your protagonist faces in the story.

Organization

noun

Definition: the act or process of putting the different parts of something in a certain order so that they can be found or used easily: the act or process of planning and arranging the different parts of an event or activity.

You must be organized. Organization is a major skill which requires mastery to achieve success. For example, the organized student has an enormous advantage over the disorganized student of similar intellectual and academic ability. This truth holds for people in all walks of life.

Would you prefer to learn your surgeon was highly organized or utterly disorganized? Apply this same question to your airline pilot, accountant, barber, hair stylist, financial advisor, waiter, etc. In fact, I can't think of a single job, career, or profession where being disorganized would be advantageous.

Organization requires discipline for the great majority of us. I suppose being organized does come naturally to some. I think this tends to be a characteristic of the "Type A" personality. When organization is taken to an extreme, I could see where it may become obstructive to productivity. An example of this might be the individual who truly suffers from obsessive compulsive disorder, and his or her need to have everything in its proper place can ultimately become a major impediment to steady forward progress. Outside of this kind of pathological need for organization, I feel this trait is a powerful asset.

If we go back to the example of the student again, you can easily envision how we often spend too much time focusing on the didactic subject matter when attempting to assist a struggling student rather than the organization skills they may need to improve upon to earn better marks. Fortunately, there are many effective resources to help us strengthen this important area. We now have a multitude of books, magazine articles, websites, blogs, digital tools, coaches, and more to aid us in building this invaluable skill set. If this is an area where you feel there may need room for improvement, don't hesitate to take concrete steps toward doing so. There are few attributes which can be more widely and often applied to the various areas of one's life.

> 66*First comes thought; then organization of that thought, into ideas and plans; then transformation of those plans into reality.*99
>
> —Napoleon Hill (1883-1970),
> American author, journalist, salesman, and lecturer

Look at your own life and candidly ask yourself if this is a place you could be stronger. Ask those around you whom you trust. If you think even for a moment your organizational skills need work, put whatever resources you must into bolstering this aspect of your personality. It will be well worth the time, money, and effort. This decision will pay dividends in terms of the quality of your life, your financial status, your happiness, your health, and the amount of free time you must enjoy with your friends and family.

Write about your organization skills and talk about where there is room for improvement, and how improving your organization can improve your success. You may find writing out a plan calls upon your organization skills. What a great place to begin strengthening this trait!

Partnership

noun
Definition: the state of being one of two or more people, businesses, etc., that work together or do business together.

Take partnership seriously. Like many of the most important things in life, partnership has its positive elements and its negative elements. Therefore, you must go into any and every partnership with a mature sensibility and some degree of caution. Partnerships may present tremendous opportunity for success, happiness, and achievement that solo endeavors cannot. For this reason, you must evaluate and consider such opportunities with a great deal of careful analysis.

My father was a physician who was in private practice for thirty-five years. He dabbled a bit with partnership early in his career, but he was never able to make such partnerships work. Ultimately, he spent the lion's share of his career in independent practice. Because of the unsavory experiences he had in his personal attempts at such cooperative efforts, one of his mantras became: "If partners are good, God would have had one." If I had a dollar for every time I heard him give me that advice growing up, I'd have been retired long ago.

On the other hand, partnerships have worked marvelously well for many people in medicine and in every other conceivable business. This likely has much more to do with the personalities involved and the agreement under which they work than the actual vocation.

The public speaker and businessman Jim Rohn was fond of bringing out the usefulness and power found in partnerships. He would often talk about how much more two or three like-minded individuals could achieve when working in harmony toward a common goal than anyone could do alone. Clearly, I believe there is truth to this way of thinking as well.

There is a story I recall hearing in my childhood years about the chief of a Native American tribe calling his sons to gather around him while he lay on his deathbed, his final moments approaching. The once powerful warrior, so frail with age and illness, bestowed upon his sons, now enjoying the robustness of their physical primes, some final advice. He gave them sage wisdom on how to remain strong within the tribe for the next generation. He drew from his quiver, which laid next to the bed, six wooden arrows. He separated one and showed it to the young braves. He said, "Look at this beautifully crafted arrow. It is new and strong and functional and perfectly built, just like each of you. But notice how easily I can snap it between my old hands." And with that, their weakened father snapped the shaft in his fragile hands.

Then, he handed the remaining five arrows to the strongest of his sons and asked him to break them between his powerful hands all at once. The muscular young man could not. He explained to them that each taken alone was much more vulnerable to attack than all of them working together and remaining close-knit as brothers should be. The braves promised their father they understood his message and would live by it for the safety and prosperity not just of themselves but for the entire tribe they would now represent as leaders.

160

This is a wonderful story about the strength we find in numbers. If you can partner with others, especially when they bring complimentary skills and abilities to the table, it is a wonderfully empowering relationship. Be cautious with whom you deal. Trust is essential. As my father pointed out, the interactions between ambitious people can be tricky to manage. Therefore, be judicious when considering new partnerships, but not to the extent that it prevents you from achieving your true potential.

> ""*I grew up watching and learning from the ultimate partnership, and that is of my father and late uncle.*""
>
> —Jonathan Tisch (1953-), American businessman and hotelier

In a story, the protagonist usually has a supporting character who helps them reach their goals. In your success story, who is your partner who strengthens your goals and resolve? Who is your partner in your attainment of success?

Plan

noun
Definition: something that a person intends to do: a set of actions that have been thought of to do or achieve something.

We have discussed making plans often in this segment, but we have not discussed the idea of planning itself. Success is never an accident. Just as Disneyland and Disney World didn't spontaneously erupt from the Earth's crust, neither will your fortune, good health, and happiness suddenly appear out of thin air. Walt Disney's ability to envision in his mind's eye unthinkably ambitious projects is legendary. He could see such these ventures in inconceivably minute detail. This was a man who was intensely fixed on bringing his goals into reality and making his dreams come true. This required profound and exhaustive planning.

If you have ambitious desires, you will need extensive plans if you truly expect to see them come to fruition. Planning takes time, energy, effort, and sometimes money. This is not a step you can eliminate from the success journey and still expect to live an exceptional life. Make the time in your schedule to work in an environment of silent solitude. This is the ideal forum for creative, imaginative, and clear thinking. I am an ardent supporter of using a journal to put down in writing all your goals, big and small. Be honest with yourself. List absolutely everything you desire. I suggest you get in the habit of doing this exercise every morning, but certainly no less than once a week. This is a very rudimentary but essential manifestation of planning.

Once you have clearly delineated and enumerated exactly what it is you want, then you can get deeper into the planning phase of executing the realization of the goal or idea. For example, you must first decide you desire a new office from which to run your business operations. General preliminary considerations may be where the office would be, how large it might need to be in terms of square footage, and when construction or development must be begun and completed. Other important planning decisions would focus on budget, funding, etc. Beyond these initial steps, you may need to enlist other specialists with expertise that would further help you bring the concept to fruition. Examples of such specialists would be bankers, mortgage brokers, engineers, architects, realtors, etc. But to think such a project could took shape without significant focus and effort would be not only juvenile but completely unrealistic.

"*Our goals can only be reached through a vehicle of a plan, in which we must fervently believe, and upon which we must vigorously act. There is no other route to success.*"
—Pablo Picasso (1881-1973), Spanish artist, poet, and playwright

Is your plan shaping up? Use this book as a workbook—or a storybook of your success! It's all in the planning, in the details. So...how are things going so far?

162

Practice

verb

Definition: to do something again and again to get better at it.

Winners practice. As a physician and surgeon, I understand well the concept of practice. Doctors practice medicine, and attorneys practice law. For me, that implies that these fields, which require years of post-graduate academic pursuit, in fact are built around a lifetime of continued learning, study, and education. That's what practice is all about—training to improve your craft and stay at the front of the field.

Every great athlete understands practice. Every great musician understands practice. Every great artist understands practice. Every great yogi understands practice (even Yogi Berra). Practice is the path to growth, maturation, enlightenment, understanding, expertise, confidence, and ability. If you do not practice within your area of your work, not only will you not improve, but your current skill set will quickly begin to decay and decline.

I remember reading about the great tenor Luciano Pavarotti still performing his daily voice exercises despite being at the very top of his profession. I have no doubt this in large part explains why he was so successful. The stories of Larry Bird and Magic Johnson and their desire to practice tirelessly are the stuff of which legends are made.

Learn to practice. Let me assure you from the outset, practicing isn't always fun. But I can also guarantee you it is a mandatory habit in developing and building a success-oriented lifestyle. Make the effort. You're worth it, and besides, there really is no other way. Whether you are performing complex open-heart procedures, selling by cold calling, or playing a violin concerto, you best be very well practiced if you desire extraordinary rewards. Only exceptional quality and quantity of practice will bring you exceptional rewards, including financial ones.

No one wants a triple bypass done by an individual who attended a weekend seminar to obtain their credentials. By the same token, no one wants an airline captain whose training was limited to a flight simulator game on their computer to fly them from New York to London. These skills take time, effort, and almost unthinkable hours of repetition to master. These professions

163

practice not only what to do when all is well, but equally as importantly what to do when there is an emergency. Avoiding bleeding in the operating room is critically important, but so too is how to control hemorrhage if and when it does occur. Every great surgeon has learned this lesson. Flying in smooth conditions with a fully functional aircraft is an important skill to possess, but so is how to handle bad weather and a mechanically disabled plane. What do you do if you lose power in an engine, if the landing gear won't come down, if the flaps won't function? Don't you assume your professional pilot has been taken through these very serious scenarios time and time again? Of course you do, and of course he has. That's what practice is about.

No matter what you do to make a living, there is no way practicing for every potentiality isn't valuable. Do whatever it takes to practice in your field regularly. This will make you an expert. This will bring you success and riches beyond your wildest dreams if you incorporate such behavior into your daily routine. Take it from someone who has walked this walk. There is absolutely no substitute for training, practice, and repetition. It is the foundation upon which every great career is built.

> ❝*Practice does not make perfect.*
> *Only perfect practice makes perfect.*❞
>
> —Vince Lombardi (1913-1970),
> American football player, coach, executive, Super Bowl champion,
> and Pro Football Hall of Fame inductee

Practice *must* be part of your success plan. Are you currently practicing— or desire to practice—a trait or a skill you wish to perfect? Talk about it.

Procrastinate

verb

Definition: to be slow or late about doing something that should be done: to delay doing something until a later time because you do not want to do it, because you are lazy, etc.

You must know how to fight procrastination like a disease. Procrastination is an affliction which is the ultimate destructive force in success, ambition, and achievement. Putting things off for a more convenient time is a nail in the coffin of productivity. Always work towards activity. Success is built upon bringing projects to their absolute completion. Any delay in this progress brings with it disastrous consequences as far as success is concerned.

One of the greatest tools in the obliteration of procrastination is time management. Time management is a vast subject which I strongly suggest you study extensively beyond the reaches of this book. There are printed materials, online resources, seminars, coaches, and more available to anyone interested in mastering this invaluable resource. Suffice it to say, for the purpose of this text, that organizational skills, scheduling, goal setting, and prioritization are *the* cornerstones of the battle against wasting time and difficulty in getting things started. One simple rule which is mandatory in achievement is you must have tomorrow planned in detail today. It is only with a sound and comprehensive plan for tomorrow's activities that you can get the most out of the day.

"Procrastination is opportunity's assassin."

—Victor Kiam (1926-2001), American entrepreneur

Be honest with yourself—do you procrastinate? Talk about where this bad habit has worked against you. How do you plan to stop this habit?

Rationalize

verb

Definition: to think about or describe something (such as bad behavior) in a way that explains it and makes it seem proper, more attractive, etc.

Successful people do not rationalize their failure; they own it and do all they can to change their behavior to a winning attitude and approach. Everyone makes mistakes, even the most highly productive individuals. The difference is, successful people do not blame the system, the government, taxes, the wage scale, the competition, foreigners, etc. for their own shortcomings; they evaluate every aspect of their life where they wish to improve and then look in the mirror and ask themselves how they are going to turn that ambition for more success into a reality.

Rationalizing things is a form of excuse-making. Don't build your life, your future, and your reputation as an underachiever on a foundation built upon piled-up excuses. This is a house certain to crumble into ruins sooner rather than later. If you're uneducated, get an education. If you can't afford one, go to the free public library; there's one in every town. If you can't read well, then practice and you will improve. Reach out for help. Every community has adult learning programs for all levels on a multitude of subjects. If you carry extra weight and fat, lose it. That sounds oversimplified, but it's not. Eat less. Eat more nutritious foods. Don't eat junk. Exercise regularly. If you cannot afford a gym membership, get on the floor and push up against it. Then turn to your back and sit up and down until your abdominal muscles ache.

I think you see my point. If you allow the excuses to do so, they will choke all the potential success right out of your body. You are smarter than that. You are worth more than that. Insist on taking ownership of every area of your life where you see mediocrity, unhappiness and failure, and then change it!

> ❝*Rationalizing is a process of not perceiving reality, but of attempting to make reality fit one's emotions.*❞
>
> —Ayn Rand (1905-1982),
> Russian-American novelist, philosopher, playwright, and screenwriter

Be honest. Rationalization is a powerful obstacle. What are you reasoning away in your life? Write it down, and face your excuses. Facing and owning up to them is half the battle of overcoming them. We all have room for improvement, and we all deserve a fair chance at being better.

Resilient

adjective

Definition: able to become strong, healthy, or successful again after something bad happens.

You must be resilient because no one wins all the time. Resiliency is all about bouncing back and continuing to push forward. Look at many of the greatest athletes if you desire inspiration in this area. Consider Muhammad Ali, arguably the greatest heavy-weight prize fighter of all time. He was the three-time undisputed champion of the world. What this impressive title tells us is he was beaten at least twice in his career. In fact, he was beaten five times. But after being beaten by Ken Norton and Joe Frazier, he was able to come back and beat both men twice in rematches. This showed his incredible competitive spirit and his tremendous resilience. There were times in his career when he could have walked away from boxing but elected not to. The world of sports, business, entertainment, etc. are replete with such stories of great comebacks after devastating defeats.

Be resilient in your life. You'll almost certainly need to be if you wish to achieve extraordinary levels of success and prosperity. Few of us, if any, can go through life without at least a few check marks in the loss column in one area or another. See these as setbacks, not final results. Have confidence in yourself, redouble your efforts, and plan to succeed when you get a second chance. As Vince Lombardi, the Hall of Fame football coach, was famous for saying, "It's not whether you get knocked down, it's whether you get up (that counts)."

66*The more obstacles you face and overcome, the more times you falter and get back on track, the more difficulties you struggle with and conquer, the more resiliency you will naturally develop. There is nothing that can hold you back, if you are resilient.*99

—Jim Rohn (1930-2009),
American entrepreneur, author, and motivational speaker

Write about the times you have shown resilience. It is good to mark those moments in your life. They will be of help to you in your future.

Watch

verb

Definition: to look at (someone or something) for an amount of time and pay attention to what is happening: to give your attention to (a situation, an event, etc.).

Successful people go through life with their eyes wide open. They want to know what is going on in the world around them. This is all about being aware of your environment both in your immediate surroundings and beyond. Winners tend to read newspapers, magazine, trade journals, online blogs, websites, academic material, etc. This is the way they keep constant watch on their world. This is how winners remain current and aware of how they can perform at their personal best always.

Be careful to watch what is going on around you. Watch what is happening in your personal life just as carefully as you keep watch on your professional life. Watch your finances. Watch your health. Watch your diet. Watch out for your family. Watch out for your friends. Watch for changes in your industry in which you must stay abreast. Watch out for potential problems and hurdles on the horizon of your life.

Always keep watch and you are far more likely to stay safe, healthy, prosperous, knowledgeable, capable, and fulfilled. Don't go through life with your eyes closed. It is nearly impossible to perform at your peak when you are unaware of the trends and tides of your culture, time, and the world at large.

"You can observe a lot just by watching."
—Yogi Berra (1925-2015),
American Major League baseball player, manager, and coach

As the writer of your success story, you must be the observer of your story as well. Focus on how you want this plan to work out. Write down your observations. Being aware is important.

168

Worry

verb

Definition: to afflict with mental distress or agitation: make anxious.

To be responsible is a virtue. To be worried is an affliction. Don't confuse the two terms. One must always be aware of one's duties and address them in a mature and timely fashion, but this must never provoke a state of anxiety. No one performs at their best when anxious. Chronic worry will ultimately lead to physical and emotional illness. Worry will sap all joy from life. No one should live unhappily.

People who achieve success assume great levels of responsibility and consistently perform at high levels. A proper attitude toward such obligation will help one cope with this lifestyle without becoming sick. One must find pleasure in their work and their personal responsibilities. The expert surgeon, pilot, or military officer must be invigorated by adversity, otherwise their careers will be short-lived.

Don't be a worrier. This is not a strength—it's a weakness. Be someone who manages stress well and produces great results under pressure. There are many tools and skills one can study and perfect through conscious effort. Examples of things you can do to improve your handling of life's stressors include meditation, yoga, and exercise. Avoiding stimulants like caffeine and excessive consumption of alcohol would also be wise. Getting the proper amount of sleep each night (ideally 6-8 hours) would most likely be helpful in your ability to manage worry as well.

Worry and stress go hand in hand. Do all you can to study stress management and to nurture an overall state of calm in your life. Like everything else, this is a process. This is a journey. There will be setbacks and rough patches. That said, if you make a conscious effort to build a peaceful demeanor, you can do it. Well-trained individuals can find tranquility in circumstances which put intense psychological strain on most people. This is the result of practice and mindful intention. Freeing yourself from worry will not happen by accident. This is a goal you must set for yourself if you wish to be liberated. Look for ways that work best for you to become a responsible individual who stands up to life's challenges without making yourself ill. Know that you can become that

169

leader whom others look to for direction when circumstances become difficult. This is a true sign of the mature and well-adjusted individual.

"*Worry is a misuse of the imagination.*"
—Dan Zadra (1946-), Author, book mentor, publisher, and consultant

What are the things you worry about? What can you do about them? Are these worries rational? Be honest. Are there things you worry about which you cannot control? If so, should your main character detach himself from such concerns? If so, how? What action does your protagonist take to relax, unwind, and find peace? Tai Chi in the park? Listening to opera? It's up to you...

Zone

noun
Idiom: in the zone

Definition: In a state of focused attention or energy so that one's performance is enhanced: also known as flow, the mental state of operation in which a person performing an activity is fully immersed in a feeling of energized focus, full involvement, and enjoyment in the process of the activity: a state characterized by complete absorption in what one does.

Successful people get in the zone and love being there. I think the zone is what Csikszentmihalyi describes as *flow*. This is that wonderful feeling that comes over us when we feel everything is going our way. Everything, work included, becomes effortless. Creativity and imagination channel through us like an eternal energy. We take sheer joy—which is a true form of euphoria—in whatever it is we are engaged in when we enter the zone.

The successful individual learns to recognize the zone and does what he or she can to prolong the experience when it occurs. The amount of productivity is massively augmented in the zone state. Efficiency and effectiveness peak. Time loses all meaning. Endurance increases dramatically. The soul feels satiated, and the body is light as a feather. When in the zone, we feel at one with our spiritual, physical, and mental being simultaneously. It is perhaps the most wonderful naturally occurring sensation a human being can experience.

Entering and re-entering the zone is a skill the highest performing individuals learn to encourage. I'm not sure anyone can get into the zone by command, but I'm certain partaking in one's favorite activities are more likely to bring on this wonderful sensation. Silent solitude is one way to stimulate entrance into the zone from a purely intellectual and visionary space for many great innovators and producers. If you have ever experienced *the zone*, you probably know it. If you don't think you have, you have something to work toward and look forward to. The most extraordinary thing about the zone is the pure simplicity and clarity it brings with it. You feel completely in touch with yourself and the world around you all at once. It's a magnificent experience when it occurs. The more you do to look inside at what really brings you joy and happiness, the more likely you are to find yourself enjoying the unadulterated pleasure only the zone can provide.

"The mind is pretty powerful. In skating, you learn to click into that zone and focus not necessarily on what you're doing but if you're doing it well."

—Dorothy Hamill (1956-), American figure skater

Write about the time or times you have been in the zone. What were you doing? How did it feel? Write about your experience.

171

Section Four:

Taking Action and Letting the Plot Unfold

T his section centers around the ideas of **Action** and **Plot**. Action is basically doing. The plot, used in this sense as a noun, is the backbone of any novel. A plan assumes details, steps to follow, a structure; a plot entails the course upon which plans run. It is what urges the action of the tale, even the action of your life. It is what you *do* from here on in that will determine your course.

In your success story, the plot will unfold, illuminating your choices and the steps you took to achieve success. The end goal here is to live a happy, successful life—on your terms. Life is made up of plot twists, and it is up to us to decide how we will react to these twists, be they made of misfortune, hard work, or a stroke of luck.

In this section, we will focus on words that, for the most part, are action words, *DO* words. We will also present some words that have to do with the plot, or course, your life takes on.

The plot thickens...

Choice

noun
Definition: the act of picking or deciding between two or more possibilities.

We all make choices. High achievers know that it is through good choices that our quality of life improves, and it is through bad choices that our quality of life takes a turn for the worse. We also know the good choices, although often fairly obvious, aren't always easy.

Do you choose to go to the gym after work or to join the rest of the crew for happy hour? Do you choose a salad with grilled vegetables and a glass of water for lunch or three slices of the meat-lover's pizza and a regular cola? Do you choose to study your most challenging subject over the weekend when there has been no homework assigned, or do you blow off the entire weekend with video games, movies, parties, etc.?

Jean-Paul Sartre said, "We are our choices." In my opinion, it's possible that truer words have never been spoken. This goes back to taking responsibility for our personal destiny. For winners, choice usually implies hard choices. And in reality, the hard choice is frequently the best choice, the correct choice. Don't be afraid to make the tough choice, the choice that requires effort, discipline, courage, and sacrifice. It is usually the path less taken that requires the greatest effort to travel, but as Robert Frost wrote, "That has made all the difference."

> ❝*But until a person can say deeply and honestly, 'I am what I am today because of the choices I made yesterday' that person cannot say, 'I choose otherwise.'*❞
>
> —Stephen Covey (1932-2012),
> American educator, author, businessman, and keynotespeaker

What tough choices have you made that you know have been for the best? What action have you taken that has helped you achieve your goals?

Development

noun

Definition: the act or process of growing or causing something to grow or become larger or more advanced: the act or process of creating something over a period of time.

Successful people have the uncanny ability to take pleasure in the challenging process of personal development. Development takes many configurations. I have already mentioned personal development, but this subject, of course, encompasses numerous subsets, including but not limited to: emotional intelligence, physical fitness, psychological well-being, financial stability, professional satisfaction, business relationships, sexual activity, educational status, hobbies and past-times, philanthropy, friendship, and family contentment and gratification.

There is also the development of a more concrete type, in other words, the building of business ventures, investment accounts, or collections of art, cars, or antiques, etc. These forms of development take attention and time to establish, promote, and expand. The developmental process can be an arduous journey, but rest assured, it is an exciting and rewarding one.

There are few things that bring such delight for the high achiever as the joy that comes with watching things grow and evolve to new heights, whether it is the amount of time spent with their spouse and children or the quality of their topspin backhand on the tennis court.

You can take great pride in seeing progress over a period of time and always striving to see dreams fulfilled through hard work and practice. Be one who is developmentally inclined. Start something new and cultivate it to a level of abundance and higher quality. Successful people are rarely satisfied with the status quo, nor should you be.

"Ever since I was a child, I have had this instinctive urge for expansion and growth. To me, the function and duty of a quality human being is the sincere and honest development of one's potential."

—Bruce Lee (1940-1973),
Chinese-American martial artist, actor, film director,
screenwriter, and producer

Talk about what you are doing. What steps have you taken that are part of the plot to your success story?

Discipline

noun
Definition: a way of behaving that shows a willingness to obey rules or orders.

Learn to understand the power of discipline. Like many of the world's great delicacies, discipline is an acquired taste. It may seem a very bitter dish when first experienced by the unsophisticated palate, but it is a dish which grows on you with time and experience.

Discipline is like a muscle; it gets stronger the more you exercise it. The more you ask of your personal cache of inherent discipline, the stronger it will grow. Discipline is like a muscle in that it is made up of what I call fast twitch and slow twitch fibers.

To explain further what I mean, think of the fast twitch fibers as those elements of discipline that can get you to do what you must right away. This is the ability to fight off procrastination and get started immediately. These conceptual fast twitch fibers of discipline are also the structures that, when developed fully, allow you to complete simple or uncomplicated jobs quickly and efficiently. Do not take forever to get simple things done. Whether this means taking out the garbage, washing a sink-full of dirty dishes, or writing and sending an e-mail response to a client, get off the mark quickly and cross the finish line like a sprinter.

The slow twitch component of discipline is what gives you your endurance—the ability to stay with a task, goal, or project for extended period of times. This is analogous to the marathoner in you. Taking projects to fruition is a classic sign of a high-achieving personality type.

Discipline is like any other skill and responds to regular practice and proper training. With discipline comes productivity, and with productivity comes reward, so assess how disciplined you feel you are and work to increase your capacity in this critically important area of personal development.

“We must all suffer from one of two pains: the pain of discipline or the pain of regret. The difference is discipline weighs ounces while regret weighs tons.”

—Jim Rohn (1930-2009),
American entrepreneur, author, and motivationalspeaker

176

Write out how you are developing your discipline. How are you starting? Keep a journal, either writing here or in your own notebook, on how your discipline is progressing.

Dividends

noun

Definition: an advantage or benefit that you get because of something you have done.

It is important to understand the value of any kind of investment that pays dividends. A dividend is like a gift that keeps on giving. The more personal, social, professional, and entrepreneurial skills you develop, the more dividends you receive in the future. To reap the reward of a dividend, by definition, an expense or advance must be paid beforehand. This may be in the form of time, effort, work, study, money, or some other significant commodity, but dividends are rarely, if ever, enjoyed without paying some price up front.

Dividends come to those who understand the concept of long-term thinking. These are fortunes usually reserved for those with the discipline and forethought to recognize the value of the eventual payoff. Again, this kind of thinking takes on many forms. It may be the planting of a seed in the soil, the reading and reviewing of material for a test, or thirty minutes of aerobic exercise three times per week for twenty-five years.

The payout is never immediate when it comes to dividends, but the prize is often delivered on the order of multiples, not a one-to-one relationship. Look for opportunities that will provide you with profits much larger than your initial contribution.

> ""*Do you know the only thing that gives me pleasure?*
> *It's to see my dividends coming in.*""
>
> —John D. Rockefeller (1839-1937),
> American business magnate and philanthropist

Think about what you are doing now and how it will reward you in the future. This will help you curtail the habit of wasting precious time.

Earnings

noun
Definition: the balance of revenue after deduction of costs and expenses.

To truly enjoy the many beautiful riches, comforts, and rewards life has to offer, you must absolutely earn it for yourself. No one can be made a winner or handed a win. The experience is simply not the same.

As one of my virtual mentors, Jim Rohn, once said: "If you found a Congressional Medal of Honor in the street, would you wear it?" I think this question says it all. I mean seriously, isn't that terrific? Would you wear it? You would have to be a real loser—or, at the very least, a misguided soul—to put a medal around your neck that someone else had earned. I still love that line. The message is so powerful.

The other thing Jim Rohn taught me was to quote people when they said something well. I couldn't find a way to express the value in earning something better than that, so thank you, Mr. Rohn, for the wisdom.

There are lots of things to earn, by the way, some of them more valuable than money. Sure, everyone thinks about earning money. Money is important. You really can't get along today without having at least some. I doubt anyone would get very far in modern society trying to make it on the barter system alone. Capital is necessary to provide food, clothing, and shelter at the very least, so it pays to earn some. But there are other things that must be earned, such as respect, trust, friendship, an educational degree, and your stripes, just to name a few. These are things that cannot be purchased, nor can they be gifted to someone.

Successful people are earners. They are never looking for a handout. The view of the ocean, the taste of a great meal, and the sound that a luxury automobile engine makes is always sweeter when you know in your heart *you* have sincerely earned the experience.

"I was offered a choice of a flat salary up front or a percentage of the film's future earnings. I took the up-front money. Nobody could have figured what Halloween would ultimately become."

—Donald Pleasence (1919-1995), English film, television, and stage actor

Write about what you have worked for and earned—a goldfish from a childhood memory, a first car, a high grade, overcoming hardship, etc.

Effort

noun

Definition: energy used to do something: a serious attempt to do something; something produced by work.

Successful people win through effort. Every highly-accomplished human being knows the truth about effort. Without great effort, there are no great results. The veracity of this statement has been tested and proven countless times in the history of mankind. The idea that good fortune is going to come knocking at your front door while you lie on the couch and watch television is a preposterous pipe dream. Free yourself of this disabling misconception if you have had the misfortune of coming to believe it.

In the end, however, we are not judged by our effort; invariably, you will always be judged by your results and effectiveness. This may seem unfair, but this is the reality of the world we live and compete in. Those who try hard with limited results will only be the recipients of limited reward. But don't let this deter you from putting forth your strongest effort at all times, because I can assure you, no one achieves significant results without trying hard and working hard. This is the only route to success, but it is not a guarantee.

Remain committed and focused on your goal, and let nothing stand in your way. Remain resolute in your determination, and good things will happen. Abandon this approach and you are certain to live a life of mediocrity at best. You have all the potential for extraordinary success within you, but it must be applied unceasingly daily for as long as you live. Never let up. *Never give up.*

It is only through a sustained effort over a prolonged period that you will outperform the average and below-average personality types.

> *"Be of good cheer. Do not think of today's failures, but of the success that may come tomorrow. You have set yourselves a difficult task, but you will succeed if you persevere; and you will find joy in overcoming obstacles. Remember, no effort that we make to attain something beautiful is ever lost."*
>
> —Helen Keller (1880-1968), American author, political activist, and lecturer

Have you made a concerted effort lately? What kind of results did it bring? Tell your story!

Evolve

verb

Definition: to change or develop slowly often into a better, more complex, or more advanced state.

It is paramount to evolve in all facets of your life if you wish to be at the top of the ladder and remain ahead of the game. This Darwinian method of thinking and approach to your life will almost certainly bear the most fruit. We are living in an incredibly fast-paced world where even our apps are becoming obsolete in a matter of weeks or months. It is essential to make every effort to stay abreast of all that is happening in your area of professional interest as well as expertise.

Perhaps the best advice here is to remain familiar with and aware of the trends developing now. Work hard to differentiate between true trends and what are better termed fads or novelties. Make no mistake: differentiating between the two is not always easy. Therefore, this may be a place where the application of type two or "slow thinking" would be most prudent. Rather than jumping on the bandwagon of every hot new idea that infiltrates your business space, take an adequate period of time to carefully evaluate the situation.

Frequently in my surgical practice, there will come onto the market a new technology, technique, or medication which is being marketed vigorously by the industry. In human nature, there is a part of us that wants to be on the cutting edge of everything new that comes along, but this is not true evolution. Evolving and surviving means making the changes that will best suit the environment and ultimately lead to health and well-being. If I were to purchase every new laser introduced to the marketplace, I would certainly be bankrupt. Evolution, by definition, is a slow process that occurs over a protracted period of time. Whether these changes involve achieving your ideal body weight or how many pushups you can do without stopping, these changes will take time. To evolve, you must make changes that will improve your chances of prospering and surviving. Gaining fifty pounds is rarely an evolutionary change for a human being who was well nourished to begin with.

What's dangerous is not to evolve.

—Jeff Bezos (1964-), American business magnate and investor

Evolve is one of the most important action verbs in this section. Evolution means to adapt; making changes allows you to thrive and move forward. Can you recall a time where you felt stuck in your life? How did you evolve? What changes did you make to get yourself out of the slump? Can you discuss how you are currently evolving?

Execution

noun
Definition: the act of doing or performing something.

Recognize that success depends entirely on execution. I have been telling everyone who will listen there are no good ideas. Ideas are worthless. The only thing that counts in this world is executing the idea through completion and having a product of value in the end.

No one will reward you for having good intentions. *Planning* to perform a complex surgery, build a tunnel or bridge, or create an app that will change the way the world does accounting is totally meaningless. The only thing anyone will ever give you credit for in any sort of demonstrable or quantitative way is action and execution. Take this message to heart. It can change your life. Remember the adage, "Deeds, not words."

"A really great talent finds its happiness in execution."

—Johann Wolfgang von Goethe (1749-1832),
German poet, novelist, playwright, natural philosopher, and diplomat

In the last section, we discussed planning at length. In this section, we discuss putting that plan into action. How are you executing your plan of action or plot?

Exercise

noun

Definition: Physical activity that is done to become stronger and healthier.

It is important to understand the value in exercise. Your body is the vessel which will carry you through life. Take good care of it. Physical activity will not only strengthen your muscles, bones, tendons, and ligaments but also your heart and lungs. Beyond the physical benefits of regular exercise, the successful individual knows that incorporating such habits into one's routine will also help maintain emotional and psychological well-being and stability. Don't be afraid of feeling great!

We live in a very competitive world, where whomever wishes to be a high achiever must endure long hours and stressful circumstances. Being physically fit will assist you greatly in taking on and overcoming such challenges. Furthermore, your peers, colleagues, and competitors will hold you in high esteem when you are in good shape. You will be seen as a person who has their "stuff" together on every level, one who leads a balanced and healthy lifestyle. This will also aid in giving you the winner's edge, as others' perception of you in a positive way can only propel you to achieve more.

"If we could give every individual the right amount of nourishment and exercise, not too little and not too much, we would have found the safest way to health."

—Hippocrates (c. 460-c. 370 BC), Greek physician

Are you exercising? How does it benefit you? If you do not exercise, write down how you can begin incorporating some exercise into your life. How will it benefit you personally? What do you think is stopping you from doing so?

Experience

noun
Definition: the process of doing and seeing things and of having things happen to you: skill or knowledge that you get by doing something: the length of time that you have spent doing something (such as a particular job).

All winners learn there is no substitute for experience. Practical knowledge is ultimately the driving force for success. Theoretical knowledge takes a back seat to real world know-how. There is an old expression that says, "Good judgment comes from experience, and experience comes from poor judgment." Nothing could be truer. With experience comes winning and losing, good decisions and misguided decisions, elation and disappointment. In the end, it must be said that if you wish to be exceptional regarding accomplishment, you must gain experience by "being in the game."

Waiting for the perfect moment to execute an idea, get healthy, launch a business, go back to school, make an investment etc., is a recipe for failure. The longer you wait to begin acquiring hands-on experience, no matter what the field of endeavor, the longer it will be until you begin to ascend the ladder of success. Find a way to get involved in the area that interests you most, the place where you intend to carve your niche and make your mark.

If you want to be one of the world's most recognized contemporary artists, don't wait. Get to work. Don't wait for the perfect opportunity or for the director of the world's most prestigious gallery to call. Simply get to doing what it is you do. Start painting, sculpting, drawing, etc. Don't wait for anyone else's permission, encouragement, or validation. You are your own person, and you are the master of your own destiny. Begin building your experience level right now. Time and again you will hear it said that top employers are looking for people with experience. So, find your experience wherever you can, even if it is at the bottom. Like it or not, that is where we all start.

"Experience is the teacher of all things."
—Julius Caesar (100-44 BC), Roman general, statesman, consul, and author

Write about your experience in the field of your choosing. Write about your experience with success.

Finish

verb

Definition: to reach the end of (something): to stop doing (something) because it is completed: to be done with building or creating (something).

Most people have difficulty starting, but successful people finish what they have started. In my medical practice for example, over the years we have built numerous divisions of services. Each of these divisions began as a dream. Using the classic paradigm for success, my team and I turned this dream into a legitimate goal by putting a deadline on it.

For a concrete example of what I mean, currently we are building a new line of services. This is the hair transplantation program at Chuback Medical Group. Because we have robust cosmetic, esthetic, and plastic surgical arms of the program, I felt contemporary hair transplantation would be an excellent fit.

Now, the successful personality never stops there. I am famous amongst my friends and family for saying, "Good ideas are absolutely worthless. The only thing that has any true value is action." I live by this philosophy, and so do most high-achieving individuals. Therefore, what we do next in my practice is take the dream of creating a hair transplantation program and set a date for it to be up and running. This date, or deadline, makes the dream an actual goal. This makes the prospect of achieving this desired outcome much more tangible.

To be up and running and serving the community by that time, many preparatory steps must be undertaken and carried out in a systematic fashion. First, we need to contact, interview, and confirm a professional relationship with qualified and experienced hair transplant technicians. Second, we must attend training programs and hands-on workshops to become comfortable with the technical aspects of the procedure, indications, potential complications, etc. Next, we need to research and purchase the necessary equipment required to perform these operations. Then we must make any changes to the physical space in the office regarding lighting, proper operating room tables, etc.

After this, we must build a website and design an advertising campaign with our marketing firm and discuss our approach to search engine optimization to drive traffic to the site and patients to the office. Also, we must visit the offices of successful colleagues to learn from their many years of experience what we think may be the best way to conduct business and care for patients. Finally, we must bring everything online and "go live" with the program and perform our very first case in the office.

This is a lot of work. We have done this time and time again as we have grown the practice over the years and made it more robust and successful. If you stall at any point along the way, the new program and any business or income that would come along with it withers and dies on the vine. It is essential to start, continue through the process of carrying out all the necessary steps, and in the end—FINISH. By "finishing" I mean getting to the end of all the preparation and doing the operation with an excellent outcome.

Winning is not for dreamers; winning is for goal-setters, doers, and finishers only. This is an essential lesson. If this lesson is lost on you, I'm afraid you have no chance at leading an exceptional life. These same rules hold true for how you must approach your nutritional regimen, exercise routine, spiritual wellness, and personal relationships. Understand the fundamental steps and begin putting them to work immediately in your life, and you will be absolutely amazed at the results this paradigm yields. Start now and insist on finishing.

Exciting real-world update: Chuback Medical Group and www. contemporaryhairtransplant.com performed its first hair transplantation operation on February 14, 2016, and we are now performing one to two surgeries per week. The program is growing beautifully—and so is the hair! We have set a new goal to do one transplant per day.

"Do not plan for ventures before finishing what is at hand."
—Euripides (c. 480-406 BC), Greek playwright

Create steps like I did above. Write them out, and go meet your goals!

Flourish

---

verb

Definition: to be very successful: to do very well.

Successful people have no intention of simply getting by or making a living. Winners are dead set on flourishing. Why not flourish? Why not be successful and live a life of wealth and abundance to share with those around you, whom you care deeply about and love? Why not enjoy all the best things that life offers? Someone will be staying in the best hotels, dining in the best restaurants, driving the best cars, living in the best homes, wearing the latest fashions, donning the finest wristwatches, etc. Why not have it be you?

Wanting to be a success doesn't make you a bad person. You can share your success with anyone you choose. Being in a position of power will allow you to give others incredible opportunities to live out their most lofty dreams. If you flourish in this life, you can pave the way for so many others to do the same. If you chose to contribute everything you earn to charity, the poor, sick children, etc., you can do that too. That's the beauty of flourishing and being successful—you become the master of your own destiny and can express your success in any way you wish.

You may choose to wear a Timex rather than a Rolex, or maybe no watch at all.

186

You may use your riches to change the lives of those less fortunate than you, to give to research aimed at curing cancer, or to donate to those who are hungry at home and around the world. The beauty of truly flourishing is the freedom it brings with it. True success carries with it liberty. This sense of absolute liberation allows the individual to do exactly as they please. You will be the boss. You will come and go as you please. You may work as much or as little as you like when you have finally flourished. Success is a good thing. You may use your personal achievements, wealth, and independence to make your life and others as beautiful as possible in every imaginable way.

> ❝*We need a place in which we may flourish and be ourselves.*❞
>
> —Timothy Radcliffe (1945-), English Roman Catholic priest

Let your imagination run wild. What would you do with your success once you have flourished? How do you see success in your life?

Follow Up

verb
Definition: to maintain contact with (a person) to monitor the effects of earlier activities or treatments: to pursue to take further action <the police are following up leads>

Follow up is key to the winning personality type. Average achievers and under achievers typically have good intentions regarding following up on things but rarely, if ever, do. The highly successful individual is compulsive about making sure things that were supposed to get done have gotten done and have been done with the level of excellence required.

Don't assume anything. Make certain things are the way they are supposed to be. The winning executive, for example, does not rely on their personal assistant to perfectly complete every task or project assigned to them. The winning executive is dogmatic about following up with their assistant to ensure what was assigned has been followed through on and is moving along smoothly. One of the great errors you can make is adopting the philosophy that says, "No news is good news." No news may mean a disaster is taking place right under your nose and you know absolutely nothing about it.

To be successful in life, nurture the sort of character within yourself that will follow up on everything, all the time. This is the kind of trait that separates the top five percent of individuals from everyone else. This behavior requires organizational skills, endurance, and great effort, but the results over time will demonstrate that it is all worth it.

> "Success comes from taking the initiative
> and following up... persisting..."
>
> —Tony Robbins (1960-),
> American motivational speaker, author, and life coach

Let's talk about the time you persisted and succeeded. Write about when you took initiative and followed up on your plans, on doing something.

Fun

noun

Definition: someone or something that is amusing or enjoyable: an enjoyable or amusing time: the feeling of being amused or entertained

Winning is fun. A real winner should have a lot of fun. Otherwise, what's the purpose of being successful? Being great at what you do, making a good living, and being surrounded with positive, upbeat, interesting people is an awesome experiential existence. Who wouldn't love being a winner? Having average results in anything will yield an average experience in life. Who wants that? Nobody. Losing is no fun. Anyone who tries to sell you on that idea needs to always be held at arm's length, as far as I'm concerned. There is no valor in coming in somewhere in the middle in life, let alone dead last.

Work hard to win. As they say, "To the victor go the spoils." Success gives access to all the wonderful trappings life offers. Don't settle for mediocrity in this extraordinary lifetime you've been given. Go for the best in everything. Work hard and play hard. Travel, see the world, see the country, visit museums, listen to great music, look at beautiful works of art, eat great food, spend time with fascinating and accomplished people. Just have fun. Never allow anyone to lead you to believe you are here to only work. Life is to be fully and deeply experienced and enjoyed. If you do that the right way, you'll have a boatload of fun.

"When you have confidence, you can have a lot of fun. And when you have fun, you can do amazing things."

—Joe Namath (1943-), American football player and Super Bowl champion

Let's talk about what you do for fun.

Generosity

noun
Definition: the quality of being kind, understanding, and not selfish: willingness to give money and other valuable things to others.

Truly successful people are generous. Successful people love to share. One of the things I have been most surprised and impressed by over the years is how willing truly successful people are to help others. In the course of my life, I have had many mentors. A mentor is someone who gives. Rarely does this have anything to do with money, but true successes tend to be charitable and philanthropic monetarily as well. A skinflint can never be a respectable person. More commonly than money, what successful individuals give is advice, guidance, and time, and these are precious commodities.

This fact comes as a surprise to many, but one of the easiest ways to learn how to be a success is to simply ask a successful person how it's done. You may be startled how frequently that person will be happy to take the time to sit down and share with you everything they did to become successful. Let's face

189

it, many such individuals have written books on the subject for no other reason than to reach out and help anyone else who is interested. This is true generosity. Giving away the ideas, the philosophy of success—this is the true gift.

I now recognize the biggest of the winning set understand there is no limit to success. There is a universe of success in which we all partake. By sharing their knowledge with you, they are at no increased risk of experiencing less good fortune in the future.

Success and achievement are not like a pizza. A pizza pie generally has eight slices. If one person eats four slices, then that only leaves half of a pie for everyone else. If there are six people at the party, either someone isn't going to get a piece of pizza, or they will be forced to share one with one of the other guests. But success isn't this way at all. The universe is endless regarding success. If you become a multi-millionaire, everyone else on your street, in your neighborhood, and in your town can too. There is no limit to how many people can become financially successful.

By the same token, there is no limit to how many people can have a happy family, good friends, or enjoy a simple walk in the park. The universe is so replete with good fortune, it just keeps on giving and giving. Successful people understand this, and that is why they are so generous with anything and everything they can give to others.

It is said the more you give, the more you shall receive. But make no mistake, for real success, this is never the motivation. The real motivation is simply the joy that comes in sharing.

"Generosity is not giving me that which I need more than you do, but it is giving me that which you need more than I do."

—Khalil Gibran (1883-1931), Lebanese-American artist, poet, and writer

Write about the time you have been generous to someone or when someone has been generous to you. How did it feel? How did it improve their lives? How did the generosity enhance your life?

190

Growth

noun

Definition: The process of developing or maturing physically, mentally, or spiritually.

Learn to embrace and nurture growth. Growth of many types is essential to getting better, remaining competitive, being the best you can be, and keeping life interesting. Without growth, there is no change, and if you are not changing, you cannot be improving. Life is a fascinating journey, and there is so much to learn. If you are learning, you are growing, plain and simple. If you are sharing, you are growing. If you are giving, you are growing. If you are receiving, you are growing. Growth is an absolute must to achieving personal development and betterment.

You may choose to grow regarding physical fitness, intellect, spiritual awareness, financial success, business achievement, personal relationships, inner peace, personal fulfillment, and satisfaction, etc. There are no limits to how you can grow; nor is there any limit to how *much* you can grow. Growing physically is an obvious aspect of childhood into adulthood. But this measurable growth should serve as a metaphor for the individual internally for the rest of their life.

For those of us who elected to pursue higher education—in my case, fifteen years after graduating high school—academic growth was a natural part of the process of getting older. That said, whether you are in school or not, you should always be growing, expanding, maturing, and developing intellectually, emotionally, and psychologically. There is an endless stockpile of resources available to all of us in the contemporary world. There are books, magazines, blogs, websites, YouTube videos, night classes, etc. I urge you take advantage of any of these incredibly powerful and empowering tools to foster your own personal growth as long as you are alive. It is the most rewarding, wonderful feeling in the world.

You are not as good now as you could be a week or a month from now. There is no limit to your extraordinary potential for growth. Accept this philosophy as your own, and tap into the energy available to all of us. Let that positive energy propel you to new heights—heights you never believed were attainable. Don't stand still. Don't stay the same. Stagnation is not the modus of super-achievers. It is the way of the ordinary crowd, and you should have no intention of being amongst them.

> *"The key to growth is the introduction of higher dimensions of consciousness into our awareness."*
>
> —Lao Tzu (604 BC–531 BC), Chinese poet and philosopher

Write about your growth—emotionally, financially, etc.

How

adverb
Definition: in what manner or way: by what means.

"How?" is a classic question in the winner's mind. How are we going to do this? How far can we go? How high can we climb? How am I doing? How can we make things better? How can I help? How can I give more? How am I perceived by my colleagues? How are you? How can we turn things around? How did we get here? How did I get so lost? How did I achieve so much? How would I like to be treated? They keep seeking answers to these questions.

The number of "how" questions is seemingly endless. How enables you to plot. How moves your story from point A to point B.

> *"It doesn't matter how slowly you go as long as you do not stop."*
>
> —Confucius (551 BC-479 BC), Chinese teacher, politician, and philosopher

Make a list of *how* questions that seem important to you in your life right now, and think hard about them. Take the time to sit alone in a quiet place and really put focused thought into each of the questions that come to your mind. Hopefully, you have been doing this throughout this entire workbook! You will be amazed at what may be brewing in your subconscious mind, and this simple activity may open the door to your consciousness and allow you to consider the best responses to the questions you have inside. I encourage you to do this soon and frequently.

192

The questions will change, depending on what you're going through at the time, but the value in the technique will prove itself again and again.

Industrious

adjective
Definition: working very hard: not lazy

Be industrious. Tremendous levels of success come from tremendous amounts of hard work. Now listen carefully: you can work tremendously hard and not be successful as well. Hard work in and of itself will not bring great riches and rewards. Wealth, prosperity, happiness, independence, liberty, autonomy, etc. will only be a byproduct of your hard work if you consciously choose that to be a goal.

You might ask, "Well, who wouldn't want that?" The answer is simple: You would be shocked how many people never set any of those parameters as goals. In fact, many people do not set *any* goals in their lives. It has been said only three percent of all adults set any goals whatsoever. Isn't that an astonishing figure? If that's true, it is no wonder why so many people never achieve what they are capable of. If you set the bar low for people, they will step over it, not jump as high as they can over it.

I have always said getting accepted into an American medical school was one of the most difficult academic challenges I have ever faced. I needed essentially a straight A average to do that. Since it was my goal to go to a fully accredited allopathic American medical school, I achieved as many A grades as I could possibly produce. In the end, my goal became a reality. But I can assure you, I am well aware of my innate desire to be lazy and to goof off whenever possible. If someone had told me I could live my dream of getting into medical school with a B average or even a C average, I wouldn't have tried nearly as hard. I jumped as high as the bar was set. It was hard as hell, but I did it.

Don't fall into the trap of setting the bar too low for yourself in life and then pretending you never wanted anything more than that. One of the great teachings I have ever heard is not to set your goals at things you believe you can achieve, but rather, set goals for yourself based on what you want. Often, what you really want out of life seems like too much or too unrealistic for

193

someone like me or you, so we quit pursuing such goals even before we start because we are afraid to fail and look foolish in front of those around us and, equally as important, in front of the mirror.

"I was obliged to be industrious. Whoever is equally industrious will succeed equally well."
—Johann Sebastian Bach (1685-1750), German composer and musician

Write about what you want. Plot and scheme and plan and do. What do you want to accomplish? Revisit this question a few times a year to see the changing answers.

Initiative

noun
Definition: the energy and desire that is needed to do something.

Take initiative. If you sit around waiting for someone else to suggest a great idea to you or push you to live up to your full potential, you're likely to be waiting a long time. As I like to say, "Don't hold your breath while waiting. Blue's not your color."

Having initiative is a great gift if it comes naturally to you, but rest assured, initiative is a skill like any other that can be nurtured and cultivated. This begins with awareness. You must be aware of the power of initiative. Once you recognize how essential it is to be the type of person who puts the energy and desire into doing things rather than just dreaming about how you would like things to be, the sooner you will be seeing real, quantifiable progress.

When you see opportunity, don't wait. Take the initiative and make something happen in real time. Possibly more important than anything is the critical understanding that there will never be a perfect time to take initiative in a new project, for example. When you decide to build a new program, a new line of services or products, let's say, it's best to just get started and handle the inevitable problems as they arise.

194

Speaking from considerable experience in launching new programs and ventures in my own practice, I can assure you nothing happens overnight. Real, productive business lines and sources of income will take years to fully develop into a mature and rewarding state. This will mean there will be changes of all kinds in the pertinent environment surrounding your business. The economy will go up and down, the competition will stiffen and weaken, technology will change more rapidly than you could have ever imagined, you will lose and gain key people in your organization, etc. You must never let these concerns dampen your spirit of initiative, as they are inescapable.

In the end, the inexorable reality of obstacles and dilemmas should be commonplace situations rather than insurmountable impediments. The individual who practices initiative is one who simply keeps moving forward at all times. It is this steady desire to progress over a protracted period of time that will result in extraordinary results. Failing to start and failing to carry on is an irrefutable recipe for utter failure.

> ff*One has to take initiative in life to achieve what he or she wants.*™™

—Donald Johanson (1943-), American paleoanthropologist

Write about how you take initiative in your life. Write about its benefits.

Instigate

verb
Definition: to cause (something) to happen or begin.

Be an instigator. Now, let me be clear here. Successful people do this in the most *positive* of ways. Unfortunately, this term has widely come to be associated with a negative connotation. Often, we think of an instigator as a troublemaker. But this by no means must be the case. On the contrary, you may be an instigator, or initiator, of so many wonderful things.

Highly prosperous people tend to be the ones to instigate a stimulating conversation, a meeting of strangers with like interests, or a highly productive new activity, program, income stream, etc. Instigators, like all high value individuals, tend to be high energy, creative, imaginative, courageous, and proactive.

Think about the people you know who behave in this way. Notice how things seem to always be happening around them. They have the capacity to energize an environment or situation. They are never satisfied with "business as usual." They are instigating that action be taken on worthwhile ideas and instigating relationships with people who possess mutually beneficial skill sets and resources. This is a key component of the leadership persona, in my opinion. These are *take charge* personality types, not *let's see what happens* type people. Instigating and implementing change for the better is the core of what these individuals do by constantly questioning the validity of the status quo and probing to find out if there is a better way of doing things. Instigators are in search of greater effectiveness and efficiency in their lives and the systems that exist around them.

Don't be afraid to be labeled, or seen as, an instigator. Rid your mind of all the negative associations this word brings with it. Instigate change in your world. Taking care to ensure this dynamic force is a positive one. Questioning preexisting paradigms and proposing new rubrics of thought may lead to unforeseen achievement for you and those in your life.

"*I'm fine with being a little bit of an instigator.*"
—Ted Ligety (1984-), American Alpine ski racing Olympic gold medalist

What have you instigated in your success story? What have you plotted and created that has brought you success? How are you an instigator in your life? Write about it!

Leadership

noun
Definition: the power or ability to lead other people.

Let's face it, if you want to win a race, by definition, you must lead the pack. You can't come in last and call yourself a winner. Now, obviously very few of us can be number one in the world at anything. Even in the Olympic Games we have medals for second and third place. But leading is essential to high achievement. If you desire great prosperity, typically it means that, ultimately, you will have others working for or with you. This station in life will require leadership.

Leading is a wonderful feeling. It gives an individual an opportunity to help others and show them the proper path in life. Leading your friends, family, co-workers, employees, teammates, etc. to higher levels of productivity, happiness, joy, education, wealth, fulfillment, satisfaction, etc. is one of the great pleasures a person can experience in this lifetime. Leadership can be a bit scary, however. Being out in front and taking on the responsibility of setting a course for someone other than yourself means you may face ridicule or criticism should things not work out as you had intended, despite having had the best of intentions.

You need not look any further than our own politicians as an example of this. It would be difficult to imagine any political figure in our society would intentionally lead his constituents down the wrong path intentionally, but sometimes the best laid plans do go awry. When the economy is off, politicians are blamed. When unemployment goes up, politicians are blamed. When the interest rate rises, politicians are blamed. And conversely, they don't always get the credit they are due when things go well.

Leadership can be a thankless job in many regards. Don't let this deter you. You must know in your heart you have the best intentions for everyone you lead. This doesn't mean the road will always be smooth or without turns. The key is to do your best. Even if you don't cross the finish line first and break the tape with your chest, be sure to give every race your all and run your personal best time whenever possible. Hopefully, those behind you will see you as an inspiration to do at least as well as you have their next time out.

Leadership is the capacity to translate vision into reality.
—Warren Bennis (1925-2014), American scholar, consultant, and author

Where and when in your life have you been a leader? How has it enhanced your life? Do you have leadership skills? In your success story, are you the leader? Are you a follower?

Let's talk about it.

Learn

verb

Definition: to gain knowledge or skill by studying, practicing, being taught, or experiencing something.

You must be constantly learning and have an insatiable desire to acquire greater understanding and evermore increasing sophistication of your preexisting skill sets. The key to this process is being inquisitive and curious about everything. A pillar of this philosophy is not simply having and nurturing the desire to know as many of the right answers as you possibly can, but, more importantly, understanding what makes the right answers right. This is about truly understanding how things work, whether you are interested in the combustion engine, the cardiovascular system, the tax code, or the politics of local government.

Always keep in mind the old expression, "Every day is a school day, and everyone is a teacher." Go into each new day with a hunger for learning as much as you can. Ask questions of anyone and everyone. You can learn from the parking attendant who works in the basement of a Manhattan skyscraper as well as the CEO of a publicly traded company who has the corner office of the penthouse floor in the same building. Engage in conversation. Look at and listen to everything around you. Read as much as you possibly can. Open your mind to the educational process every situation offers.

Use your mind like an old transistor radio, but rather than being tuned in to only one bandwidth on the receiver dial, open your consciousness to every station simultaneously as if your brain were composed of a thousand separate radios receiving signals simultaneously. This may seem overwhelming or even impossible, but, in fact, it's not. The reason it is feasible is because your extraordinary mind is a biological supercomputer with the unimaginable capacity to filter out trash and white noise at light speed. If you stay tuned in

198

to your environment and all the learning possibilities all the time, your conscious mind will automatically hone in on the material most valuable to your personal growth and development. Try it. Be more awake and alert as you go through your day. Don't just stroll down the street absent-mindedly. Be on the lookout for information and knowledge of use to you. Approach each day like this and you will be mesmerized by the forward progress you make in a very short period of time.

> ""*I am always doing that which I cannot do, in order that I may learn how to do it.*""
> —Pablo Picasso (1881-1973), Spanish artist

Learning is an excellent action word, one we should all engage in every day.

What did you learn today? What must you learn to achieve your personal brand of success?

Marketing

noun

Definition: the activities involved in making people aware of a company's products, making sure the products are available to be bought, etc.

Successful people are marketers. If you are to be prosperous, you must bring some service or product to the market. Your profits will ultimately be based on the value you bring to the marketplace. If you had little or no exposure to the consumers within a given population, it would be impossible for you to provide the service or product you possess, no matter how excellent the quality.

In some cases, the most important thing the success-oriented personality can market is themselves. Examples that stand out in my mind in contemporary times include figures like Donald Trump, Bill Gates, Steve Jobs, Warren Buffett, and Martha Stewart. These individuals carefully positioned themselves as personalities with which their service or product has been strongly linked. By liking, respecting, trusting, or being impressed with the personality behind the brand, the public develops a seemingly insatiable desire to support, promote, and purchase what each of these people are selling.

Marketing is about public awareness. Remember, if no one recognizes you or your company's existence, they cannot access what you are offering, although it may be superior to your competition. Make the effort to figure out a solid, effective, and honest marketing strategy to fulfill your potential in a very competitive modern-day business environment.

> *"The aim of marketing is to know and understand the customer so well the product or service fits him and sells itself."*
>
> —Peter Drucker (1909-2005),
> Austrian-born American management consultant, educator, and author

What is your brand? How do you want to go about creating (doing, plotting) a marketing plan for what you want to offer the world? Get some ideas started, or develop the ideas you already have.

Mastery

noun

Definition: knowledge and skill that allows you to do, use, or understand something very well.

In whatever you choose to do, you must achieve mastery. Sustained productivity, success, and prosperity cannot be built on pomp and pageantry. There has never been, nor will there ever be, a substitute for quality and ability. In the final analysis, no matter how well you promote yourself to gain the attention of the consumer, the product or service being offered will always speak for itself. If, for example, you build a beautiful dining room with professional waitstaff but serve poor food at high prices, the restaurant is certain to fail.

I had a professor when studying cardiac surgery who repeatedly advised the residents under his tutelage to, "Get your ducks in a row." What he meant was, there were to be no shortcuts in our education or in our pursuit of appropriate certification and accreditation. He insisted we all achieve complete mastery in the field of cardiac surgery from every point of view: technical mastery, intellectual mastery, emotional mastery, and academic mastery. If we were to fall short in any of these areas, it would soon become painfully obvious in the highly competitive world of open heart surgery. Mastery was the bare minimum level of competence required to even begin to expect to find professional success.

Set the bar high for yourself. Never sell yourself short. Get whatever training, education and practical experience required for you to be regarded as a true master in your field. We live in a world far too challenging to think mediocre skill sets, in any field, will be adequate to bring you to the top of your game. Training to achieve mastery requires hard work over a protracted period of time. The process of acquiring and maintaining the status of a master in your area of expertise is ongoing and never-ending. The sooner you come to terms with this unwavering reality, the sooner you may find yourself traveling the path to the head of the field.

"If people knew how hard I worked to get my mastery, it wouldn't seem so wonderful at all."

—Michelangelo (1475-1564), Italian artist, architect, poet, and engineer

What do you want to master? Write it out, and write out the steps you need to achieve master status. How many years of school? How many years of practice? How many hours of service? How many reps? How many clients?

Meditation

noun
Definition: the act or process of spending time in quiet thought.

201

Learn to recognize and exercise the power of meditation. Surprisingly, many people are intimidated by the idea of meditation. Meditation is easy. If you can think, you can meditate. If you think meditation means developing the ability to stop thinking, you're wrong. We are always thinking. Our minds are highly active and always functioning. In meditation, learn to focus the mind while at the same time relaxing the mind. One of the simplest forms of meditation revolves around focused breathing. Focusing on your breathing requires thinking about your breathing. Also, other thoughts will naturally come to the forefront of your mind. This is okay. Don't judge yourself too harshly if you are not completely focused on your breathing every moment of the process. Just let the unplanned thoughts float out of your mind as easily as they came in, like leaves floating down a stream. The process should be calming and rewarding. It should not be stress inducing.

If you start with only five or ten minutes a day and work up to thirty minutes, I think you will find your ability to focus and relax will steadily improve. Over time, this focused relaxation will open a new stream of creativity, energy, drive, and desire within you, which can then be put to work achieving your various goals. This is almost like stretching or yoga for the mind. It is a wonderfully rewarding process.

There are many forms of meditation and many tools to help you get started. Again, this practice is not about right and wrong, nor is it about being judgmental about your ability. Like all other skills and exercises, with practice will come expertise. See if it adds something to your daily life. If, after a reasonable period of time, you feel it has not enriched your existence, you can always leave it for a while and come back to it a later time. Of course, if it doesn't seem to add value for you at all, you can give it up altogether, but I ask you to at least give it a chance for a while. It has helped so many people achieve so much and get so much more out of our day-to-day experiences.

"Half an hour's meditation each day is essential, except when you are busy. Then a full hour is needed."

—Saint Francis de Sales (1567-1622), French bishop of Geneva

Did you meditate? Try it, then write down how it felt.

Now

adverb
Definition: at the present time.

Recognize the power of now. Now is all we have. Yesterday is gone. Tomorrow is not here yet. All we ever have, all we have ever had, and all we will ever have is right now. Time is an illusion. It appears to be a continuum, and you can think of it that way in a sense. But, in fact, time is only now. Our existence is always in the present. There is nothing else. If you elect not to live in the present, then you cease to exist during those periods of time.

Successful individuals comprehend the value of now. Now is where all action can be taken, all feelings can be experienced, all thoughts can be had, all life can be lived. Wasting any of the now regretting or reminiscing about the past is shameful, in my opinion. Using any of your now on fear of the future is a terrible misuse of your precious time. Make every effort to live fully in the now. Make every effort to act on things now. Planning to act in the future is called procrastination when something can be done now.

Too many times I hear people say things like, "Yeah, I'm planning to do that," or "I've been meaning to do that," or "I have to find the time to do that." Make no mistake, you cannot *find* time. More time isn't hiding in a closet somewhere. Time is always right under your nose. Time is always right here, right now, and nowhere else. You can never find more time. You can only decide to allocate the time you are living in presently to do what is most important immediately. This is how highly productive people spend their seconds, minutes, hours, days, weeks, months, years, and lives—*forever in the now.*

One of the most instructive descriptions of how to take full advantage of now was described in *The ONE Thing* by Gary Keller. In this excellent work, Keller basically says we should have goals. I totally agree. Well then, you say, isn't setting goals dreaming of the future, living in the future, and breaking the rule of living in the now? Good question, but listen to what Gary Keller says about this. What I took away from reading his book is one should have a goal of where he or she would like to be in ten years. This may be financially, professionally, personally, health-wise, whatever. Remember, ask for a lot. Don't be shy. Aim high. The world is full of abundance, and you were put here to live a rich, joyous, fulfilling, happy, and rewarding life. Think as big as you possibly have the courage to do.

Once you have decided exactly where you would like to be in ten years, you must ask yourself, "For that to be true, where would I have to be in five years to make that happen?" Then you ask, "And for me to be at that point in life five years from now, where would I need to be in one year?" Once you've figured out where you need to be in one year, you ask yourself where you would need to be and what you would need to be doing in six months. For your six-month ambition to take place, figure out what you will have had to achieve in one month. One month isn't very far away, so logically, it's critical to calculate in your mind how you will need to be positioned in one week for the one-month goal to become a reality.

Next, ask yourself what you need to do by the end of today to bring your one-week target into being. And finally, ask yourself the most important question of all: "What is the ONE thing I need to be doing right NOW, right this minute, right this second, to achieve by the end of today what I absolutely need to get done to make my huge ten-year ambition come true?"

This is what truly living in the now is about. Think hard about this. Once you fully digest and internalize this powerful concept, your effectiveness will skyrocket. Don't underestimate the extraordinary effectiveness of this very simple tool.

> "*Change your life today. Don't gamble on the future.*
> *Act now, without delay.*"
>
> —Simone de Beauvoir (1908-1986),
> French writer, philosopher, political activist, feminist, and social theorist

This concept is firmly planted in both Plot and Do. Give yourself time and space to work on this one. Write it out here.

Performance

---

noun
Definition: the act of doing a job, an activity, etc.

Recognize the value in high quality performance. Like it or not, we are judged and rewarded in the marketplace based not on our intentions, wishes, or desires, but rather on how we perform. This tends to make low level performers unhappy.

Whether we look at the system of "grading" which has become accepted in school, standardized testing, or any other quantifiable metric, whether you like it or not, the fact remains these are parameters by which we will all be judged. It's easy to point fingers of blame at the "system" and make arguments about why it is unfair, biased, antiquated, or flawed. That's all fine and dandy, and in some cases true. That said, my advice is for people to spend as much time, effort, and energy on performing well within the guidelines of the existing rubric of evaluation and reward as they do on changing the system into something that suits their personal strengths and needs better.

The reality is there are certain requirements and guidelines within which we all must function to succeed. Just as it would be ridiculous to think if you came in dead last in the one-hundred-meter dash you should win a gold medal, it would be preposterous to think any other avenue of life should treat you differently. If you plan to go through life complaining about the net being too high in tennis or the hoop being too small in basketball, you are in for a lot of angst.

My advice to you—and you can take it or leave it—is to focus more on bringing your personal performance up to snuff in the areas you find meaningful rather than waste a lifetime of promise and possibility by blowing against the wind. Work hard at building a skill set that has high value in the marketplace. When you build such a treasure trove of ability, you will see far less impropriety in the standards of excellence set by "the system" and spend most your free time enjoying the bounty of the fabulous crop you have sown.

"In business, the idea of measuring what you are doing, picking the measurements that count like customer satisfaction and performance...you thrive on that."

—Bill Gates (1955-),
American business magnate, philanthropist, investor,
computer programmer, and inventor

205

In your success story, where do you want to see your performance level? Where is it now? How do you get from where you are now to where you want to be? How can you improve upon your performance?

Precision

noun

Definition: the quality of being very accurate and exact: very careful and exact about the details of something.

Learn to love precision. One of the most important concepts is successful individuals decide exactly what they want and then they go after it. Great singers are precise in the notes they hit, surgeons are precise with their scalpels, naval pilots are precise about their aircraft carrier landings, a classical guitarist is precise with their fingers, an orator is precise about the words they choose to speak, and so on. Great engineers, physicists, mathematicians, and accountants should be precise in their work and attitude toward their calculations.

Unfortunately, too many of us live by the *good enough* philosophy, a cornerstone of mediocrity. I had a professor in my general surgical residency years who used to teach, "Don't become a good enough surgeon." This was a powerful lesson. If you are sewing an arterial anastomosis, it needs to be precise. In a situation like that, an individual's life depends on the job being perfect.

There are times when *good enough* simply isn't good enough. I know this philosophy has served me extremely well over the years, and I know it will do the same for you if you decide to adopt it and live by it.

"I have an over-achievement to precision, which is why I've sold more magazines than any man alive."
—Felix Dennis (1947-2014),
English publisher, poet, spoken word performer, and philanthropist

206

Look at your life, both professional and private, and honestly ask yourself where you may have made the mistake of being too imprecise in your choices, decision making, planning, goal setting, and actions. If you do this, you'll be able to identify areas which can easily be improved upon if you will just take the time and make the effort to be precise rather than careless.

Proactive

adjective

Definition: controlling a situation by making things happen or by preparing for possible future problems.

Successful people either learn to be proactive or are born with such an inclination. Being proactive is what I like to call "being a pusher." A pusher is one who is always moving oneself, those around him, and a given project or effort toward completion at all times. Time is so precious; it should never be wasted. The individual who possesses successful traits knows it is their obligation to constantly encourage progress at every stage of any undertaking. With experience, you learn that standing by and waiting for things to develop organically will almost always bring a gradual, but unmistakable, halt to any ambitious process.

This is an essential characteristic of leadership. You must continue paddling and shouting words of encouragement through a megaphone at the bow of the ship. Most people, even those with the best of intentions, will stop rowing unless given constant prodding to do so. This so-called encouragement may at times be unwelcome and result in some unhappiness to members of the team. For this reason, it is wise to temper such instruction with equal helpings of approbation and praise whenever possible.

"Real freedom is creative, proactive, and will take me into new territories. I am not free if my freedom is predicated on reacting to my past."

—Kenny Loggins (1948-), American singer-songwriter and guitarist

207

In your success story, where have you been proactive? In what areas do you think there is room for improvement? You are the main character of your success story; create yourself the way you want to be seen.

Rainmaker

noun

Definition: a person (as a partner in a law firm) who brings in new business; also: a person whose influence can initiate progress or ensure success: person who produces or attempts to produce rain by artificial means.

Strive to be a rainmaker. Successful people simply take action, resulting in causing good things to happen. Many times, I have been around individuals who possess seemingly identical skill sets but produce vastly different results. This is one of those areas where it is a bit more difficult to advise or instruct someone in this ability.

In some ways, this tool tends to fall more into a characteristic which is more commonly believed to be a gift. That being said, it is the purpose of this book to help the reader in every way possible to put to good use each of the words presented. So, on that note, my advice would be that if you are by nature a rainmaker, that has certainly become obvious to you and those around you already. My advice to such individuals is to recognize, embrace, and nurture this tremendous ability with every fiber of your being.

If, on the other hand, you are a person who seems to lack the rainmaking gift, that realization also is essentially important. This understanding will allow you to make every effort to develop this powerful ability. The most important advice I can give you is that to become a rainmaker, you must have the desire. Nothing will happen regarding your success, productivity, and financial wealth unless you begin with the wish for it to improve. This may sound a bit simplistic, but many people simply float through life hoping for the tide to take them to some exotic, exciting, and beautiful destination. I can assure you the chances of finding success by employing this technique is about as likely as hitting the Powerball lottery.

Therefore, you must truly want to be a rainmaker before it can happen (assuming you weren't one of the lucky few born with the gift). Then, you begin by watching and studying rainmakers you know, and you can begin to emulate them. Go where they go, do what they do, speak as they speak, study what they study, share the company they share, etc. Now, you need not worry that you will become a clone of some other highly prosperous individual you know.

No matter how hard you try to be just like them, you will never become them. You will always be you, hopefully just a better, more successful, more financially secure version of yourself.

American Indian tradition exalts the Rainmaker. The Rainmaker used magical powers to bring the rain to nourish the crops to feed the people.

—Jeffrey J. Fox (1945-), American author and consultant

So, are you a rainmaker? If not, think of the people you know; do you know anyone who *is* a rainmaker? What attributes do they possess that you would like to emulate? How can becoming a rainmaker help you reach your goals?

Read

verb
Definition: to look at and understand the meaning of letters, words, symbols, etc.

There is an adage that says, "Readers are leaders." I believe that, although this is a catchy quip, we should probably look at it a bit more closely. I have certainly known a lot of voracious readers in my life. Few of them are leaders of any kind. Therefore, the first thing to recognize is reading in and of itself will not ensure leadership qualities.

Furthermore, some of the best-read people I have ever known are not particularly prosperous when it comes to financial wealth. Think, for example, how many teachers—from grammar school to graduate school level—will read more than the vast majority of the general public. Typically, such individuals will earn an honest living that will sustain a stable lifestyle, but rarely will such individuals realize any sort of notable wealth in their lifetime. Obviously, there is nothing at all wrong with that, as monetary independence is not a goal shared by everyone.

The flip side of this coin is I am certain there are some people who become rich who are truly illiterate. Therefore, reading and financial success are not necessarily linked in any kind of absolute manner. That said, many if not most highly successful individuals do read almost compulsively. This may be in the form of books, magazines, professional journals, or online in the form of blogs, websites, tweets, etc. Let's face it, the more you know, the more interconnections they can make intellectually and philosophically. These cerebral "cross-links" allow your mind to expand, especially in the areas of imagination and creativity. As we have already discussed, these qualities are fundamental underpinnings of the exceptionally prosperous lifestyle. The more new and good ideas you have, the more likely you are to act on them and start the success process in motion.

I strongly suggest you read every day as much as you can. This can come from any source. Some of this time should clearly be spent in your area of professional expertise, while some should be focused on leisurely interest-based reading. I would strongly advise against reading garbage. Just as I wouldn't eat garbage, I wouldn't read it either. Ingest material which will nourish and help to develop your incredible mind. It is truly an organic and physiologic supercomputer. The more valuable data you feed your brain, the more brilliant ideas will spring forth from it. Perhaps not every reader is a leader, but if you intend to be one, read as much and often as you can. This is one piece of advice I feel certain can never steer you down the wrong path in life.

"A truly good book teaches me better than to read it. I must soon lay it down, and commence living on its hint. What I began by reading, I must finish by acting."

—Henry David Thoreau (1817-1862),
American author, poet, philosopher, abolitionist, naturalist,
critic, surveyor, and historian

What can you read that will nourish and propel your success?

210

Recover

verb
Definition: to become healthy after an illness or injury: to return to normal health: to return to a normal state after a period of difficulty.

Not only is this section focusing on what a successful person must *do*, I would like to spend some time in this segment discussing what successful people should *not do*. Successful people have the capacity to recover from failures, disappointments, and untoward results. They also make time in their otherwise hectic lives to rest and recover from labor. A successful person is essentially always a hard worker. This means many hours performing their occupational duties, often for long stretches of time.

Many highly successful people learn through experience there is a limit to this way of life. Of course, the big danger here is what is commonly known as "burnout." For this reason, one must learn to rest and recover. Recovery is essential. We see this philosophy practiced more and more among world-class athletes. We have also seen this over the years in the training of top thoroughbred race horses. No trainer with any expertise would over-work a million-dollar thoroughbred. Experienced breeders, owners, and trainers know this will break an animal down over time. There must be a perfect balance of high quality excellent work mixed with high quality excellent rest.

Another classic example of this approach to maintain and foster optimal production is that of the Major League baseball player. No manager would ever allow his ace starter to pitch every game. The physical toll on the shoulder, wrist, and elbow would be too much night after night. And that doesn't consider the psychological and emotional price an individual in the spotlight pays by performing in front of a crowd made up of tens of thousands of cheering, or jeering, spectators.

A pitcher typically can't come up with "the stuff" for an entire nine-inning game. The pitching coach keeps a very close count of the number of balls he throws, and he knows when the quality and effectiveness is bound to fall off precipitously for each starting big-league star. Carefully monitoring and limiting this vital statistic well can be the difference between winning on any given night and over the course of a season. We are all subject to such physiologic limitations. To think otherwise would be foolish and naïve.

211

The second key component to understanding recovery, after recognizing it is necessary, is learning how to incorporate this behavior into the lifestyle of the highly productive individual. Typically, the super-achiever would sincerely like to take some time off and vacation, for example, but they find they simply don't have time for that sort of thing. This is a very common, and precarious, mentality. The highly successful person normally says something along the lines of, "I'm going to take a break and get away for a few days, as soon as I can find the time."

Of course, the key word here is *find*.

The take-home lesson in this passage is you will never *find* the time to recover. You must *insist* on making the time to retreat from work and let the mind, soul, psyche, and body fully recuperate. This is an essential practice. You must learn to make time, that is, allocate time in your hectic schedule for restoration of the self.

This concept of creating time for important elements of your life is not limited to recovery. Just as you make time for meetings, the workday, or lunch, you must also make time for exercise, relaxation, seeing the dentist or doctor, etc. I can assure you, if an individual excludes this philosophy from their lifestyle, they will be nowhere near as happy, healthy, wealthy, or fulfilled as if they did. You will not necessarily die from non-stop work, but frankly, if that's the case, what the heck is the point in living?

Work hard and get regular doses of rest. Do not overdo it. This will make you much more productive, energized, engaged, creative, and prosperous in the long run. This is hard for top performers to accept at first, but I can assure you it has been proven to be true time and time again. Besides, you're worth it. You deserve to enjoy this life just as much as the next person.

"I didn't give myself enough breaks during the training year to recover. I didn't understand the power of periodization."
—Alberto Salazar (1958-),
Cuban-born American track coach and world-class long-distance runner

212

What do you do to relax and recover from hard work? Do you allow yourself periods of rest to recharge your batteries? Have you ever gotten to the point of being run-down because of being overworked?

Resourceful

adjective
Definition: able to deal well with new or difficult situations and to find solutions to problems.

It is best to be resourceful because life is not always cooperative. One of the fundamental things successful individuals recognize, embrace, and accept is the path to greatness will be strewn with stumbling blocks and impediments. To think otherwise is to be unrealistic, immature, even foolish. Essentially, every single day, life will present situations which are potentially obstructive to our forward progress and the realization of our goals.

You must learn to take such challenges in stride. The winning personality type expects such unwelcome turbulence in their personal flight toward achievement and prosperity. You must learn to curtail an excessively negative response to such circumstances. Of course, it is unrealistic to think anyone would celebrate such difficulties, but a middle ground regarding your emotional response must be found. This is called maturity. This is emblematic of inner strength and professionalism.

Responding to problems in a hysterical or panicked manner is always counterproductive. Logic, thoughtfulness, and measured action must prevail when stressful events come to pass. Do all you can to avoid reacting to these instances as crisis scenarios. To deal with the trouble of day-to-day life, you must develop a toolbox of resources you can use to sort out any situation. These resources may take the form of financial commodities, education, people, advisors, specific skillsets, etc. The more resourceful you can become, the more successful you will be.

If you fail to develop a robust cache of resources, you will be hamstrung in your ability to methodically work through trying times and, in the end, will be left as a member of the larger pack. Typically, association with this group means mediocrity in one form or another.

❝Life's too short to hang out with people who aren't resourceful.❞
—Jeff Bezos (1964-), American business magnate and investor

Plotting and planning the steps towards success has much to do with being resourceful. Write about how your skill at being resourceful has helped you along in reaching your goals. How does your resourcefulness help develop your success story?

Risk

---

noun
Definition: the possibility that something bad or unpleasant (such as injury or a loss) will happen.

Risk is a valuable component of success most highly productive individuals understand very well. It is difficult to make significant progress without putting something at risk. You may put any number of commodities at risk to break free of the main pack and get out in front of the rest of your peers and competitors.

This may mean money, of course. Often, financial risk is taken when one hopes to get ahead in life. This may mean money spent on an education. Some people decide to leverage dollars at an early age, sending their children to private schools from the outset. This is a big investment and a calculated risk. Here, one is betting that laying out cash in exchange for a better education will, in the end, in one way or another, pay some sort of dividend. This payout may mean a higher paying job or profession, but it may mean other rewards as well.

Being well educated gives you a different set of skills, allowing you to be more creative and imaginative, and those tools can be put to work to make the world a better place for all of us. Again, paying a premium for an education, especially at the primary and secondary school level, is risky, because no one can really assure the investor that this financial sacrifice will have any demonstrable or quantifiable advantage in the end. That said, many highly successful individuals will take this chance in the hopes of giving their children some advantage in a highly competitive world.

214

Another common risk people take is to put money into some sort of entrepreneurial endeavor and start their own business. For many of us, this gamble represents the opportunity to be free of the constraints that come because of being employed by another individual or entity.

> ❝The biggest risk is not taking any risk…In a world that's changing quickly, the only strategy that is guaranteed to fail is not taking risks.❞
>
> —Mark Zuckerberg (1984-),
> American computer programmer and internet entrepreneur

What risks have you taken in the pursuit of success? Did they pay off?

Self-Destructive

adjective
Definition: acting or tending to harm or destroy oneself.

Learn to avoid self-destructive behavior and thought at all costs. There are far too many negative forces at work in the world to be hampered by to add to the ever-growing list. You should be a champion for your own cause. Your responsibility when it comes to forging your own path to success is to take the best care of yourself as you can. Your job is to eat well, exercise, read, surround yourself with the best people, study, learn, add new skills, and so on.

It is not your place to do anything harmful to your person. You want to avoid obesity, laziness, ignorance, poverty, weakness, ill health, loneliness, trouble, and unhappiness. This is a choice. This is not an accident. Decide in your mind today you are going to rid your life of any self-destructive behaviors or thoughts. Decide today you are going to focus all your energy on building up your strength and diminishing your shortcomings. It is up to you to make this very definite conscious decision. No one can do it for you. We all must ultimately stand on our own two feet. Come to terms with this and accept it as one of the great truths life offers. Through proper decisions about your

215

daily routine, you can choose self-development as your personal philosophy rather than the dead-end street known as self-destruction.

"When we meet real tragedy in life, we can react in two ways—either by losing hope and falling into self-destructive habits, or by using the challenge to find our inner strength."

—Dalai Lama (1935-), Tibetan monk

Let's discuss your self-destructive behavior. How does it hinder your success? How do you deal with this obstacle? How would the hero or heroine of your story overcome self-destructive thoughts and behavior?

Sell

verb

Definition: to exchange (something) for money: to make (something) available to be bought.

Everyone is a salesman, like it or not. You may be selling a product or a service, or you may just be selling yourself. Keep in my mind that's a hell of a lot different than selling out. That's a hell of a lot different than selling your soul to the devil. That's also a hell of a lot different than scamming, cheating, and stealing.

Selling is a word often associated with something unsavory, unethical, or seedy. In fact, although it certainly can be, it usually isn't. Everyone requires products and services from others. That's just the way it is. Very few of us are truly independent, disconnected, living off the land, and removed completely from the so-called grid. If you're not intentionally screwing someone and taking advantage of them, there is nothing wrong with making an honest living by putting in hard work, adding value, and trading one commodity for another so you can continue to survive in a very costly modern-day environment.

Whether you are selling yourself to a new acquaintance at a cocktail party by offering a firm handshake and a warm smile, or you are selling a

216

reliable vehicle thoroughly prepared for road travel on a used car lot, you haven't committed a sin. Everyone is selling something, whether it's a philosophy or an object. Embrace this reality, and be responsible when it comes to your personal approach to this truth. Never try to take advantage of someone, and be cautious not to be exploited by an unscrupulous individual, either.

Know you will need to buy many things in this lifetime to be safe, healthy, and comfortable. By the same token, you will need to pass along goods or services at a fair price to others. The objective should be to create a win-win scenario whereby no one feels they have been taken advantage of and everyone feels they walk away from the exchange a bit richer, although they have had to give something up in exchange.

> *People often remark that I'm pretty lucky. Luck is only important in so far as getting the chance to sell yourself at the right moment. After that, you've got to have talent and know how to use it.*

—Frank Sinatra (1915-1998), American singer, actor, director, and producer

What skills or wares have you to sell? Is selling a part of your success story? Talk about it here.

Strategy

noun
Definition: a careful plan or method for achieving a goal usually over a long period of time: the skill of making or carrying out plans to achieve a goal.

You must have intention in everything you do, especially when undertaking the difficult task of designing a success strategy. You must first fantasize about what it is you truly want out of this incredible life we have been given and then go after it full force, head on and without fear. Paint a mental picture in great detail in your own imagination. But this must be followed up with a definite strategy to achieve what you desire. You must create a list of steps to get you moving in the direction of your dreams. You cannot expect the universe to simply reveal the end goal to you without making deliberate moves in the direction of your deepest desires. You need to plot, to strategize.

If you will formulate this strategy and begin walking down the path to your own personal greatness, doors will open and clues will somehow reveal themselves to you along the way. But you *must* walk the path. You cannot expect these revelations to present themselves while you are disengaged from the process. The answers will come as a result of doing the work and carrying out the steps you have delineated as your personal strategy.

> ❝*Strategy is about making choices, trade-offs; it's about deliberately choosing to be different.*❞
>
> —Michael Eugene Porter (1947-), American university professor

Write out your strategy. Have you put any of it to action? Write about that experience.

Thorough

adjective
Definition: to include every possible part or detail: careful about doing something in an accurate or exact way: complete or absolute.

Successful individuals are thorough in their work and bring projects to full completion, fulfilling each step along the way to the best of their ability to arrive at a superior result. Just as we would expect a professional airline pilot to be thorough in going through his pre-flight checklist, or a surgeon to be thorough in reviewing your medical record prior to entering the operating room to perform a surgery, we must all be thorough in our personal work every day.

218

To be half-hearted in our approach to doing anything of importance is to set ourselves up for a sub-optimal outcome. Being thorough is one of the easiest ways to tip the scales in your favor for success. As a resident in surgery, I was taught that to do a perfect operation, no matter how complex, it is simply a matter of doing each component step perfectly. Rushing through certain aspects of the procedure—or, worse, skipping vital elements which may seem trivial or non-essential—is a blueprint for potential disaster in the operating theater.

Be thorough in your preparation of any task at hand, and be thorough in the execution of the project. This attitude will forge a path of success in your life. This way of approaching any assignment or responsibility will also help to define a reputation of professionalism and excellence around you in the circles in which you travel and beyond. Take your work seriously, and leave no part undone. Be thorough and you will be thoroughly rewarded with a life of abundance.

66*There is no shortcut to achievement. Life requires thorough preparation—veneer isn't worth anything.*99

—George Washington Carver (1860-1943), American botanist and inventor

Let's discuss how and if you have been thorough in your execution of tasks. Are you thorough in your studying? In your meal plans, for example? Are you mindful of your precision in the workplace? Is there room for improvement? Write about it.

Work

noun
Definition: a job or activity that you do regularly, especially to earn money: the things you do especially as part of your job.

Successful people recognize that smart and effective work is the sword that cuts the path through the overgrown jungle of mediocrity to the expansive

Your Blueprint for Success

beauty of the coastline we call prosperity. I've always said work is a four-letter word. I've also been known to say hard work is two four-letter words back-to-back. That being said, work remains a necessary comrade in the fight for personal and financial liberty. No one has ever rested their way to the top.

Mihaly Csikszentmihalyi has done extensive research, writing and teaching on the subject of work and how it can be related to *flow* and *happiness*.

If you haven't studied any of his work, I suggest you do. His teachings remind each of us that if we find the right occupation, we can be lost in the pleasure of performing our work. This is what Earl Nightingale used to refer to as being a river person. In my opinion, there is no greater gift regarding your job than to find the vocation which fills you with happiness and a sense of great self-satisfaction.

The pursuit of finding work which makes you a river person, I believe, is a wonderfully worthwhile ideal or goal. The river person is one who does their daily work feeling as if they were simply being carried by the never-ending strength of a swift current. The work is getting done with what feels like little or no effort of the individual performing the task at hand. Time seems to have no dimension under such circumstances. The participant literally gets lost in the joy of doing the work and loses all sense of time. I have certainly had such wonderful emotions and experiences in the operating theater. Hours can pass where the focus is so intense and all-consuming that, at the end of the surgery, the operating room team has no concept of time. Half a day can go by without eating, drinking, or using the restroom, but the body feels full of energy, at ease, and perfectly in harmony with its surroundings. This is a fabulous, meditative process when it occurs.

I wish for all people to find this river in their life and then jump in. Make it one of your highest priority goals to find out what you love doing, and then be sure to become a part of that field. This will make all the difference in the rest of your life. You will never regret you did it, and you will wish you had done so sooner.

> ❝*Opportunity is missed by most people because it is dressed in overalls and looks like work.*❞
>
> —Thomas A. Edison (1847-1931), American inventor and businessman

220

One of the most important words in this section, *work,* is definitely an action word.

What work are you currently engaged in that is propelling your dreams of success? What can you do that allows you to lose yourself for hours upon hours? Write about your work.

Section Five:

Finishing—The Ultimate Payoff of Motivation

What do you feel you need to persevere? This fifth and final section focuses on finishing up and sustaining the motivation it takes to run that last mile to the finish line. Motivation is not always a straight line, just as writing a success story is not written from beginning to its end. Many writers write the ending first, which is your goal. Some develop characters and circumstances first and do not have an idea of where they want their story to go.

Your success story may have its stops and starts. Here is a group of words to keep in mind. Hopefully, they will inspire you to keep moving towards your goals, to finish what you've started, and to see your success story to completion.

And speaking of completion…

Completion

noun
Definition: the act or process of completing: the quality or state of being complete.

Complete task and projects. Everyone has ideas. Everyone starts projects. I tell everyone I know: great ideas are useless. The only thing that has any value is a completed project.

Surgeons get no credit for starting a great operation and never actually completing it. Airline pilots get no kudos for a great takeoff and a smooth ride at altitude without a successful landing to complete the journey safely. Dr. Porsche did not become internationally respected because he had a great idea for an automobile. Bill Gates is not a billionaire because he had an idea that every household should have a computer in America; he's a billionaire because every household in America has at least one personal computer.

Have you ever said you wanted to write a book? What happened? Did you take the project to completion, or did it die as an idea in your head? Did it languish as a few sheets of paper on your dining room table? Did it wind up a simple outline? Did you perhaps get through the introduction or the first chapter? Your dreams and goals are terrific, but they must be carried out completely to have any real impact in the world.

Successful people know how to complete tasks and assignments big and small, whether it means cleaning out the garage, organizing your closet, or building a new business. This concept, when fully adopted as a personal philosophy, can turn anyone's life around, no matter where they find themselves at the moment. Don't be known as an "idea man" (or woman); be known as the person who gets stuff done. This is the reputation of all the top performers, regardless of their occupation.

> *"Good business leaders create a vision, articulate the vision, passionately own the vision, and relentlessly drive it to completion."*
>
> —Jack Welch (1935-),
> American business executive, author, and chemical engineer

Think about your protagonist in your story; what task must they complete to be recognized as a success? Let's look at your life. When did you see a plan through to its natural end? How did that experience help you in life? Are there any ideas you have shelved that you regret not having had come to their completion? Write about them—you may find you are inspired to continue!

224

Determination

noun

Definition: a quality that makes you continue trying to do or achieve something that is difficult.

As Brian Tracy says, highly successful individuals are "unstoppable." Where others may be deterred, the super-achievers continue to forge straight ahead. There are so many obstacles in life, so many potential pitfalls. It seems every day when we get out of bed there is someone or something attempting to discourage and dissuade us from achieving our full potential.

Do not be hindered or impeded by these negative forces. Understand that they are simply a normal part of everyday life in the real world. Life is not a rose garden. In fact, as you travel deeper into the garden of life, the more thorns, vines, and thickets you will encounter. Don't allow these frustrating and aggravating obstructions to impede your momentum in any significant way. A determined attitude is like a razor-sharp machete hacking through this metaphoric jungle of brush, thistle, and bramble.

Determination is that force which keeps the victorious few always treading forward. This is an essential element of the success-oriented personality because the wind will not always be at your back in life. There will be many times when the headwind may seem endless and oppressive, but never stop putting one foot in front of the other. With time, the winds always change direction, and you will enjoy good times when your sail is full and taut. Always find the fortitude and will to proceed in a positive direction even when the progress seems minimal. Remain determined and, over time, unexpected breakthroughs will allow for sudden bursts of headway in your personal voyage toward an exceptional life. It is perfectly okay for things to get in your way—just do not let these things win.

"*Failure will never overtake me if my determination to succeed is strong enough.*"

—Og Mandino (1923-1996), American author

Where has your determination gotten you in the past? Do you recall a time when you gave up entirely, then wished you had started back on your journey towards success? Remember that time and write about it.

Effective

adjective
Definition: producing a result that is wanted.

It is essential to be effective. Otherwise, without an effective outcome, no matter how much work or effort is put into a project, you are only generating heat. Heat is lost energy, and that is never good—unless you are trying to lose calories! The desired result must ultimately be achieved if effectiveness is to be realized.

To be effective, you must learn to be goal-oriented. You must understand clearly where the finish line is. Coming up six inches short in a marathon is not adequate, unfortunately. We have seen this so many times. Think of the people you have known who took a year or two of college and then dropped out, the friend who had a fantastic idea for a business that never opened its doors or sold a single product, the associate with a genius idea for an invention but who never went through with the patent application and approval process. Perhaps they just decided to go a different route in life, but, usually, these are the common acts of ineffective individuals. This again has to do with completion and follow-through. Good ideas and good starts have little to no value if they are not seen to completion. It may sound harsh, but the only thing that ultimately counts in this world is where things finish.

No one cares about a smooth airplane flight that comes up one hundred yards short of the runway and puts you in the harbor. This is not an effective job of piloting. No one cares about who leads in the first four hundred and ninety-nine miles of the Indianapolis 500 or who wins the first two stages of the Triple Crown thoroughbred racing series. Effective individuals are finishers. This is an imperative facet of the high achieving personality, the ability to demonstrate effectiveness again and again over the course of a lifetime.

❝*The most effective way to do it, is to do it.*❞

—Amelia Earhart (1897-1937), American aviation pioneer and author

Think about the ways in your life your actions have been effective. You studied hard and got good grades? You practiced and practiced a skill and got really good at it? You pushed yourself to achieve at work and you got a promotion? You battled and conquered an addiction, an illness, or made the right choices and left an abusive relationship? There are *many* ways one can be a success in life. Write down where your actions have been most effective.

Endurance

noun
Definition: the ability to do something difficult for a long time: the ability to deal with pain or suffering for a long time: the quality of continuing for a long time.

Understand the indispensable need to develop endurance. Perhaps the first rule of winning should be: success is an ultra-marathon, not a 100-yard sprint race. In fact, in working toward, pursuing, and achieving success, there is no finish line.

Charlie Munger, vice chairman of Berkshire Hathaway Corporation, is now ninety-one-years-old, has an estimated net worth of $1.3 billion, and still goes to work every day, along with his eighty-four-year-old chairman, Warren Buffett, who is currently worth $67 billion. These are men who have built their fortunes on the concept of value investing: buying quality companies and being in it for the long haul.

Whether you are building a business or a sound personal relationship, it takes commitment, hard work, and, above all, time. Do not delude yourself into thinking you will be an overnight success. The stories of such individuals, although exciting and seductive, are often false or, at best, wildly exaggerated and oversimplified. In fact, the most prosperous individuals owe many of their accomplishments to their stamina, grit, and mettle. Having the capacity to tolerate struggle over many years is the mark of a seasoned expert or professional.

Backbone is developed from standing resolute through many storms. The pertinacity born as a result of enduring the long hard fight serves winners well in a highly competitive and often harsh work environment.

> *“The first virtue in a soldier is endurance of fatigue; courage is only the second virtue.”*
>
> —Napoleon Bonaparte (1769-1821), French emperor and military commander

Your success story relies upon endurance. Write about how you have endured and pushed through difficult times.

Excitement

noun
Definition: a feeling of eager enthusiasm and interest.

Get excited about things! Do you have an innate enthusiasm about something that gets you started on a project immediately and keeps you interested in it? If your work is drudgery and associated with a feeling of emotional pain or deflation, there is only so far you can take the process of achievement.

When studying the lives of big-time success stories, you will learn, again and again, almost without exception, those folks love what they do and are excited to go to work every day. It is difficult to find examples of truly exceptional individuals who don't like, or even hate, their work.

Just as with enthusiasm, excitement about what you are doing is a key component to success in any avenue. If you find yourself in this position, you must either find a way to love what you do by seeing all the positive aspects of it, or change what you do. Not enjoying your profession, method of weight loss, or chosen sport, etc. will hamper how far you can take your own personal achievement in that field. Being competent does not mean you love what you do.

Be true to yourself and follow your heart. You know deep down inside what you want to be and who you want to be. Listen to that voice, heed its advice, and make your dream a reality. The sooner you make those changes, the sooner you will be on a meteoric rise to the top of your field. You'll be excited about living every tomorrow and every today. That is the most glorious way to live one's life.

"Get excited and enthusiastic about your own dream.
This excitement is like a forest fire—you can smell it,
taste it, and see it from a mile away."

—Denis Waitley (1933-),
American motivational speaker, consultant, and author

Let's discuss what is in your heart. What do you love doing? What do you get excited about? How do you see your successful self in your story? Joseph Campbell once said, "Follow your bliss." Where is your bliss?

Faith

noun
Definition: strong belief in someone or something.

To succeed, you must have complete faith in yourself. You must have faith in your plans, that you will complete and fulfill any goals you have set out to achieve. This is essential. Having faith in your own ability, work ethic, self-worth, skill, talent, creativity, imagination, and inherent right to be a big success in this world is common to all success. To reach the heights of greatness, you must be convinced of your value and ability as a human being and as an individual. Lacking such faith in yourself is a non-starter and is a handicap that must be recognized, addressed, and overcome prior to the realization of any expectation of uncommon success. Self-doubt is a crippling disability which must be purged from your mind to become a highly productive person.

229

"None of us knows what might happen even the next minute, yet we still go forward. Because we trust. Because we have Faith."

—Paulo Coelho de Souza (1947-), Brazilian lyricist, novelist, and musician

Let's get honest—do you have faith in yourself, in your dreams and your talents?

If so, write about it, celebrate it. If not, write about it and think of ways you can improve your confidence and faith in yourself and your own success.

Follow-Through

noun
Definition: the act of completing an action or process.

To be successful, you must be all about follow-through. Whether you are looking to win a golf tournament, a tennis match, or the company sales contest, you better master the concept of follow-through. Great hitters in baseball are not known for having the most spectacular bunt; they swing at the ball and follow-through to hit shots out of the park. This goes back to the concept of finishing. You can't achieve big things by taking half-swings or being known for a long list of incomplete projects.

Follow-through is *essential* to success.

You will see this rubric for success outlined and defined again and again in this book, but I don't believe the blueprint can be overstated. First, you begin with a dream: what it is you want to accomplish in your life in one area or another. Second, you put a deadline on that dream and force it into being what we call an actual goal—e.g., I will graduate from law school by June of 2020. Third, you create a plan regarding how you can achieve that goal. Fourth, you set out on undertaking the various steps of the plan. Last, and perhaps most importantly, you follow through and complete all the necessary tasks required to achieve the goal. That's how successful people outdo the competition, again and again. They apply this simple formula to every facet of their lives, whether it is losing two pounds or putting away $25 million in their retirement account. Decide to be a winner. Follow through.

230

"I can give you a six-word formula for success:
Think it through—then follow through."

—Eddie Rickenbacker (1890-1973),
American World War I fighter ace and Medal of Honor recipient

Record here the times when follow-through worked in your life. Think about where you want to be in the future. What will you need to see to fruition to succeed?

Habit

noun
Definition: a usual way of behaving: something that a person does often in a regular and repeated way.

Work hard at developing and maintaining good habits. Something you do habitually is something you do routinely and with regularity. The mature mind knows this is the key to results. Now, notice I simply say *results*, without qualifying what type of results. Good habits, or healthy habits, are behaviors practiced on a routine basis and will yield good results over time. Bad habits, on the other hand, are behaviors practiced on a routine basis that will ultimately yield poor results over a prolonged period of time.

Examples of such habits would be taking a thirty-minute walk every morning after eating a nutritious breakfast versus smoking a pack of cigarettes every day and overeating a low nutrient diet. The overwhelming likelihood of where these behaviors will lead the individual who practices them is blatantly obvious.

Constantly analyze your status and measure against your habitual behavioral patterns. Take stock of any parameters you can on a steady basis. For example, your goal is to lose weight and regain your health. You begin by knowing your body weight. You must also know your BMI (body mass index). Know your body fat percentage. Know your current blood pressure. Get tests done at the doctor and know your cholesterol and triglyceride levels. Also, know your LDL (lousy) and HDL (healthy) cholesterol levels. Know your fasting blood sugar level. That's for your physical health.

What about your financial health? Know your checking account balance. Know your retirement account balance. Know what percent your money is earning in your investments on average. Get an idea on when you can retire. Learn how to effect change in any of these parameters, and others, when you recognize data points with which you are dissatisfied.

If your body weight is too high, you can go to work on correcting it immediately through a new set of habits. A lower calorie diet and more exercise ensues. Understand these behaviors must become habitual and be implemented over weeks, months, or even years to have any sort of measurable impact. But that is okay, because as a high achiever, you are a long-term thinker. You are not deluded with the false notions of instant gratification and reward.

The wealthy individual does not become rich overnight. They analyze their investment accounts and see where the bottom line stands. If the number is too low to ensure a comfortable retirement at a reasonable age, then more dollars go into the account and fewer dollars are spent on frivolity. This is the mindset of the successful personality type. The success-oriented philosophy is a disciplined one and an analytical one. Conscious adjustments are made to daily behavioral patterns to chart a course for triumph rather than defeat.

This concept is essential to living a regarding and enjoyable life. Look at where you stand, and compare these results to your daily rituals.

"Psychological studies reveal that ninety-five percent of everything we feel, think, and achieve is a result of a learned habit!"

—Darren Hardy (1971-),
American publisher, motivational speaker, and author

See if you cannot make modifications to the choices and actions you make every day to improve results over time. I think you certainly can, but don't put it off to a better time. Begin today. Begin right here, right now.

Happiness

noun

Definition: the state of feeling pleasure and enjoyment because of your life, situation, etc.

If you are truly happy, you have won. This is the ultimate barometer of success. This is far more important than your bank account, the size of your home, the type of car you drive, etc. There are countless people who have large amounts of material success and are empty inside.

On the other hand, there are others who have very little quantifiable wealth but lead rich, fulfilling lives.

If a simple skewer of shish kabob and a crust of bread while surrounded by friends and family is enough to fill you with joy, then you need look no further for success. Happiness is an experience unique to each of us. How we arrive there is a complex path which mankind has been searching for since the beginning of time.

Happiness is a feeling, an emotion. When you have it, you know it. And when you don't have happiness, you'll know that too. Presence or absence of the feeling is not a mystery. It's obvious. Being happy is the most beautiful feeling in the world. It is worth the effort to find it and to do everything in your power to maintain it. This often requires a somewhat convoluted admixture of elements for most of us to achieve. The formula typically involves components of hard work, ambition, desire, achievement, money, friendship, love, sex, passion, struggle, faith, spirituality, companionship, solitude, enlightenment, challenge, physical exercise, and intellectual discourse. Ultimately, the alchemy required to achieve true happiness is determined by the perfect balance of these various ingredients. Finding the proper amount, intensity, and duration of each is key to the process. In many ways, that process is called life. Awareness of the path we are on and keeping the ultimate goal of happiness in the forefront of our thoughts and daily routine is paramount if we are ever to have any realistic hope of arriving at the pure happy emotion.

"Be happy for this moment. This moment is your life."

—Omar Khayyam (1048-1131),
Persian mathematician, astronomer, philosopher, and poet

233

Your protagonist in your success story wants the story to have a happy ending. How will you go about achieving that happiness? Do you possess happiness already? Name and describe that which makes you happy. Relationships, sports, exercise, self-expression, a musical hobby, charity, etc. Explore it all here.

Joy

noun

Definition: a feeling of great happiness: success in doing, finding, or getting something.

Life is beautiful. We are here to have a joyous existence. No matter how much wealth, education, power, or professional success you achieve, if you cannot feel joy in day-to-day life, you are missing the entire point of the process. Joy is something which must be shared. Joyful occasions, joyful interactions, joyful experiences, this is what adds the true richness to any person's life.

If you aren't experiencing joy, you are doing something seriously wrong. Changes must be made. You are missing out on the essence of life. Do what you must to experience joy in your daily routine. Take joy in work, take joy in exercise, take joy in eating, take joy in your friends, family, and lover. Don't let anyone convince you that you must be suffering to be valuable. Each of us must find our proper place in this big and very complicated world.

If you find the day-to-day drudgery unbearable, start planning today how to change that. Remember, that process begins with looking deep inside and asking questions. Who do you want to be? Where do you want to be? With whom do you want to be? What do you want to do? These are the first questions to ask. If the answers are not in harmony with your actual existence, make the changes *now*. If not now, *when*? You are worth it. You can live the life you dream of, but you *must* have total clarity on what that means and then put a plan in place to go after it.

"*Pilots take no special joy in walking. Pilots like flying.*"

—Neil Armstrong (1930-2012),
American astronaut, engineer, moonwalker, aerospace engineer,
naval aviator, test pilot, and university professor

234

You have been asked plenty of important questions above. Time to answer them!

Legacy

noun

Definition: something that happened in the past or that comes from someone in the past.

Many successful people leave behind a legacy of success in one form or another. Not every winner is remembered by society at large, but probably many wouldn't mind if that were the case. Certainly, to qualify as a winner of any magnitude there should be some individuals who knew you personally who have good memories of your deeds when you have departed this world.

Leaving behind a legacy is about leaving a mark on this world that will live on beyond your own years. For me, this book is an example of my legacy. Whether it ever becomes a best seller, I believe in it. I know that each of my children and my nieces and nephews will all have a copy in their possession to carry with them throughout their lives. Hopefully, that will mean that their children and grandchildren will hold a copy of this book in their hands one day and think of me, many years after I have left the realm of the living. What a wonderful thought, to live in their eyes and hearts and minds well past my own mortal existence. This is the kind of thing money cannot do.

That is not to say you shouldn't plan to leave some dollars to those you love, but think of how you personally can do more. Can you write a book? Can you donate a library in your community? Can you create a foundation to serve those who are less fortunate than you when you have passed on? By nature, we are mark makers. Basically, what every artist does is mark making, whether it's a pencil on a piece of paper, a brush stroke on a stretched canvas, a notation on sheet music, chisel marks in stone, or a hand print on an ancient cave wall.

Throughout history, we see signs of great civilizations made up of great individuals. We have the pyramids in Egypt, the Colosseum in Rome, the Acropolis in Athens, and Persepolis in Iran. We look at these awe-inspiring remnants of mankind's glorious past as mighty symbols of inspiration for what we can do now and in the future. Think about what, if any, mark you may leave behind. It's certainly not an obligatory requirement of every great person, but it certainly might be nice. Consider what the Carnegies, Rockefellers, Eastmans, Fords, and Gettys of American history have left behind and how these contributions have helped to shape our great nation. These families and scores more have created opportunities for future generations in fields including, but not limited to, economic opportunity, higher education, public policy, art and culture, K-12 education, and the preservation of Americana.

A great legacy need not be on such a grand scale. Leaving each of your children, siblings, spouse, etc. a hand-written note that was set aside just for them to be read at the time of your death may have an impact greater than you could ever imagine. A well-cared-for and organized family photo album, whether analog or digital, is of indescribable value to your family for generations to come. Annotating these records with names, dates, description of the events and locations, etc. would provide information that would otherwise forever be lost. That would be a great tragedy. I know that for the past several years, my own father, who is now eighty-eight and retired from medicine, has been working diligently on a daily basis converting his lifetime collection of motion pictures and photos to a digital format. Much greater than any money he could ever leave his four children, this will be the real treasure our family will always have and hold as our personal history. What an incredible inheritance that will be for us—and a beautiful legacy for him.

> ❝*Proud about my father? What am I most proud of?*
> *I think I'm proud of the legacy he left, I think is what it is.*
> *He has left us so much.*❞
>
> —Ziggy Marley (1968-),
> Jamaican musician, singer-songwriter, voice actor, producer, and philanthropist

In a powerful story, the main character leaves behind a legacy, much like historical figures. In your story, with you as the main character, what do you want your legacy to be? How does your story finish, and what do you leave behind—for children, students, family, employees, friends, etc.? Does the idea of leaving a legacy motivate you?

Liberty

noun

Definition: the state or condition of people who can act and speak freely: the power to do or choose what you want to.

When given liberty, you can do what you do best. Liberty allows the innovative, productive individual the latitude to express themselves to the fullest extent. The creative mind can be unleashed in such an environment and allowed to act on elaborate goals and dreams that drive a culture forward. Being unimpeded, the mind can activate its full potential of imagination and ambition. When successful people gather in a society built on liberty, ideas can be shared and flow freely between great minds. This interaction between uninhibited individuals moves the overall productivity of the group forward at a much more rapid pace. The ability to network freely and work in a symbiotic manner is one of the great strengths of any nation or organization built on a true foundation of liberty.

Liberty is not dependent only on external force, however. Mankind has been fighting tyranny from all sorts of political and social oppressive forces for millennia, but perhaps the most crippling of all entities is the highly disabling internal propensity for self-doubt. One of the most tragic things one can witness is the person who, while living in a free society established in the name of liberty, mentally handcuffs themselves from living life to their full capability and worth. Too many of us have been convinced, one way or the other, we are somehow inferior or inadequate in some way. These feelings of self-deprecation are probably the greatest impediment to extraordinary achievement we shall ever face.

Please recognize the indescribably valuable gift we have all been given living in a free society, and make every effort to take full advantage of it. When you catch yourself feeling incapable of achieving great things, stop yourself immediately and remind yourself that each one of us was born to be great. It is your birthright as a human being to achieve exceptional levels of success and to contribute wonderful things to your family, community, country, and world. Doing anything less, given such extraordinary liberty and opportunity, would truly be beneath someone like you.

❝We hold these truths to be self-evident: that all men are created equal; that they are endowed by their Creator with certain unalienable rights; that among these are life, liberty, and the pursuit of happiness.❞

—Thomas Jefferson (1743-1826),
principal author of the Declaration of Independence,
third president of the United States of America

How does your liberty influence or motivate your decisions?

Love

noun

Definition: a feeling of strong or constant affection for a person: attraction that includes sexual desire.

Love people and love life. Who you love and what you love is up to you. But what is for sure is: without love in your life, there can be no real success or achievement.

The highly successful individual will be hampered if they do not love their work. This is where love and passion go together so harmoniously. If you are not surrounded by loving people outside of the workplace, then what is the purpose of being prosperous? There is no feeling more satisfying and gratifying than sharing your wealth with others. By definition, a loveless life is a poor one, and a life filled with love is a life filled with the greatest riches of all. Never lose sight of this essential principal of how one can truly live "the good life." I've met far too many people who lost sight of this concept along the way and found themselves alone, miserable, and emotionally bankrupt.

❝We are born of love; love is our mother.❞
—Rumi (1207-1273), Persian poet, theologian, and Sufi mystic

238

Let's talk about love. How does love motivate your actions? Talk about the love in your life. What or who do you love? It can be a garden, a music collection, your pets, friends, community, your country, your profession, your vocation, your studies, your lover, your family—list the things you love.

Loyalty

noun

Definition: the quality or state of being unswerving in allegiance.

Learn to understand loyalty, for love and loyalty go together. You must be loyal to those you love, loyal to your profession, loyal to your company, loyal to your co-workers, and loyal to your personal code of ethics. But most important of all, in the end, one must be loyal to themselves. If one abandons one's oath to be true to themselves, all other forms of loyalty will, in turn, disintegrate and collapse. Experienced and highly accomplished people know that this isn't always easy, but it is fundamental to long term happiness, prosperity, and self-respect.

"Success is the result of perfection, hard work, learning from failure, loyalty, and persistence."

—Colin Powell (1937-),
sixty-fifth United States Secretary of State, retired four-star general,
and national security advisor

We discussed who you love. Let's discuss to whom you give your loyalty. Write about how important loyalty is to you.

Momentum

noun

Definition: the strength or force that something has when it is moving: the strength or force that allows something to continue or to grow stronger or faster as time passes.

Learn to generate and sustain momentum. It is the only way to properly finish what you have started. Momentum implies forward motion. It is a fundamental key to success to always keep moving forward.

The speed is far less important than the perpetual nature of momentum. This brings to mind one of the great childhood stories of the tortoise and the hare. As the story teaches, slow and steady wins the race. Just keep going forward at all times. When others stop, stray laterally, or even go backward, you must maintain your forward momentum.

The key to this concept is that sustaining a forward direction requires much less energy and effort than initially creating forward momentum, so every time we get hung up in life and come to a complete stop, it becomes very difficult to get going again. We've all had such experiences, I'm sure. Think of how difficult it is to return to school in September after that delightful summer vacation. If you've ever quit going to the gym for a while, you know how hard it is to start up again. If you've ever stopped watching your nutritional and caloric intake for a while, you know how difficult it is to find the discipline to get back on track. Such examples are numerous. If you've taken some time off from your formal education with the plan to resume later, you know how daunting a task it can suddenly become. It takes what seems like a Herculean effort to get the ball rolling once again.

On the other hand, Newton's first law of motion teaches us an object at rest tends to stay at rest and that an object in motion tends to stay in motion, with the same direction and speed. This is a physical law of the universe. There is one caveat though: for this to be true, this system must exist in a vacuum. Remember, in a vacuum, there are no external forces. In the real world, there are a lot of external forces. These forces can be quite troublesome when it comes to achieving real success.

One of the greatest forces to impact your momentum either positively or negatively is people. Do everything in your power to get around—and stay around—good people. Expose yourself to individuals who possess and express positive energy. If you don't believe in the energy people can radiate, I'm afraid to tell you, you have absolutely no idea what you're talking about. The idea of energy, vibrations, and chemistry between people is as real as the sun and moon in the sky. Although you can't touch them, they are without question *very* much there. Feel for this energy; be open and receptive to it. If you sense negative or obstructive forces being emitted from a certain

240

individual, do all you can to avoid them. This is an individual who will break your momentum. If, on the other hand, you encounter an individual who gives off positive energy and with whom you share good chemistry, embrace this relationship and treat this person well. This is an individual who will put wind in your sails and help you get to where you're going with less effort needed.

People are not the only forces. Your environment, your place of employment, your level of education, and the breadth and depth of your personal skill sets are all entities that can either propel you forward or retard your progress. Open your mind and your eyes to this very important set of principles. Do all you can to get going and stay going where you want and with the wind at your back.

People who succeed have momentum. The more they succeed, the more they want to succeed, and the more they find a way to succeed. Similarly, when someone is failing, the tendency is to get on a downward spiral that can even become a self-fulfilling prophecy.

—Tony Robbins (1960-),
American motivational speaker, author, and life coach

Momentum can be thwarted by external and internal forces. Name the things and people you feel act as obstacles, hold you back, and drain you of your momentum. Decide right now to avoid these influences in your life. Call them by name first. How do they get in your way? How (if so) did you overcome them?

Motivation

noun

Definition: the act or process of giving someone a reason for doing something: the condition of being eager to act or work: a force or influence that causes someone to do something.

Do everything you can to remain motivated. Winning is a perpetual process. It's not about a single goal, deadline, or finish line. Anyone can "get up" for a single big event, opportunity, or contest. That's not success. Success is when an individual repeatedly digs down deep and finds the ambition, desire, energy, and fortitude to give it their all again and again. This is what being motivated is all about. It's about maintaining the will to act and achieve. This skill can be developed and honed. This is what separates the proverbial men from the boys.

The truly motivated individual doesn't perform based on the score. What I mean is, the motivated individual remains eager to give it their best in good times and in bad. True champions are not only hungry to train and practice when they are on top, but are equally driven after defeat and disappointment. This explains why a man like Muhammad Ali was the undisputed heavy weight of the world on three separate occasions. He suffered devastating defeats between these infamous reigns as champion. But that wasn't enough to keep him down for very long. He found inspiration and motivation in the idea of making a great comeback and regaining his world championship title.

Perhaps the best example of this that I have seen in the world of sports is Roger Federer. For years, at an advanced age (for his sport of tennis, that is), he has toiled, fought, and scraped to remain at the top of the world rankings. On numerous occasions when the pundits had counted him out and predicted his retirement, this extraordinary competitor returned to fight another day. He currently remains number two in the world and has made valiant attempts to win more Grand Slam events as he still routinely makes it to the final round.

One can take great inspiration from this highly-motivated individual. Emulate such people. If you are honest with yourself, you will find you possess this same character trait deep down inside yourself. Don't let others deter or dissuade you from staying on the path to your ultimate greatness.

"Of course, motivation is not permanent. But then, neither is bathing; but it is something you should do on a regular basis."

—Zig Ziglar (1926-2012),
American author, salesman, and motivational speaker

When you look towards the finish line, what is motivating you to finish? Where is the motivation in your story? What spurs your protagonist on? Is it the love of the game? Is it money? Is it to beat your personal best? Write about it! Chances are, when things get tough, you will need to revisit this part of the book to see what motivates you.

Passion

noun
Definition: a strong feeling of enthusiasm or excitement for something or about doing something.

Does your passion drive you? To truly reach your full potential, you should be engaged in activities you are passionate about. You can be successful in something you dislike or simply tolerate, but whatever that level of success, it would be far exceeded by you if you were involved in a field that you absolutely loved. If you have ever known a person who had a "fire in their belly" for their work, then you know what I'm talking about. These are the people who say they feel as though they have never worked a day in their life. These are the individuals who feel fortunate to get paid at all for what they are doing. That's how much they love their job. I have known people like this. This feeling is one of life's greatest gifts. This is, in my opinion, the holy grail of work life. It doesn't matter how much money these people actually earn, as their employment is as satisfying to them as any other activity they could engage in. This should be a goal for each of us to achieve.

Imagine the wonderful feeling of going to sleep at night, exited to get to work in the morning. Imagine feeling totally happy, fulfilled, and at peace while performing your daily duties in the workplace. This is a dream-like scenario.

66*There is no passion to be found playing small—in settling for a life that is less than the one you are capable of living.*99
—Nelson Mandela (1918-2013),
South African anti-apartheid activist, politician, philanthropist,
president of South Africa

243

In your success story, what are you doing? Do you see yourself loving it so much, it doesn't feel like work, it doesn't feel like a chore? Passion motivates—write about it! This will be another section that will keep you motivated.

Patience

noun

Definition: the capacity, habit, or fact of being able to remain calm and not become annoyed when waiting for a long time or when dealing with problems or difficult people: the capacity to do things in a careful way over a long period of time without hurrying.

Success requires patience. Most people who get labeled "overnight successes" have worked for many years to finally see their hard work culminate into some sort of financial, personal, or professional payoff which appears to the outsider to be quite sudden. There are numerous adages which have stood the test of time to illustrate this point. Simple examples are: "Rome wasn't built in a day," and "Slow and steady wins the race."

Patience and persistence tend to go hand in hand. When I look back at my own professional success, I can easily remember the grueling effort required just to complete my formal training in cardiovascular and thoracic surgery. My journey was, at the time, the most abbreviated path one could take to become an open-heart surgeon. Despite this, it still took fifteen years after high school to accomplish—fifteen extremely difficult years. This is broken down as follows: four years of college, four years of medical school, five years of general surgery residency, and two years of cardiothoracic surgical residency. For many of my colleagues, it took even longer. Some took time off between high school and college or college and medical school, for example. Some got master's degrees or PhDs along the way.

Others did one or more years in the laboratory, doing scientific bench research. The point is, there was no fast track.

Keep in mind, at the end of this process, most of us were well into our thirties and then just beginning to look for our first real job. Many of us had as much as several hundred thousand dollars in student loans. It was difficult, but it was the path we chose. Years later, when individuals like myself enjoy a comfortable lifestyle, others may see someone in their early forties enjoying the finer things in life and think, "How lucky he is to be so well-off at such a young age." Well, although I do feel very fortunate to be in the position I am in and live the life I do, I also know how hard I worked, not only to get to where I am, but to stay here as well. As my old professor used to say, "Nothing hard is ever easy."

Be patient when it comes to success. Except for hitting the Powerball, Mega Millions, or being born into a huge trust fund, I think just about everyone who is successful has worked long and hard for it. One needs to be patient in watching this success grow and develop along with the individual. By the way, I'm not sure the lottery winner or the recipient of an enormous inheritance is a success for those reasons. They may be rich, but that's different from being successful. That's not to say one couldn't be both, but I think you understand my point.

Don't be in a big rush to win big. If you are, you're likely to be frustrated and disappointed a lot of the time. Take your time and just keep chipping away at your goals and your destination. Earl Nightingale, radio personality and writer, to name just a few accolades, was fond of comparing this journey to that of a cruise ship on the high seas. That ship might only be doing twenty knots, but it keeps going, on course twenty-four hours a day, day after day until it arrives safely in port. Whether the seas are rough or calm, the engines keep running and the propellers keep turning tirelessly.

On the ocean, it sometimes appears no progress is being made at all, but the captain stays the course and, ultimately, makes the port of call on time, with exceedingly few exceptions. Live your life like that and you are bound to have an amazing, fulfilling, and rewarding journey.

> "*Have patience. All things are difficult before they become easy.*"
>
> —Sa'd' (1210-1292), Persian poet

Are you a patient person? Do not mistake patience for passivity. You still need to move forward; you are not just sitting on your haunches, letting things just unfold. You must find a balance between making things happen and allowing things to unfold, to have the patience to allow things for which you have worked very hard to fall into place. You must practice patience—it may not come to you without effort. Write about where patience has paid off in your life. How did you stay motivated to the finish line?

Persistence

noun
Definition: the quality that allows someone to continue doing something or trying to do something even though it is difficult or opposed by other people.

Be persistent in your goals. Don't give up. Successful people keep on trying when others have quit and moved on to something easier. Highly successful people are not dissuaded because the road becomes difficult. This is a rare gift that comes naturally to some, but it must be learned by most of us.

Those with highly productive mentalities continue forging ahead despite any problematic environmental conditions. Like a great mountain climber, continue to put one foot in front of the other to reach your goals, no matter how steep the ascent, how thin the air, how extreme the temperature, how hard the wind blows, how brutally the rain or snow falls, etc.

Be persistent and relentless in your pursuit of your dreams and goals. At the core of persistence is not only an insatiable desire to succeed, but also a deep contempt for defeat. There are numerous excellent motivational quotations demonstrating the importance of the personal attribute.

A classic and instructive adage came from Napoleon Hill, author of the timeless book on personal development, *Think and Grow Rich*, who said, "Persistence is to the character of man what carbon is to steel." I couldn't agree more. One of the most important things my colleagues and I took away from our many years of grueling training was the value of a persistent character. It was this persistence which carried us through the many challenging years of education, not only in the classroom but on the wards and in the operating room as well.

The trait of being persistent may mean the difference between life and death in the field of medicine and surgery. One doesn't quit when trying to control hemorrhage or when attempting to resuscitate a lifeless patient until absolutely every tiny grain of hope has been lost. I can recall many times in my life working tirelessly for hours under such dire circumstances when patients presented in extremis after gunshot or stab wounds. Every experienced surgeon you meet can share with you stories of people they brought back long after others on the team felt any chance for survival had passed. And it is with this attitude that each of us should approach our own personal and professional lives.

It is never too late to get in better physical condition—just keep trying. It is never too late to lose weight if need be—just keep trying. It is never too late to complete your formal education, learn another language, start your own business, or build a rewarding intimate relationship—just keep trying. Always remember the words of the British educational writer William Edward Hickson, who popularized the following proverb:

'Tis a lesson you should heed:
Try, try, try again.
If at first you don't succeed,
Try, try, try again.

Apparently, this quote can be found earlier in *The Teacher's Manual* by Thomas H. Palmer and was meant to inspire children to work hard at their lessons and homework. If taken to heart, this seemingly childish phrase could change your life dramatically.

"*The big talent is persistence.*"
—Octavia E. Butler (1947-2006), American science fiction writer

Let's talk about how persistence has manifested in your life. Talk about the times you gave up. Talk about the times you did not. How do they differ? If you can do things differently to get to the finish line, how do you think you should proceed?

Purpose

noun

Definition: the reason why something is done or used: the aim or intention of something: the feeling of being determined to do or achieve something: the aim or goal of a person: what a person is trying to do, become, etc.

Motivation will come to you when you behave with purpose. Taking a haphazard approach to life is sure to result in frequent disappointments and overall underachievement. Be purposeful in all your endeavors. Know what you want to do and why. Always be architecting your life's plan. Where would you like to be in ten years, and how do you plan to get there? These are very important questions. You may, or may not, be surprised how few people ask themselves such questions in any sort of serious manner.

Any good surgeon, pilot, civil engineer, choreographer, or building contractor will tell you that, to realize high levels of success, you must act purposefully. You must have a game plan, a blueprint, a flight plan to follow if failure and personal catastrophe are to be averted.

The questions to ask yourself (in the journal segment at the end of each word) will lead you quickly to your major purpose in life. These are powerful and important questions. The answers to such questions will tell you a lot about yourself—perhaps things you didn't fully understand previously.

I strongly encourage you to find your purpose and then live by it, through it, and for it. This will add new heights of meaning, pleasure, fulfillment, and value to your very existence. Never underestimate the worth of a purpose-driven lifestyle.

> *"The purpose of our lives is to be happy."*
> —Dalai Lama (1950-) Tibetan Buddhist monk and author

Ask yourself, what is my purpose for getting out of bed today? What do I wish to accomplish? Where am I now, and where do I want to go? What are my motivations for my ambitions? How much money do I wish to earn and why? Where would I like to live and why? What occupation would I like to involve myself in and why? With whom do I want to do business and why? With whom do I wish to socialize and why?

Reason

noun
Definition: a fact, condition, or situation that makes it proper or appropriate to do something, feel something, etc.

You must have a reason to succeed. Success-oriented people tend to be driven largely by a very specific reason. The reason need only be important to the individual themselves. Friends, relatives, and colleagues may not understand the motivational nature of another person's reason, but that is completely irrelevant. Each of us needs to find our own reason for why we do things and why we wish to be exceptional in one way or another.

Every individual who is determined to achieve great success in their life is motivated by something. Without a reason, there will never be enough enthusiasm, desire, persistence, and discipline generated to produce extraordinary results. The possibilities are endless, but the following list is a few examples of what may inspire certain people to achieve greatness in one area of life or another.

If you were born into poverty, you might want to gain wealth so you never have to live under poor circumstances again. You may also strongly desire to break a cycle of poverty so your children do not live that way. Another example might be if you were born into the so-called middle class. You might perceive this as mediocrity. Not everyone will feel this way, but for those that do, they may resent it and develop an appetite for greater abundance, education, travel, experiences, etc. You may be fortunate to have been born into wealth or a highly-educated family, or both. Your primary reason for wanting success may be to maintain such a lifestyle throughout your lifetime. You may also be motivated to show those around you that you are a high-quality individual and your prosperity is not simply a byproduct of your birthright.

You may want prosperity for financial freedom. You may not want to work for anyone else. You may have certain objects you desire like cars, watches, homes, etc. You may want to achieve a certain level of education so you can find a cure for cancer. You may want to gain great wealth so you can donate it all to charitable causes. The choice is yours, but the great likelihood is, if you lack a good reason to excel, you will not.

Jim Rohn used to say, "When the *why* is big, the *how* becomes easy." A classic example of this, which I believe really helps someone understand what I'm talking about, is as follows. If I were to place a steel beam twelve inches across, twelve inches high, and twelve feet long on the floor and place a $100 bill on one end, would you walk across the beam to pick it up? If you could do so successfully, I would allow you to keep the $100 dollars. If, on the other hand, you stepped off and put your foot on the floor, I would put the $100 dollars back in my wallet. I would hazard to guess you would take this challenge. The reward is high for the effort and risk involved. In other words, the *why* is big, and the *how* is easy. I also have no doubt that just about any able-bodied person could successfully complete this task without ever coming close to losing their balance and stepping off the beam and onto the floor.

Now, how about if I were to place this same beam between the rooftops of two five-story buildings, fifty feet in the air, and asked you to walk across to retrieve your $100 bill? Would you do it? You know you could physically. You will have already proven you could walk on a twelve-inch beam without falling. But in this scenario, something tells me you would not step out onto the beam when the risk of a misstep would almost certainly cost you your life. Here, the *how* looks much bigger, and the *why* has become much smaller.

Let's look at a final situation. The beam is still between the roofs of the five-story buildings, but I've replaced the $100 bill with your baby in a bassinet. And I've added one new variable: the building your baby is nearest to is on fire. If you don't go get the baby, he will either be burned to death, or the building will eventually collapse, and he will fall to his death. Would you walk across the beam now? I know you would. Here, the *why* gets enormous and the *how*, although still sizable, is immediately overcome. This is the power of the *why*. This demonstrates why we all need a very good reason to succeed. Once we find that, we can do practically anything. Certainly, we can do much more than we may have believed we were capable of prior.

*❝We have forty million reasons for failure,
but not a single excuse.❞*

—Rudyard Kipling (1865-1936), English short-story writer, poet, and novelist

Talk about what your reasons are for wanting to succeed. You will see, your story will be very inspiring to you. Everyone has a story, and here is your opportunity to tell it. Your reason for wanting to achieve will motivate you!

Receptive

adjective
Definition: willing to listen to or accept ideas, suggestions, etc.

Your receptivity to ideas is fundamental to success. Being willing to receive new information, concepts, and philosophies is central to personal growth, development, and achievement. The cornerstone of this behavior probably rests upon listening. Successful people are wonderful listeners. This invaluable skill does not always come naturally to the highly productive personality type, however. Often, such individuals are so focused on having their voices and opinions heard, they leave very little time to take in new data. We can learn both through speaking and listening, but it is critical not to leave either facet of communication out.

Being open to novel thoughts and suggestions is a very important part of intellectual enlightenment as well as professional and financial expansion. Think of yourself as a gigantic net, eager to take in anything the sea of knowledge can offer. At the end of the day, you must reflect on all you have seen, heard, and read, and then wade through it. The trash can be disposed of, the little fish can be thrown back into the water, but the big fish are the keepers.

These are the thoughts, observations, and notions that should be transferred into one's notebook—or, ideally, right here within *this* book— and carefully filed for application in some project or endeavor down the road. If all you do in a day is spew words incessantly into the ocean of life,

251

your net is sure to be empty at the end of the day. That will ultimately lead to intellectual, emotional, and financial bankruptcy. There is, after all, a reason why those who fish are usually quite quiet on the waters.

> ❝Seeking means: to have a goal; but finding means: to be free, to be receptive, to have no goal.❞
>
> —Hermann Hesse (1877-1962), German-born poet, novelist, and painter

Here is your chance to write down the things that have inspired you or changed your thinking. What stands out? What did you hear, see, or read that inspired you to change your job, move to a different place, change your eating habits, or strengthen your body? What did you receive from the universe that encouraged you to pursue your desires? Keep coming back to this segment, add paper, and keep notes on what knowledge you have acquired. It will encourage you to keep moving towards your finish line.

Recognition

noun
Definition: the act of accepting that something is true or important or that it exists.

Recognize others for their achievements and contributions. Highly successful people recognize they can only go so far, ascend the ladder of prosperity, and do only so much by themselves. The greatest opportunity to succeed will present itself when exceptional individuals work together creating a synergistic movement toward a particular goal.

It is essentially impossible to attain any significant amount of abundance, fulfillment, or happiness when you attempt to do so without the help of others. You must not be consumed with the question of who will get the ultimate credit for any given feat. Furthermore, understand the power of not only recognizing the contributions of those around you, but also be certain to reward such collaborators in kind. Trying to take the whole pie—whether it be monetarily or regarding praise, accolades, and publicity—is a grave mistake. This approach will invariably tarnish your reputation and quickly put you in a position of almost complete isolation.

Without the aid of an excellent team of participants, no project of any significant scale can be carried out to completion. To be victorious in the game of life, you must build a spectacular team around yourself and be sure to hold any trophies won in the air as a unit, not as an individual. The more you work at sincerely recognizing the efforts and excellence of those around you, the sooner you will taste the fruits of prosperity you desire in your life. Share in the banquet of success. No one likes to sit at the dinner table with a greedy, selfish pig. I cannot put it any more plainly than that.

"There are two things people want more than sex and money: recognition and praise."

—Mary Kay Ash (1918-2001), American businesswoman

Every story has supporting characters who influence and help the main character along on their journey. Write about those who have played a part in your success story. Give credit where credit is due!

Relentless

adjective
Definition: continued without becoming weaker, less severe, etc.; remaining strict or determined.

Be relentless in pursuing your goals. Whether this is related to losing weight, training for a marathon, completing your MBA while raising a family and working full time, keep going after what you desire. The source of this drive is internal. It is a difficult behavior to teach, but I believe it can be learned. One of the best ways of developing this habit is through observation of highly successful individuals in the world around you. Look to the people you admire for inspiration and motivation.

Who is the fittest person you know? Do you respect them? Do you envy them? Would you love to go through life fit, strong, and attractive? Would you like to feel comfortable in your clothing or in a bathing suit in front of others? I think most of us would. What could the downside of being in good health and good physical condition possibly be? For most of us, this is something we would truly love to achieve deep down inside. So, who do you know who seems to have mastered this area of their life? Surely you know someone that you revere for their physical wellness. Write about them below!

Once you have determined who that person is in your world, begin to look at how they behave and consider emulating their lifestyle when it comes to good health and physical conditioning. Watch what they eat. Observe how much they eat. Ask them to share with you their personal exercise routine and their attitude toward conditioning. See if you can begin to incorporate some of these rituals into your own daily routine.

This practice will typically reveal a significant degree of relentlessness in that individual's life. You'll commonly hear them say things like, "I exercise six days a week," or "I almost never eat pasta or white bread." You wouldn't be surprised to learn these highly successful people typically don't consume processed foods or that water is their primary beverage choice at every meal. We all know people like these, so why not elevate them in our minds to the status of a role model for that particular area of your life?

Then, we can look at someone who has excellent relationships and emulate those activities and behaviors. Here, you might come to find out the person you know with a wonderful family life, "Never misses his daughter's softball games," or they insist on taking three family vacations every year, no matter what. They are relentless in their approach to fostering and maintaining healthy and rewarding personal relationships.

The same will be true for each category of success. Finances will be no exception. You might not be surprised to find out the most fiscally responsible person you know puts away ten percent of every paycheck they earn, no exceptions. They are relentless in building economic stability and security, no matter what the economy is doing. These are the people we must look to for guidance regarding our own actions if we want to achieve similar results.

Key to this process is the reason why you would like to have any of these things, whether it is good health, fitness, wealth, or sound personal relationships. If you don't care whether you are obese, then you will continue to be so. If, on the other hand, you would like to lose weight to improve your health and enhance your life experience, or so you will be around to dance with your son or daughter on their wedding day, that might be just the motivation you need to become relentless in your pursuit of such noble goals.

> 66 *Whether you're shuffling a deck of cards or holding your breath, magic is pretty simple: it comes down to training, practice, and experimentation, followed up by ridiculous pursuit and relentless perseverance.* 99
>
> —David Blaine (1973-), American illusionist and endurance artist

Are you relentless in your pursuit of knowledge and advice? Who in your life illustrates the skill of being relentless? How does it help them reach their goals?

Resolve

verb
Definition: to make a definite and serious decision to do something.

Learn to have resolve. This is an enormously important distinction that separates highly successful individuals from everyone else. Almost everyone has within them wants, desires, wishes, fantasies, dreams, etc. Far fewer people develop a plan outlining how specifically they are going to go about getting everything from life they really want.

Of those people who do outline a well-defined strategy regarding how they are going to create the lifestyle the really want, even fewer begin to work at that goal in any serious manner at all. And then, of the small number who begin that process, almost none have the resolve to stick with the program through actual realization.

In the end, it is the resolve which is the most valuable attribute one can possess. This is the ability to continue trying as all the ups and downs of real life create a steady turbulence which knocks most people off course. Success is not easy. In fact, attaining unusual levels of productivity and prosperity typically requires extraordinary effort put forth over protracted periods of time. This, in and of itself, is a pretty darn good definition of resolve. Resolve is about the personality that can "keep on keepin' on" when it seems all hope is lost and the proverbial deck is heavily stacked against you. This is the attitude the successful person must adopt. This philosophy is heavily steeped in faith, optimism, and grit. Look deep inside yourself and ask if you have true resolve.

Ask yourself if there were times when you quit too early and now you regret that choice. Did you quit school too early? Did you quit dieting too early? Did you quit exercising too early? Did you quit on an intimate relationship too early? Write about it below. If you're anything like me, the answer to at least one of these questions is *yes*. If not, good for you. But if the answer to this or any number of important questions you might ask yourself is yes, don't worry. It is often not too late to show resolve and pick up where you left off or start fresh with a new beginning on a new path. Remember, winners never quit, and quitters never win.

> "*You must bring great resolve to your work.
> It's not all a bed of roses.*"
>
> —Douglas Conant (1952-), American businessman

So, when did you quit? What did you pick up again? Talk about your resolve and how it helps.

Results

noun
Definition: something caused by something else that happened or was done before.

Winning and losing is important. It's not just how you play the game. Don't let anybody try to convince you otherwise. You need to see positive results. If you were to be told by your doctor that your weight, blood pressure, or cholesterol were dangerously high, and you implemented some changes in your lifestyle habits but saw no change in the measurable results, that wouldn't be okay, would it? The answer is: "Of course not." That would be life-threateningly dangerous. We would need to implement and try a new plan—perhaps more exercise and fewer calories, perhaps some medication if those modifications yielded no improvement.

Again, don't let people lull you into a false belief system that teaches that results are meaningless. That kind of thinking is a recipe for disaster. It is impossible for one to achieve their true potential without looking at and analyzing results. For example, what would you do if you put your hard-earned money in the hands of a professional financial advisor and you saw that over a reasonable period of time there was no growth in the monetary value of the account? How would you feel about that? How would you judge the effectiveness of that so-called professional? It would be hard to accept, wouldn't it? Even worse, what if you saw your account dropping in value? How would you feel then? How would you feel about those results?

Albert Einstein is purported to have said, "Insanity is doing the same thing over and over and expecting different results." He also said, "People love chopping wood. In this activity, one immediately sees results." Obviously, in the mind of one of history's great thinkers, results held a very important place. Interestingly, his theory of relativity has been, and continues to be, tested exhaustively through scientific experimentation, and to date, every aspect that can be tested shows his mathematical calculations are correct. Only recently has the existence of gravitational waves been proven through empirical testing. I'm sure the white-haired professor would be tickled pink to learn of these results.

The importance and value of results is evident in business-related matters as well. Jack Welch, former CEO of General Electric, said, "Culture drives great results." During Welch's twenty-year tenure at GE, the company's value rose some four thousand percent. Those are phenomenal objective results regarding a business's performance. The eighty-year-old retired businessman's personal wealth has been estimated at more than $700 million dollars. That's not a bad result, either, from a financial independence point of view.

I suggest you become a results-oriented individual if you are not one already. Look at quantitative as well as qualitative parameters in your life and take stock of how you are doing. What is your waist size, your body mass index, fasting blood sugar, blood pressure, and cholesterol level? How many friends do you have? What is the quality of those relationships? When was the last time you called your parents, your siblings, your cousins, etc.? How does your bank account look? How does your retirement account look? Are the kids' college accounts fully funded? Have you even opened one yet? These are the kinds of questions we must ask ourselves if we expect to generate good results or improve upon where they are currently. Use the writing space below to answer these questions and write about your findings.

Don't bury your head in the sand. Look at your personal results in every category you can think of, and then deal with them. Give yourself a pat on the shoulder where you are doing well and a kick in the backside where you are not.

"There is no such thing as failure. There are only results."

—Tony Robins (1960-), American motivational speaker, author, and life coach

Self-Control

noun
Definition: restraint exercised over your feelings or actions.

Strive to develop high levels of self-control in all areas of your life. As you progress on the road to enlightenment and fulfillment, it becomes clearer and clearer that understanding and connection with oneself is essential to this process. Spinning out of control never leads to high achievement.

There are many examples of this, but let's use several common and simple-to-understand illustrations. A few of the top areas of self-control would include food, alcohol, and sex. These are areas where mankind has had trouble finding balance since time immemorial. There are inherent desires that seem to drive us toward excess regarding these specific activities. Perhaps the genetic blueprint has survival of the individual and the species at the core of this yearning when it comes to food and sex. As a trained biologist and physician, my professional opinion would be that that is probably the case. Regarding alcohol consumption, this is probably driven by the pleasure area of the brain and the stress relieving desires we seem to possess innately.

That said, most adults with any semblance of real life experience quickly learn that the urge for excess in these spaces best be tempered, lest one wish to be in one kind of trouble or another. Moderation seems to be the best medicine regarding these three particularly ubiquitous fields of endeavor. Abstinence has been exercised by some individuals, but it is seemingly not the most practical approach for most of us. Regarding food, starvation is literally incongruent with life, so that is not a viable option.

There are many examples where self-control is critical to a highly productive and rewarding life. These include, but are in no means limited to: work, gambling, illicit drugs, greed, spending, saving, exercise, sleep, and so on. Depending on the activity, you sometimes need to have self-control to exercise complete avoidance. Sometimes self-control is in the form of moderation, and sometimes it means doing more than one has become accustomed to. Finding this balance is up to you. Those who are the most skillful in the application of these choices and decisions are much more likely to be the ones who enjoy the most fruitful and joyous lives.

“The intelligent want self-control; children want candy.”

—Rumi (1207-1273), Persian poet, scholar, theologian, and Sufi mystic

Let's discuss self-control. Do you have it? If so, how does it help in reaching your goals?

Solution

noun
Definition: something used or done to deal with and end a problem: something that solves a problem: the act of solving something: a correct answer to a problem, puzzle, etc.

To succeed, you must be solution-oriented. Identifying problems is essential for success, but this is a skill set that most of us possess in abundance.

259

The issue with this is that many people begin to falter when they come up against any type of dilemma. It is easy to become demoralized, deflated, and derailed when obstacles present themselves. The modestly successful individual will too often determine any problem is bigger than them and, rather than fight through it, they quickly elect to quit. Success behaves differently.

The success-oriented personality recognizes and accepts that hurdles, barriers, and complications are naturally occurring phenomena. It is foolhardy to believe the climb to the summit in any field will be smooth. In fact, there is an instructive allegory stating that, without the outcroppings, crags, and crevices along the side of a mountain—the rough spots as it were—it would be practically impossible to climb. One needs a few jagged points and overhangs upon which to get a foothold from which to push off. Rocky and rugged places are needed so one can firmly grasp with one's hand to remain connected to the mountain and on which to pull and assist in one's ascent.

Don't fear the irregular nature of the face of the mountain. Instead, I suggest you embrace it. These course features are what we refer to in life's journey as experience. And, as long as you do not make any foolish and dangerous decisions, it is these experiences which will ultimately make you an expert climber. Don't fear the zenith, and don't fear the harsh passages in the journey. You will be better for it in the end.

Be a problem solver. Be the solution-minded leader others look to for answers. Remember, just about anyone can define the problems we face. They tend to be self-evident. Navigating those difficult moments is the key to unlocking real expertise and value in the marketplace. Remember to never panic. Remain calm and look for the solutions. This habit and characteristic will help you like no other in building a reputation of competence, courage, and administrative command. Problem solvers are needed everywhere. If you develop this ability, you will always find yourself in unfathomable demand.

“As an entrepreneur, you work out solutions.”
—Les Wexner (1937-), American businessman and philanthropist

260

Discuss how you have discovered a solution (or solutions) to get out of a conundrum and on to the finish line to success.

Stamina

---

noun
Definition: great physical or mental strength that allows you to continue doing something for a long time.

You must possess great stamina because success is not a sprint race; it is an ultra-marathon. When I think of my own life and my own professional success, I recognize I cultivated a personality designed for endurance. It often comes as a surprise to people, when they ask about my education, that I didn't finish my formal schooling until I was thirty-three years old. That means that after completing twelve years of high school, I then did another fifteen years. The final fifteen were much more grueling and demanding than the first twelve, that's for sure. But I, like those around me, just kept going. It brings to mind the old advertisement for the Eveready bunny. He "kept going, and going, and going..." That is how the vast majority of people build their success. It is a process of practically incessant hard work carried out over a very protracted period of time.

Consider that, in my case, those thirty-three years weren't spent getting me to the finish line; they were the prerequisite to get me on the starting line of my career. It wasn't until that point that I could even to begin to work toward creating a successful surgical career. That is called commitment. This requires patience and persistence. And all that is built upon a solid foundation called stamina.

Albert Einstein is quoted as saying, "It's not that I'm so smart, it's just that I stay with problems longer." There's a hell of a lot of truth to that. And I'm living proof you can achieve extraordinary things if you just stick with it and refuse to quit, no matter how difficult the journey becomes. I can assure you, there were innumerable times along the way when I was dying to quit. But I didn't, and neither should you. Work hard to build your personal stamina; in the end, it may be the greatest resource you have. It is far more valuable than intelligence quotient or even money when it comes to getting things done.

⁶⁶*More than a half, maybe as much as two-thirds of my life as a writer is rewriting. I wouldn't say I have a talent that's special. It strikes me that I have an unusual kind of stamina.*⁹⁹

—John Irving (1942-), American novelist and screenwriter

Give examples of the stamina you possess.

Strength

noun

Definition: the quality that allows someone to deal with problems in a determined and effective way.

To succeed, you must be strong. Being successful does not mean you live a life devoid of problems. Successful people do not win all the time. Everyone deals with setbacks, defeats, losses, disappointments, troubles, and obstacles of all kinds. Coping with, solving, and overcoming such issues requires strength. That's as simple as I can make it. That is just another one of those realities you must accept if you wish to live an abundant lifestyle.

Anyone who tries to convince you that you can be weak and successful is either disingenuous or delusional. Being weak in any way is one of those attributes I really can't see any redemption in. Would you like to be physically weak? Would you like to be mentally weak? Would you care to be emotionally weak? How about financially weak? Intellectually weak? Academically weak? Morally? Ethically? Professionally? I highly doubt it.

Be strong. Work hard to get strong and stay that way. As the popular contemporary mantra professes, "Live strong." This will give you your best chance of succeeding in a highly competitive world and marketplace. Anything short of this will likely leave you short of your true ambitions, desires, wishes, and dreams.

"Strength does not come from winning. Your struggles develop your strengths. When you go through hardships and decide not to surrender, that is strength."

—Arnold Schwarzenegger (1947-),
Austrian-born American actor, model, producer, activist, businessman,
investor, writer, philanthropist, professional bodybuilder, politician

Talk about your strengths and weaknesses. How does your weakness keep you from success? How does your strength serve to keep you motivated? How has your strength aided you in finishing a task, project, or completing a goal?

Strive

Intransitive verb
Definition: to try very hard to do or achieve something.

Strive to be your personal best. This is largely an internal process. It is one thing to fight hard to overcome the external hurdles that present themselves in this ever-changing and complicated contemporary climate; it is something altogether different to struggle to live up to our internal yearnings and objectives. This is the greatest challenge of all. This is where you must really push to constantly go the extra mile in everything you do. This is what separates the top three percent of all successful people from the top one percent in their field, for example.

It has been said, "The best thing about going the extra mile is there are never any traffic jams out there." Undoubtedly, this is true, but the effort it requires to push oneself out into that rarified air is exponentially more difficult than what is required to be simply above average.

It is the pain you sometimes experience that makes all the difference in the end. I am once again reminded of my own life experience as a

263

trainee in general and cardiovascular surgery. We all had to dig deep down inside to push far beyond whatever we thought was humanly possible. It was not unusual to go thirty-six or forty-eight hours without sleep while functioning at an extremely high level of mental acuity, manual dexterity, and physical capacity. In fact, there were several occasions in those years where I was forced to push myself for seventy-two hours without any rest at all. This is what was required to succeed, and there were a small handful of us willing to make the personal sacrifices required to take care of a very active surgical service comprised of many seriously ill patients. We strived to be the best we could be while providing the treatment necessary, day or night.

The first four years I was in private practice as an open-heart surgeon, I took a grand total of five days of vacation. This is what the job required, and so that is what I did. It was certainly not for everybody.

Each of us must look deep inside and find out what we are made of. We must ask who we want to be and how we are going to get there. Are you willing to do absolutely everything it takes to do something extra-ordinary? If the answer is yes, then do it. It's as easy as that. The formula isn't complicated; it's the actualization of the formula that is the difficult aspect of the equation. Many people who have achieved greatness in their respective field will tell you it is an extraordinary experience to learn about yourself and how hard you can push and how far you can go. There is a kind of self-enlightenment inherent in this process that will otherwise be a mystery to you.

Perhaps one of the greatest regrets people have at the end of their life looking back is when they ask themselves silently, "I wonder what I could have really achieved had I tried a lot harder than I did." Now, not everyone will possess this sort of introspection, but it seems many people do. Take the opportunity now to leave it all on the field, as the adage goes. You don't want to have to wonder what you were capable of at the end of your life. I think you would prefer to know you got everything out of this journey that you possibly could.

"You are capable of more than you know. Choose a goal that seems right for you and strive to be the best, however hard the path. Aim high. Behave honorably. Prepare to be alone at times, and endure failure. Persist! The world needs all you can give."

—E.O. Wilson (1929-),
American biologist, researcher, theorist, naturalist, and author

It is a tall order, but are you managing to do it? Talk about how you are doing so far in keeping yourself motivated and staying on your path. Your writing will motivate you, whether you are already striving to meet your goals or just starting to write your success story.

Teamwork

noun

Definition: work done by several associates with each doing a part but all subordinating personal prominence to the efficiency of the whole.

Understand that only through teamwork can you fulfill your true potential. Big projects and big undertakings typically require more than one person to accomplish. Skyscrapers in Manhattan cannot be built with one pair of hands. Such an effort requires a team. Brain surgery cannot be done by one person; it requires a team. Building a business of any kind necessitates a team be put in place. Even seemingly solo occupations, like writing a book, mandate there be a team of professionals in place. You need a literary agent, an editor, a publisher, a printer, a distributor, a group of retailers, advertisers, etc.

Nothing of significance can be achieved in a vacuum. You must learn to build and maintain relationships with other individuals in the community with whom to develop and complete tasks and projects. As the old expression goes, "No man is an island." Reach out to those around you, and learn to work in harmony with other valuable individuals. Everyone brings something to the table of vital importance. Nurture your capacity for forging ethical, honest, mutually respectful relationships with other talented people, and this will greatly increase the efficiency with which you achieve substantial progress, regardless of what type of goals you have set out for yourself.

If you make the common mistake of trying to be the head chef, maître d'hôtel, dish washer, waiter, *and* busboy, you will soon build a reputation for having an awful restaurant and be out of business faster than you can say soup du jour. You must appreciate that delegating responsibilities to other capable individuals is a natural and necessary aspect of growth and development in business of any kind. Accept the fact that you are not, in fact, the best at everything, and even if that were the case, it would be impossible for you to do all things required to finish a venture once it takes on any sort of meaningful scope and scale.

66*Teamwork is so important that it is virtually impossible for you to reach the heights of your capabilities or make the money that you want without becoming very good at it.*99

—Brian Tracy (1944-),
Canadian-American motivational speaker, entrepreneur, and author

Whether your goal is body building, building self-esteem, building a business, or building relationships, you will find you are not going it alone. Talk about the team you have created and how each person plays an important role in motivation, resolve, persistence, and keeping you on the right path.

Tenacity

noun

Definition: the quality or state of being very determined to do something: not easily stopped: firm or strong: continuing for a long time.

To succeed, you must have tenacity. As I mentioned earlier, Albert Einstein was quoted as saying, "It's not that I'm so smart, it's just that I stay with problems longer." Now, although I'm quite certain that Professor Einstein was much smarter than I am, I am also sure his tenacity had just as much to do with his prolific and prodigious academic, mathematical, and scientific career.

The reality is, hard things take time to bring to any sort of meaningful and productive conclusion. As my professor at Sloan Kettering, Dr. Valerie Rusch, used to say, "Nothing hard is ever easy." After many years in surgical practice, I can say I agree with my teacher. When you take on challenging and meaningful work, successful completion necessitates that you commit to sticking to the job at hand. Too many of us quit before we get to where we wish to go. The truth is, typically, all that is needed to accomplish a lofty goal is to continue putting one foot in front of the other. A good example would be the difference between running a mile, a 5K race, and a marathon. The technique is always the same: putting one foot in front of the other. The difference is in the endurance. The endurance is a byproduct of having the tenacity to keep training so you develop the stamina required to go the longest distances.

Try to remind yourself of this simple philosophy when times get tough and you begin to feel like you may quit short of the finish line. Just as Dr. Einstein didn't scribble out his now famous theory of relativity overnight, neither should you expect to reach your personal summit in a day, a week, a month, or even a year. The reality is, the serial winners just keep on keepin' on. Before you know it, you will have gone the extra mile. And as someone once said, "The best part about going the extra mile is that there are never any traffic jams out there."

Let me tell you the secret that has led to my goal. My strength lies solely in my tenacity.
—Louis Pasteur (1822-1895), French chemist and microbiologist

Tenacity, resolve, endurance—they all have many things in common, not the least is they are characteristics all successful people possess. Be honest with yourself and write about how these strengths manifest in your life. Are they helping you achieve your goals? What are you putting into practice to hone your tenacity?

Thrive

Intransitive verb
Definition: to grow or develop successfully: to flourish or succeed.

You want to thrive, not simply survive and subsist. I strongly believe this is what is intended for us. Nature encourages an oak tree to grow as tall and strong as it can possibly be. The eagle is meant to soar amongst the clouds. The cheetah is designed to run as fast as it possibly can. And we are built to thrive.

We are created with such extraordinary intellectual prowess, creativity, and imagination, it seems improbable, if not impossible, we would be expected to live a life of mundane ambitions and mediocre results.

There are so many beautiful places in the world to see. There are vistas that can you're your breath away. There are homes adorned with the most lavish and lush furnishings. There are automobiles that are works of art combined with genius engineering, handling, and performance. There are concert halls that produce sound in perfect harmony and vibration with the human ear and soul. If these things and other such experiences and objects exist, and they do, who are they for? Hopefully you think the answer is *you*. I certainly think the answer is you. I also think the answer is *me*. I believe we are all intended to enjoy the full bounty mankind has created in all its wisdom and ability.

Someone is going to live in that fabulous lakeside home, why not you? Aren't you deserving of such trappings? Someone will drive the Porsche, the Bentley, the Rolls-Royce— why shouldn't it be you? Are you somehow inherently less worthy than the Prince of Wales, or the artist formerly known as Prince? I don't believe you are. I think you have all the potential in the world to drive the world's finest automobiles, take your loved ones on the finest vacations, fly first-class getting there, and stay at the most luxuriously appointed hotels. They built the hotels, didn't they? There is a first-class cabin, isn't there? Do you automatically assume those amenities are expressly for someone other than you? Someone more deserving perhaps? Someone of greater value somehow?

I certainly hope those are not your sentiments. That would be awfully sad. I hope you think much more highly of yourself than that.

Tragically, almost all of us have been programmed to think of ourselves in this way. We have been led to believe we are in some way inferior to those who live such lifestyles. Why is this? Who made those rules? These thoughts come to us from our parents, our friends, our co-workers, our siblings, and just about anyone else we can think of. They have us convinced we deserve a sensible and reliable car and a safe home that's clean with a roof that doesn't leak. A solid education and three square meals come with this consolation prize of a lifestyle we've been sold. How pathetic is that? Well, I'm not having it. I won't stand for it, and neither should you.

If someone is going to enjoy all those wonderful things, I want to be one of them. I'm not inferior to anyone. I don't give a damn who their father was or how blue their blood is; I could not care less how well they sing, act, or hit a baseball. I'm just as valuable as they are in my own way. I want to thrive. As far as I can tell, we only get one bite at the apple. I'm going to make mine as big and sweet and juicy as I can. You do what you want, but my advice is to do the same. If you don't, someone else certainly will.

"My mission in life is not merely to survive, but to thrive; and to do so with some passion, some compassion, some humor, and some style."

—Maya Angelou (1928-2014),
American poet, civil rights activist, dancer, filmproducer, playwright,
film director, author, actress, and professor

Do you feel deserving of these things? Try the exercise where you see yourself as the main character of a novel. What would you like this character to have? Are they worthy of thriving?

Tough

---

adjective
Definition: physically and emotionally strong: able to do hard work, to deal with harsh conditions, etc._

Winners are tough. This is typically true because they have done a hell of a lot of hard work along the way. Often, the trail of the successful individual is littered with years of sacrifice, exertion, strife, practice, repetition, risk taking, growth, stretching, straining, pain, anguish, introspection, failure, and rejection. If words like those have become familiar to you through personal experience, the likelihood is that you are doing pretty damn well.

One area of employment requiring toughness is sales. Sales can be a very rewarding profession in many ways, but it can also be brutal. It has been suggested that, in the end, everyone is a salesperson. I agree. We are all selling a service or product of some kind. If not, we are selling ourselves in the sense that everyone wants to be liked. We must convince others that what we are offering is of value and they would be wise to accept. The big problem with sales is the experience of rejection. No one likes to be rejected. Rejection is painful. It just hurts.

One of my favorite anecdotes about selling is as follows. I don't know the origin of the story or whether it's true, but it certainly serves as an excellent teaching tool. The story goes, a gentleman owned a company based on sales. He did all he could to encourage his sales force to increase revenue and close sales. He used threats of being fired, reduction in pay, reduced commissions, and rewards for the highest number of sales. Little seemed to change. Then it occurred to the man that he should create a sales contest at the office whereby the salesperson who could prove the greatest number of denials or rejections would win $500 per week.

After implementing this idea, sales skyrocketed. The idea was that suddenly every salesperson's apprehension was dismantled. They were no longer afraid to call on prospective clients and offer their goods. They happily said, "And if you're not interested, for in any reason, Mr. Jones, just please kindly sign this form that states you absolutely, positively don't want to buy anything, and I'll never bother you again." Of course, the sales team was off and running, knocking on doors and cold-calling like crazy. Typically, the same individual who had the most rejections at the end of the week also had the most sales. You see, the rejection lead to exposure of the product and more sales. The sales force was emboldened with this technique. They were made tougher. They could swallow the word "No!" with a smile on their face. The toughness gave them the confidence they needed to take on the most inhospitable of client with ease.

270

Remember this little tale when you are feeling intimidated or weak. Imagine you'll be given $500 for being rejected most, and you'll find your real rewards will be far greater than that in your life.

"Every quarterback can throw a ball; every running back can run; every receiver is fast; but that mental toughness that you talk about translates into competitiveness."

—Tom Brady (1977-), American football player and Super Bowl MVP

Are you tough? Write about it. What toughened you up? How has it served you and your goals?

Triumph

noun

Definition: a great or important victory: a great success or achievement: the very happy and joyful feeling that comes from victory or success.

Get into the mindset of expecting to experience triumph regularly. No one spends their life planning to fail. No one puts in the effort and preparation so they can fall short of the finish line. I have never met a single individual who dreamed of a life of pervasive mediocrity as a child. Successful people triumph. Those are simply the facts. This may be a bitter pill to swallow, but it doesn't make it any less true.

I regularly play tennis with one of my very dear friends. We are well-matched on the court and are both fiercely competitive. We enjoy our time together immensely. The rivalry is certainly fraternal in nature, but nonetheless, it can be quite intense. I can assure you, neither of us wants to lose. On those days when I am defeated, I will say something to my friend like, "Well, second place isn't too bad, huh, buddy?" or, "I can't wait to go home and show my mother my silver medal. It's almost as shiny as your gold one." Of course, we both lose it and crack up at this point. It's all in good fun, but the underlying point is clear. In tennis, like in so many things in life, there is no second place.

Like it or not, you must set triumph as your goal. Victory is much sweeter than the alternative. Obviously, this doesn't mean any of us can always come in first place, but I do think it's a worthy goal to set. Who wants to enter any sort of competition with the intention of simply finishing—or worse yet, participating? That would be a pretty sorry way to go through life. I mean, can you imagine sitting down to study for a test with the aim of getting a nice solid C? That would put you in the fat part of the curve. What's wrong with that? You could be like most people; that's okay, isn't it? Let's face it, most people are truly wonderful. And I don't mean that facetiously. I mean it sincerely.

That said, no matter what parameter you use as a measuring stick, mathematically speaking, half of all the people you ever meet will be average in many ways. Most people have an average amount of wealth, make an average income, have an average education, live in an average house in an average neighborhood, and go on average vacations an average number of times of year staying in average hotels. If that statement makes you upset, I'm sorry, but that is what we call reality. Only a few people can be an exception to any of those rules. As I frequently advise people, only five percent of people can be in the top five percent. You can't squeeze ten percent into the top ten percent. The question is, "Where would you like to be?" Do you want to be average? How about below average? Statistically speaking, fifty percent of all the people you'll ever meet fall into that group.

Wouldn't you prefer to be above average? Exceptional? Excellent? How about extraordinary? That's up to you, but something tells me that, in your heart of hearts, you would like to be a top-tier individual. This will require triumphant behavior. You'll need to succeed in school, in the work place, in the market place, etc. if you truly want to live a life of abundance, joy, freedom, and pleasure. Think about it. You don't have to choose this path if it seems unappealing to you. The middle of the pack tends to be extremely accommodating. I'm certain they'll make room for someone like you. You decide. The choice is all yours.

"The harder the conflict, the more glorious the triumph."

—Thomas Paine (1737-1809),
English-American political activist, philosopher,
political theorist, and revolutionary

What do you think about this? Are you happy and content with where you are? That's perfectly all right if you are! Let's discuss it.

Will

Transitive verb
Definition: to determine by an act of choice

Successful people develop a steadfast will to succeed. Will is most valuable when you meet with obstacles and setbacks. When riding a bicycle, it takes little effort to coast downhill. Unfortunately, in the world of achievement, essentially all the bounty lies along the uphill journey. This requires lots of pedaling. The higher you go, the thinner the air becomes. Not everyone is built to push to the summit. This requires an enormous amount of will. Again, the will is based largely on the reasons you wish to succeed.

Great will is typically associated with varying degrees of discomfort and pain. If you never experience such emotions, it is likely you will never realize your full potential. Remember, if you are coasting through life, it is basically impossible you are headed in the right direction. Again, what matters most here is what you personally want out of life. If you have chosen to be satisfied with small goals and are content with the quality of your life, then this may not be a problem for you.

I want to point out that I am not being facetious here. Some people set low goals and have low expectations of their life experiences and standard of living. This is perfectly okay. Again, that's what makes a country like America so great; you have the right to choose how you wish to live and then behave accordingly. If you wish to live in the valley, then coast.

On the other hand, if you dream about living in a beautiful house on the hill with a beautiful view of the valley, you'll have to cultivate the will to pedal hard and steadily until you get to a perfect lot where you can stake your claim. I suggest you try the latter. It's a fabulous process. I strongly believe that if you take my advice, you'll be happy that you did.

273

❝The will to win, the desire to succeed, the urge to reach your full potential...these are the keys that will unlock the door to personal excellence.❞

—Confucius (551-479 BC), Chinese teacher, politician, and philosopher

Are you happy where you are right now? If you want to change things, do you have the will to do it? How do you think you can strengthen your will or resolve? It is probably decision time in your life, or you probably would not even have this workbook in your hands. You would be surprised how many successful people thought, at first, they did not have what it took to reach their goals. In life, you *can* surprise yourself in the most wonderful ways.

Zeal

noun
Definition: a strong feeling of interest and enthusiasm that makes someone very eager or determined to do something.

To demonstrate great zeal in a project you choose to be involved in, you should have a passion for what you are doing. If you don't have tremendous enthusiasm for whatever it is you do, it is not possible to produce exceptionally good results.

You must love what you are doing and have tremendous desire and ambition driving you each day to outperform your fellow competitors—plus, seriously, it's good to love what you do! This is why the so-called river person, who is simply being carried along by the sweeping current of their personal vocation or avocation, tends to do so well.

The message here is simple: If you know in your heart you aren't genuinely zealous about what you do each day, you absolutely must make a change if you ever wish to live a life of true abundance and happiness. You cannot fake it. The adage, "Fake it 'til you make it," is a recipe for mediocrity. If you can be sincere in your passion for your occupation, you will, truly, never work another day in your life. Now, there's an aphorism to live by.

Think of the greats like Walt Disney and Thomas Edison, for example. Those are individuals who achieved extraordinary success by being completely immersed in their daily endeavors. I can assure you, you must possess zeal to produce exceptional results in your life. If you are simply going through the motions, working for the weekend, and trying to hammer out a living, you will never have the joy of realizing your immense, innate potential.

"Experience shows that success is due less to ability than to zeal."

—Charles Buxton (1823-1871), English brewer, philanthropist, and politician

On which note would you like to conclude your success story? Get passionate about your life and what you can do with it! Write about yourself as the hero or heroine of your own success story. Be as creative and as wonderful as you can possibly imagine. It feels great to do it, doesn't it? If you are skeptical, keep writing until you *do* feel great about yourself and your goals. Face each challenge ahead with confidence and a positive attitude.

Conclusion

I hope you›ve enjoyed working through this book and that this was a deeply introspective experience. You are now on your way to becoming all that you can be.

You have learned a lot about *winning* and *success* in these pages. It has been said, "The greatest triumph one can achieve is victory over oneself." In truth, the only person with whom you compete is yourself. Who are you today as compared to yesterday, and who do you wish to be tomorrow? Those are the essential questions. Always remember, if you are progressively working toward a worthy goal, you *are* a success. Where you stand along that path is irrelevant.

If you have completed the written exercises, you have drafted a blueprint for a character, a setting, and a plot which you will now transform into reality through action. I assume you have written a story of happiness, loving relationships, excellent health, abundance, and financial independence.

I would like to leave you with two closing quotations. The first is from Elbert Hubbard, who wrote, "He has achieved success who has worked well, laughed often, and loved much." The second is from John Stuart Mill, who said, "Those only are happy who have their minds fixed on some object other than their own happiness; on the happiness of others, on the improvement of mankind, even on some art or pursuit, followed not as a means, but as itself an ideal end."

Always keep these statements in mind and you are sure to enjoy the richest possible style of living. I wish you all the best on your personal adventure. May it be replete with great challenges, triumphs, and treasure of every kind.

Index of Essential
Power Words

Index of Quoted Individuals

Made in the USA
Middletown, DE
07 September 2024

59974053R00168